Subversive
Action

Subversive Action

Extralegal Practices for Social Justice

Nilan Yu and Deena Mandell, editors

WILFRID LAURIER UNIVERSITY PRESS

This book has been published with the help of a grant from the Canadian Federation for the Humanities and Social Sciences, through the Awards to Scholarly Publications Program, using funds provided by the Social Sciences and Humanities Research Council of Canada. Wilfrid Laurier University Press acknowledges the financial support of the Government of Canada through the Canada Book Fund for its publishing activities. This work was supported by the Research Support Fund.

Library and Archives Canada Cataloguing in Publication

Subversive action : extralegal practices for social justice / Nilan Yu and Deena Mandell, editors.

Includes bibliographical references and index.
Issued in print and electronic formats.
ISBN 978-1-77112-123-1 (paperback).—ISBN 978-1-77112-086-9 (epub).—
ISBN 978-1-77112-085-2 (pdf)

1. Social justice—Case studies. 2. Social service—Case studies. 3. Social change—Case studies. 4. Human rights—Case studies. 5. Social workers—Legal status, laws, etc. 6. Public welfare—Law and legislation. I. Mandell, Deena, [date], author, editor II. Yu, Nilan, 1969–, author, editor

HM671 S92 2015   303.3'72   C2015-903246-6
                                         C2015-903247-4

Cover design by Blakeley Words+Pictures. Front-cover photo by Gabrielle Easter (2008): *Banksy: Girl and a Soldier,* Bethlehem, West Bank. Text design by Janet Zanette.

© 2015 Wilfrid Laurier University Press
Waterloo, Ontario, Canada
www.wlupress.wlu.ca

This book is printed on FSC® certified paper and is certified Ecologo. It contains post-consumer fibre, is processed chlorine free, and is manufactured using biogas energy.

Printed in Canada

Every reasonable effort has been made to acquire permission for copyright material used in this text, and to acknowledge all such indebtedness accurately. Any errors and omissions called to the publisher's attention will be corrected in future printings.

No part of this publication may be reproduced, stored in a retrieval system, or transmitted, in any form or by any means, without the prior written consent of the publisher or a licence from the Canadian Copyright Licensing Agency (Access Copyright). For an Access Copyright licence, visit http://www.accesscopyright.ca or call toll free to 1-800-893-5777.

Dedicated to Adrian Vicary – mentor, friend, and colleage.

– Nilan

Dedicated to courageous activists everywhere.

– Deena

Contents

Acknowledgements   ix

Introduction   Social Work and Salt Making ▸ *Nilan Yu and Deena Mandell*   1

Chapter 1   Social Justice and Social Work: Convergence and Divergence in the Wake of the Toronto G20 Summit ▸ *Deena Mandell and Alex Hundert*   9

Chapter 2   Challenging State Aggression against Indigenous Australians ▸ *John Tomlinson*   25

Chapter 3   Politicizing Welfare and Humanizing Politics: Social Workers Opposing Apartheid South Africa's Policies ▸ *Thérèse Sacco and Jeanette Schmid*   41

Chapter 4   Social Workers, Resistance, and Martial Law in the Philippines: A View from Below ▸ *Mary Lou L. Alcid*   61

Chapter 5   Medha Patkar's Environmental Activism and Professional Social Work in India: Mass Legitimacy and Myopic Structures ▸ *Manohar Pawar and Venkat Pulla*   77

Chapter 6   Challenging the Authority of the State and Reclaiming Citizenship: A Case on Eviction and Deportation of Pavement Dwellers in Bombay, India ▸ *Purnima George and Ferzana Chaze*   99

Chapter 7   Non-violent Resistance: The Landless Rural Workers Movement of Brazil ▸ *Wilder Robles*   119

Chapter 8   Subversive Education in Ethiopia and Canada: Turning Coercive Encounters into Transformative Possibilities ▸ *Martha Kuwee Kumsa*   145

Conclusion   Rights, Justice, the Law, and Extralegal Action
             ▸ *Nilan Yu*   165

About the Authors   177

Index   181

Acknowledgements

Putting together this volume was a journey that took several years. The idea for the book started with just one story and I was stuck with it for more than a couple of years. Initially, I thought of a volume that mainly featured the life and work of such legendary figures as Gandhi and Martin Luther King, Jr. But it was Jim Midgley's counsel for me to stay clear of larger-than-life and worn cases that led to the reconceptualization of this volume to what it is – a book of stories of life-sized people grappling with challenges they confronted. Hopefully, these stories speak to contemporary practitioners of social work, social pedagogy, community work, and all those who are involved in the promotion of human rights and social justice.

The one story became two when a colleague, Carole Zufferey, introduced me to the work of John Tomlinson, one of the authors in this volume. Jeanette Schmid, who authors a chapter here with Thérèse Sacco, introduced me to Deena Mandell, who helped move the project forward in many ways. Apart from writing a chapter here with her son Alex Hundert, Deena was instrumental in finding one additional contributor as well as in introducing me to our friends at the Wilfrid Laurier University Press. Her insights, drawn from previous experiences, helped steer this project in her role as co-editor of this volume. It was an utter delight and comfort working with her.

We would like to thank the Wilfrid Laurier University Press for embracing the idea and encouraging us to pursue what was, in a sense, uncharted territory. The support and guidance that Ryan Chynces and then Lisa Quinn gave us were invaluable.

To Nina who joked about how she, together with her older brothers Awin and Laya, had caused the delay of this project for some years – it was actually the hope, joy, and inspiration the three of you gave me that saw this through.

And, of course, the heart of this book comes from the contributors who graciously shared my vision and invested their time and talents in realizing it. I feel profoundly privileged to have been part of this fellowship. It was such a joy meeting each and every kindred spirit who joined the pilgrimage and shared their inspiring stories. The countless exchanges we had over the course of this project were utterly stimulating to both mind and spirit. The journey was as fascinating as the destination.

Nilan Yu

When my involvement in this collection went from contributor to co-editor, it was a pragmatic partnership for which Nilan and I were both grateful. It came at a time when Nilan's vision for this volume resonated very powerfully with my own questions about social work and social justice and thus quickly moved beyond pragmatism for me. Nilan graciously made room for me in the project and he was a joy to work with. I greatly appreciate the thoughtful exchanges we had about each chapter; I always trusted our shared wish for the intellectual and critical integrity of the book to be the compass for any directional choices we needed to make.

Working with the contributors to this book was for me an experience of being in the company of greatness. I have been moved by the courage, humility, and fierce commitment at the heart of all their stories. Writing our own story with my son, Alex Hundert, has had many meanings for me, all of them deeply gratifying. I am proud and happy to have done this work with him.

Deena Mandell

INTRODUCTION

Social Work and Salt Making

Nilan Yu and Deena Mandell

On 5 April, after twenty-five days of marching, Gandhi reached the sea at Dandi, not with his seventy-eight followers behind him but with thousands.... At first light, he led a few into the water for a ceremony.... Then he waded out and felt his way up the beach with his spindly legs to a point where a thick crust of salt, evaporated by the sun, was cracking. He bent down and picked up a chunk of the crust and in so doing broke the British salt law.

Kurlansky, Salt: A World History

So began the salt rebellion instigated by Gandhi against the British Empire. The British had, for over a century, imposed heavy taxes on salt and forbade the making of salt in areas with hundreds of years of history of salt making in a bid to monopolize the salt trade and protect British salt producers. The ban imposed by the colonial rulers was so restrictive that traditional salt makers were forbidden from making salt even for their own family's consumption. They could not pick up crusts of salt lying right at their feet without risking severe punishment. Traditional salt makers were forced to leave their families starving at home as they searched for work in other parts of India. Although so-called salt rebellions had sporadically occurred for decades, Gandhi's action inspired hundreds of thousands in many parts of India to challenge the colonial regime by violating colonial law through the act of salt making, instigating widespread repression that put into question the legitimacy of British rule in India and eventually led to Indian independence.

▶ ABOUT THE BOOK

This volume represents an effort to identify and examine the experiences of "salt makers" and the place of "salt making" in social work. The book features cases involving extralegal social action by social work professionals and citizens in response to challenges to social justice and human rights. One would occasionally encounter the mention of the likes of Gandhi and Martin Luther King, Jr, in discussions about the promotion of human rights and social justice (see, e.g., Ambrosino, 2008; and Ife, 2010, 2012). Gandhi's struggle against the British Empire and the drive for civil rights led by Martin Luther King, Jr, embody the discourse on social justice and human rights that we find in some of the most widely accepted definitions of social work today; such as the one adopted by the International Federation of Social Workers (IFSW) (2014). But while many definitions of social work fashion it as a profession devoted to the pursuit of social justice and human rights, standard social work texts (see, e.g., Wilson, 2011; Thompson, 2009; and Zastrow, 2010) hardly make mention of the traditions laid down by Gandhi and King. Much less explored in social work texts are the extralegal dimensions that accompanied these traditions. There is occasional treatment of the notion such as with Spech's (1969) discussion of disruptive tactics in social work and the appropriation by some social work practitioners of Alinsky's (1972) model of practice. But extralegal action arguably does not occupy a central place in mainstream conceptions of social work. And yet we speak of challenging structural oppression, discrimination, and disadvantage that in many cases occur within particular political economic orders where legitimate action – legal action – is defined and redefined at will by those in positions of power. It would then be difficult to speak of the promotion of social justice and the liberation of people, as the IFSW's definition of social work does, without confronting the possible necessity for extralegal action.

By extralegal action for social justice, we mean action intended to subvert and/or resist oppression, discrimination, and disadvantage through a suite of strategies ranging from skirting the law or breaking the spirit of the law without breaking the letter of the law to what may be considered patently illegal in particular political-economic contexts.

The presentation of the cases in this volume is not meant to showcase good practice as much as to evoke questions about social work and what it represents. These questions arise because of the unique place of social work in the community of professions. Social work, like all recognized professions, operates on a claim to legitimacy within the political economic contexts in which it is practised. Unlike other professions, however, social work espouses discourses such as social justice, social change, and emancipation that, if carried to their limits, can mean the challenging of the foundations of the social order in which such practice is undertaken. In other words, social work can potentially involve actions that run counter to dominant ideology and practice and question the legitimacy of the social order within which the practice of social work derives legitimacy of professional status.

This book offers eight stories from around the world of what can be regarded as extralegal action by social work professionals and citizens in the pursuit of social justice and human rights. In gathering and presenting these narratives together, it is not our intent to suggest generalizations or invoke judgments, nor do we particularly wish that the reader do so. On the contrary: the highly localized contexts of each story – political, historical, cultural, and subjective – are not meant to offer conclusions but to raise questions and induce reflection. Taken as a whole, these stories perhaps raise more questions than they answer. We see this as a good thing: for what *is* a critical perspective, if not one that raises difficult, often uncomfortable questions and eschews easy, definitive answers? Why do some social workers see themselves compelled to "push the limits" and others not? What mix of political and historical context and timing, individual social location, and personal proclivities or vulnerabilities contributes to different stances? What role does "professionalization" of social work have in discouraging subversive social action on the part of social workers? Under what circumstances do we begin to feel that a social worker may have gone "too far," and how do our own subjectivities and (perhaps unacknowledged) allegiances shape such a determination?

We, as editors, sometimes had very different responses to the individual narratives – not just stylistic ones, but perspectival as well. We have had some fascinating exchanges about what we respectively saw as the strengths and weaknesses in a particular piece and what those differences might reflect about our own politics and notions about the scope of the book's topic. We hope that this volume will provoke similar discussions among readers and colleagues.

▶ THE STORIES

The stories featured in this volume involve what can be regarded as extralegal action by social work professionals and citizens in the pursuit of social justice and human rights.

In chapter 1, Deena Mandell, a senior social work academic, and Alex Hundert, a committed radical social activist, recount a story of state repression and the criminalization of dissent surrounding the Toronto G20 Summit protests of 2010. The state crackdown on protest and radical groups led to Alex's incarceration for a total of nine months plus severely restrictive house arrest for over a year. To the initial very serious charges of conspiracy were added charges of breaching his bail conditions, after Alex participated in two university panel discussions on the implications of G20 policing for activist groups. One of those panel discussions was held in Mandell's Faculty of Social Work, where undercover police were present. Alongside Deena's outrage over state violation of the academic space and criminalization of dissent was the crucial fact that Alex is her son. Their dialogue begins with her disappointment at the lack of response within the university to the oppressive police incursion. It grapples with questions about the essential conservatism and privilege of professional social work and social work academics in North America and the perception of its limitations by non-professional workers for social justice.

In chapter 2, John Tomlinson distills a national story of injustice toward Indigenous peoples into the tale of one social worker (aided by a few administrators) who acted in the early 1970s to subvert that injustice for the sake of one child, Nola, and her family. The act of returning Nola to her family against explicit directions was both specific and symbolic, and it ignited a strike by Tomlinson's fellow social workers in protest – the first social workers' strike in Australia – when Tomlinson was suspended for acting against orders. Although the author's focus is on the operation of the child welfare system as a mechanism of colonization and systemic discrimination, we cannot help, in reading his unembellished narrative, but wonder about what motivates one individual to take up a stance of resistance when others do not. The collective response of John's colleagues tells us that his extralegal act resonated sympathetically, the strike itself representing a kind of expanded resistance to prevailing policy. What individual histories, values, beliefs, and social identities foster the courage to take personal risk on behalf of social justice? We are given a few clues by Tomlinson in relation to himself but we can all reflect on this question in relation to ourselves since systemic injustices actively continue, not only in Australia but in all of our respective countries.

In Thérèse Sacco and Jeanette Schmid's powerful chapter recounting the resistance strategies of social workers under apartheid in South Africa – from secret meetings and covert acts of protection to highly public protests and support of vulnerable communities – we learn about how a network of social workers devoted themselves to bringing down the system of apartheid. As surveillance and the severity of consequences increased, the social workers' activities became, de facto, increasingly illegal and personally more risky. They also became increasingly diversified, ingenious, and daring. The authors allude to painful memories and experiences that we are left to wonder about. They do not talk about their own extraordinary courage, but we as readers cannot help but register it and reflect upon what made this ongoing involvement in this ultimately successful process of collective resistance possible. Do extreme social, political, and economic conditions breed extreme courage and determination to resist them? Is some specific social identity required in the social worker to impel him or her towards active resistance? Finally, we cannot help but ask what the power of collective commitment and courage might achieve in our own particular contexts.

In her chapter, Mary Lou Alcid talks about the subversive action by social workers under martial law in the Philippines as part of the struggle of resistance against the Marcos dictatorship. Based on life histories of selected social workers, Alcid shows how the imposition of martial law in the Philippines influenced some social workers to engage in transformative social work – subversive action in the eyes of the state. She explores the meanings, critical elements, and processes of transformative social work as articulated by the social workers and the attendant risks and challenges.

In chapter 6, which gives an account of the environmental activism in India of Medha Patkar, Manohar Pawar and Venkat Pulla outline the challenges to human rights and social justice posed by heavy-handed governance and the responses that evolved out of Patkar's integration with grassroots communities. With Patkar's assistance, communities threatened with physical and economic displacement as a result of government-administered dam construction projects learned to mount struggles of resistance covering a very broad range of strategies that include the use of unconventional tactics in line with the non-violent social action method of *satyagraha* – literally, the force of truth – laid down by Gandhi. Pawar and Pulla suggest that Patkar's professional social work education may have had a role in the shaping of what has become her life's work, but they also note with concern the social work profession's apparent indifference to her cause. This, for them, raises critical questions about the social work profession in terms of the discipline's ability to respond to issues affecting the poor and marginalized in line with its espoused values of human rights and social justice in restrictive and repressive political economic contexts.

The chapter by Purnima George and Ferzana Chaze revisits 1980s Bombay/Mumbai, when the state began executing a plan to evict and deport pavement dwellers from the city. In this inspiring narrative, we learn how social workers and social work academics, along with their students, led a coalition of 23 organizations aimed at resisting the government's plan. The coalition's activities included research and dissemination of information designed to foster public support for the pavement dwellers and culminated in the illegal occupation of a symbolic public space, a racecourse. Ultimately, a court-based challenge to the state's authority to conduct the evictions was launched, using the university's research to build the case. Having provided a detailed sketch of the economic and social landscape in which the threat of eviction and the strategy of resistance unfolded, the authors offer penetrating reflections on the conditions that led them and their colleagues to become involved in the unique ways that they did. Readers are bound to reflect, in turn, on opportunities – both those taken and those missed – to wield the powers of privilege in the service of social justice.

Wilder Robles writes about the work of the Movimento dos Trabalhadores Rurais Sem Terra (MST), the famed landless peasant movement of Brazil. With a membership base of 1.5 million spread over 23 of Brazil's 26 states, MST is quite possibly the largest social movement in Latin America. This peasants' organization is known for the extralegal occupation of idle farmlands in the name of agrarian reform. Robles examines the extralegal strategy of the MST in the context of the broader social order and the issue of land rights and agrarian reform in Brazil. Robles argues that government inaction in the face of widespread poverty and stark social inequality leaves very limited options and thus necessitated MST's use of extralegal means in promoting the rights and welfare of landless peasants.

The last of the eight stories is that of a social work educator reflecting on her personal and professional journey from being a political prisoner in Ethiopia to being a social work educator in Canada. Martha Kuwee Kumsa talks about creative social actions intended to turn coercive encounters into possibilities of social transformation. She frames these actions as "social working" to dispute the complicities of social work education in the injustices of nation-states. She tells us of her experience of being imprisoned under a repressive totalitarian regime in Ethiopia and the practice of pedagogy that she went on to develop in prison. Her reflection focuses on what these experiences offer in her current work as a social work educator in a liberal democratic societal context. Although the contexts in these two countries seem stark contrasts, Kumsa argues that the coercive encounters entrenched in both contexts reveal a "false" dichotomy when it comes to the pursuit of human rights and social justice. She concludes by positioning subversive pedagogy as holding out creative possibilities of social transformation and blurring the multiple "false" binaries constructed between the West and the rest, local and global, national and transnational, legal and illegal, bondage/imprisonment and freedom, past and present/future.

These stories are meant to be instrumental in allowing us to examine the place of extralegal social action in social work practice. Some of the important considerations in examining these cases are the actors, the issues involved, and the political-economic contexts in which the actions were undertaken. Two of the stories feature non-social-work professionals: Alex Hundert, identified as a "radical activist" in chapter 1, and the landless rural peasants that make up the MST in Robles's account. One might question why these voices are included in a volume intended to stimulate critical reflection in the profession. Such argument, in a way, suggests that discussions about social work should be confined to accredited professionals and that the work of non-social-work professionals has nothing of value to offer to the profession. By this logic, however, we might dismiss from consideration the life and work of Gandhi, Nelson Mandela, and Martin Luther King, Jr, something that would be unthinkable to most of us. Many a social worker can only dream of (borrowing from the IFSW's definition of social work) "empowering" individuals and communities to enable the kind of "liberation" and "social change" that the stories of Alex and the Landless Rural Workers Movement of Brazil demonstrate. On the basis of mainstream conceptions of social work that confine it to the activities of specifically educated and credentialed professionals, we argue that these stories about the work of non-professionals can offer insights for professional practice in relation to the questions raised in this volume. But more importantly, these stories open up the question about how we conceptualize social work, the question that is central to the theme of this book. Does social work, as the International Federation of Social Workers defines it, actually reflect the promotion of "social change, problem solving in human relationships and the empowerment and liberation of people" or is it all that but contingent on whether or not the actors have the establishment-endorsed qualifications to do such work? We include these stories because they contribute to the aim of the volume; doing so is an intentional step outside of the restricted realm of mainstream conceptions of social work and allows us an opportunity to conceptualize practice beyond the dominant paradigm.

In the concluding chapter, Nilan Yu problematizes conceptions of social work grounded in claims of professional identity and mandate in the light of discourses on empowerment, liberation of people, and social change embodied in many definitions of social work. He points out how mainstream conceptions of social work, embodied in the drive toward professionalization, embed social work in the politico-legal framework where practice is carried out. This, he points out, raises a question on the bounds of legitimate action in situations where discrimination, oppression, and disadvantage form an integral part of the economy of and is sanctioned by the established order. Yu asks, "Is there a place for 'salt making' in social work?"

References

Alinsky, S. (1971). *Rules for radicals*. New York: Vintage.
Ambrosino, R. (2008). *Social work and social welfare: An introduction*. (6th ed.). Belmont, CA: Brooks/Cole Cengage.
Ife, J. (2010). *Human rights from below: Achieving rights through community development*. Sydney: Cambridge University Press.
Ife, J. (2012). *Human rights and social work: Towards rights-based practice*. (3rd ed.). New York: Cambridge University Press.
International Federation of Social Workers. (2014, August 6). Global definition of social work. Retrieved 25 June 2015, from http://ifsw.org/policies/definition-of-social-work/
Kurlansky, M. (2002). *Salt: A world history*. London: Vintage.
Specht, H. (1969). Disruptive tactics. *Social Work, 14*(2), 5–15.
Thompson, N. (2009). *Understanding social work: Preparing for practice*. (3rd ed.) New York: Palgrave Macmillan.
Wilson, K. (2011). *Social work: An introduction to contemporary practice*. (2nd ed.). New York: Pearson Longman.
Zastrow, C. (2010). *Introduction to social work and social welfare: Empowering people*. (10th ed.). Belmont, CA: Brooks/Cole Cengage.

CHAPTER 1

Social Justice and Social Work

Convergence and Divergence in the Wake of the Toronto G20 Summit

Deena Mandell and Alex Hundert

The authors of this chapter are, respectively, a progressive social work educator (Deena) and a radical activist (Alex); we are, respectively, a free woman and an imprisoned man. Alex is serving nine months in prison as we begin writing this chapter;[1] prior to his sentencing on charges related to the G20 protests of 2010 in Toronto, he had already spent nearly five months in detention centres and eighteen months on house arrest. For the past number of weeks, Alex has been in solitary confinement because he has been deemed a "security risk" by the prison. He has continued to dictate an ongoing political blog over the phone to supporters who transcribe and post each instalment. Deena lives in her lovely home and works at the university where she has been a full-time faculty member since 1998.

How, then, do we come to be writing this story together? We are mother and son. Our worlds beyond the family collided when Alex was rearrested (while on bail) for participating in two post-G20 panel discussions, one of which was held at the Faculty of Social Work where Deena works; in fact, she had facilitated the booking of the event at the request of a group of students and community activists. Undercover police attended both events and rearrested Alex on his way home from the second event, which had been held at a different university.

In our story, "legal" became a moving target as the state reacted violently and extralegally to protests against the austerity agenda of the G20 Summit in Toronto in June 2010. Initially, Deena was a horrified and alarmed bystander to the unfolding story. Both her sons were arrested, twenty-four hours apart: one was taken from a peaceful street protest and the other (Alex) from his own home in the middle of the night, at gunpoint. The number of arrests in Toronto over the course of one weekend reached an estimated 1,100 people, roughly 1,000 of whom either never had charges laid because there were none or ultimately had their charges dropped. The abusive treatment of most arrestees in crowded cages under appalling conditions was the subject of outrage and further protest among many Canadians. Alex was one of seventeen people who did face charges – and the prosecutor was so intent on making an example of Alex and two of his co-accused as "ringleaders" of a conspiracy that the Crown actually appealed their release on bail. "Release" meant house arrest, the conditions of which were so remarkably constraining that a major Canadian human rights organization stepped in to protest them. The conditions that garnered the most attention were the prohibition against attending any demonstration and the prohibition against posting or being quoted in the media. As Alex's right to protest was removed, Deena exercised hers more than in all her own (1960s) undergraduate days.

The failure of Deena's university, as an institution, to respond aggressively to the incursion of the police into its (the university's) legitimate domain was shocking. The reframing by the police and the Crown of a legitimate university activity as illegal in order to pursue an unconstitutional agenda was unfathomable. That the university did not push back initially seemed equally unfathomable. The president of the Faculty Association did write a letter to the minister of justice, when asked, and so did the president of the provincial association of university faculty members. Both of these associations are akin to labour unions and tend to be more inclined toward activist stances. A majority of social work faculty members and some of Deena's own students signed a similar letter of protest (which Deena initiated). Although members of the social work faculty and staff were individually sympathetic and personally supportive to Deena and Alex, the absence of a coherent, outraged response was profoundly disappointing. Calls to action were met with responses that ranged from none to limp. Willing partners were ultimately found, however, among activist faculty members and graduate students in other departments and a conference called "Speak Up! Speak Out! Public Dialogue and the Politics of Dissent" was organized for the university and the broader community. It was held in the same auditorium where the fateful panel discussion had taken place as a symbolic reclamation of the space. Where were the social workers whose espoused raison d'être is social change and social justice?

In this chapter, we explore together the questions about the positioning of social work as a profession, along with social work academics as their ideological seedbed, as potential forces for radical resistance and change. We understand "radical" in this sense to reflect its original Latin meaning, "of the root": change that not only gets at the root of underlying issues, but also emerges from – is envisioned and enacted by – the grassroots of communities.

Since it is not possible for us to speak with a single voice about the politics of anything, we have chosen to write this chapter in the only way we know for sharing our ideas with one another: We speak our minds and ask each other questions.

Deena Writes

Of necessity, this dialogue has taken the form of letters since, at the time we begin writing, Alex is incarcerated. I write to him on my computer, he writes to me with a stubby pencil on lined paper from the prison canteen. We worry that when his mail is screened (as it regularly is), the book's title *Subversive Social Action* and the theme of our chapter will raise a red flag for the security officers. I tuck my letters between photocopied crossword puzzles and magazine articles about the politics of Kraft Dinner to increase the likelihood that they will go unnoticed.

Shortly after Alex entered prison, I attended a stimulating gathering of international social work academics in the United States, where a discussion unfolded among the group on the question of how social workers contribute to change in the world. My jaded contribution to the conversation was that in North America it is not social workers who help change the world. In Canada and the United States, social workers' preoccupation with professionalization is a clear sign that we are invested in a system of privilege and alliance with power that makes true push-back unlikely. (I am certainly not the first to identify this; I was merely the first to say it in that discussion group.) Our social work system is too dependent on state funding for social workers to act freely as agents of conscience. But what about social work academics, who hold tenured positions and thus have highly protected social and economic privilege within an institution founded on the notion of free speech? There is a long history of universities as places of resistance and change, but that is not what happened here.

The question of how this story fits within the frame of extralegal or subversive social action feels very slippery to me. On the one hand, there was nothing illegal about the panel discussion – it was a typical university/community event, attended by students, faculty, and community members. My role in facilitating the booking of the room and posting ads was by the book and had been run by the dean beforehand. I was particularly cautious about following procedure, which in itself is telling, I think. The conference on the politics of dissent was also a perfectly legitimate university/community event; nevertheless, my subjective experience was that I had crossed a line, that I was being scrutinized and assessed. Indeed, when I was questioned in court as a potential legal surety for another activist seeking bail, the Crown prosecutor demanded to know how far my "progressive" leanings go and did my colleagues and I teach violence to our students? The lawyer acting for that same activist urged me not to speak out publicly after I became a surety, lest I jeopardize that individual's legal position. It seemed both ludicrous and dangerous at the same time, rather Kafkaesque – as so much of those events did. How do you understand this shifting landscape?

Alex Writes

I believe that to understand the nature of this "shifting landscape" requires a picture of the scene both before and after the shift, so that we can clearly identify that which has shifted. And in describing such a scene, the identity of the actors becomes of vital importance. You and I are both white, cis-hetero,[2] upper-middle class people, and our expectation of being is not to be criminalized. This expectation is central to understanding criminalization and how it can, as you say, "shift" landscapes. People of colour, Indigenous people, poor, queer, and disabled people in this country can have very different expectations (than what I might be used to) regarding what types of actions will be criminalized.

One of the dynamics that I spoke about during the panel discussions in question was that many people are targeted for criminalization by virtue of their very existence as people whose being and presence can undermine the hegemony of the dominant norms and identity of the culture. For example, people of colour in a society where whiteness is dominant, Indigenous people in a settler society. This dynamic is important to understanding the shift we are talking about. What shifts in between the before and the after pictures of the landscape? The laws have not been rewritten, nor has society been reconstructed. So what has changed is only the relationship of the actors to society vis-à-vis "the law." To understand that shift, I believe we need to interrogate the nature of "the law" and what it is for.

You have talked about a "subjective experience," a feeling that accompanies and embodies the shift we are examining. I would say that it is the experience of a moment in which your role in society, in relation to "the law," shifts. And it is in these moments of transgression, I think, when we can recognize, feel, and know what "the law" actually is and what it is for. The law is not a consensus or an agreement among the members of a population that it is said to apply to, nor is it a contract for the mutual protection of people; it is not something we have willingly entered into, consented to follow, or participated in shaping its terms, nor does it do anything to protect us. Strong legal codes do not make most people safer, and making people safe is not the interest of the law. "Law" is about upholding and enforcing a particular set of interests and a particular order. "Law" protects property and the order of a particular hierarchy – a white, patriarchal, colonial, and capitalist power structure. That is what "the law" is for and what laws have always been for.

The reason, I think, that you experienced a shift is because an otherwise legal action – a panel discussion and a conference on a university campus – became events that challenged and undermined that dominant power structure at a particular historical moment. Such challenge, regardless of its form, given what "the law" is for, will always be criminalized and targeted in response.

The panel discussion at Wilfrid Laurier University was the precursor to a larger panel event held three days later at Ryerson University in Toronto; it was after the latter event that I was rearrested. The panel was framed as a post-G20 discussion on prospects and imperatives for ongoing organizing for social change, titled "Strengthening Our Resolve: Movement Building and Ongoing Resistance to the G20 Agenda." The event sought to bring together theoretically diverse movements and featured noted speakers from migrant justice, anti-poverty, Indigenous sovereignty, queer liberation, feminist, union, and anarchist movements (with emphasis on the overlapping and intersectional nature of their relationships). Part of the framing of the discussion included the premise of a need to unite "the left" and heal from divisions that occurred within "the movement" as a result of, among other things, tactical disagreements surrounding the protests against the G20 Summit and the brutal police crackdown against these protests.

I had recently been released from jail on bail, with charges including an assortment of "conspiracy" offences stemming from my role in organizing against the G20 Summit. Eventually, through examination of the evidence against the "G20 Main Conspiracy Group," as well as peripheral documents (some obtained through Freedom of Information requests), it became clear that law enforcement's ferment and furious overreaction to a very typical anti-summit "riot" (quite tame by global standards) was but part of an intensive sustained operation designed to attack a burgeoning network of activists from various intersecting social justice movements (particularly Indigenous sovereignty, migrant justice, and anarchist). Identifying this attack and emphasizing the need for us to continue to build and expand these networks was the core of my contribution to the panel discussions, and the events functioned as a very clear subversion of the state's intent in its attack on protests following the G20 "riot," that goal having been, in addition to discouraging dissent, to create and exploit division and fear, thereby weakening movement networks. The panels were targeted because they subverted the interests of state "law" enforcement. The conference you and others organized in response to that targeting was a continuation of that subversion.

As people who entered this landscape as actors with a tremendous degree of systemic privilege, it is in these moments when it becomes possible to recognize something that people from targeted communities experience constantly: the feeling of being targeted. The subjective experience of being scrutinized and assessed is something that many people have to live with on a day-to-day basis, just for being Indigenous, black, or trans (for example) in a white heterosexual patriarchal settler society. In the cases of people from targeted communities, the reaction of "the law" to perfectly legal activities, or even a person's mere presence in society, will often serve to transgress the hegemony of dominant norms, to upset order. Something similar happens when the content of discussion or conferences similarly challenges that order – when dissent, in itself, becomes resistance.

One of the things you mentioned in leading up to the question about shifting landscapes was a reference to the academy as "an institution founded on the notion of free speech." And while it is true that universities and student movements have played very important roles in the history of modern social change, I think it is necessary to problematize the notion of their being founded on free speech. It has been suggested by people much more learned than I that the academy is, rather, one of the primary sites where the dominant order is reproduced through the authorized production of knowledge. The notional respect given to "free speech" is part of how that authority is maintained, simultaneously maintaining the societal conception of power as democratic. And I would suggest that part of what made the events so dangerous was the fact that their taking place on campus served to introduce their content into that *authorized* body of knowledge that is the product of academic discourse.

The bail condition that I was alleged to have breached by participating on the panel was to not be a part of any "public demonstration." It is obvious that neither panels nor conferences are what we normally consider to be public demonstrations. But in order to enable "the law" to serve the interests of dominant order, a "demonstration" became defined for the purpose of my bail conditions as "any public meeting in which any political or moral views are expressed" and the police and Crown attorneys in turn asserted the authority to police – to surveil and curtail – campus-based discussion as if it were a rally or street protest. This is another part of the shift that occurred. It is important to recognize that a much broader, deeper, and more significant shift occurred in the wake of 9/11, when the activities of Muslim academics became severely scrutinized and assessed by "law" enforcement.

You have talked about the response of the university administration and faculty as "profoundly disappointing." But I wonder if they ever understood what was happening. Do you think there was a collective recognition that something was shifting, that university activities were coming under the gaze of "law" enforcement? If not, what does that mean? If yes, then I wonder why the response was so, as you put it, "limp"? Is it possible for academic or professional social work to respond in a more confrontational or otherwise more meaningful way, given their respective relationships to the system? And if it is, why did that not happen in this case? In what ways have you (and the Faculty of Social Work) responded to the ongoing and pre-existing criminalizations that are always taking place according to the system and its order?

Deena Writes

You are asking the question that I have asked myself for the past three years: Did my colleagues and the administration fail to grasp the implications and portents of what was happening, or did they understand it and choose not to confront it? In grappling with this question it is tempting to distance myself from the cynicism and/or apathy I initially inferred from the behaviour of colleagues and the administration. Some of my colleagues who don't carry the range of privileges that I do may, I'm sure, have shrugged off the horror of a middle-class white, heterosexual faculty member as obnoxious naïveté. There was no new story here for them, and they need their energy for their own struggles.

Your other question, however – the one about how I and my faculty have responded to ongoing and pre-existing criminalizations – compels me to interrogate my own patterns of response and non-response. I cannot know what kept the Faculty of Social Work as a collective from rising up, and I have no right to try to interpret my colleagues' experience. What I can do is try to formulate some understanding of why I was moved to rise up on this occasion and have failed to do so at other times, around other subversions of justice. Since the time of the mass arrests, the unlawful detentions and treatment of protesters and bystanders, I have felt acutely aware of how my personal privilege has protected me from having to acknowledge what happens daily to those without such privilege. My outrage about the targeting and arrest of both my sons and their friends and about the aggressive, unjust treatment to which they were subjected is the outrage of every mother whose children have been targeted in some way. My outrage was not just about "How could this happen here?" but "How could this happen to *us*?" Our family had never before encountered "the system" in a way that we couldn't ultimately navigate successfully. Over and over, the response from family, friends, and colleagues to the G20 story and images was "Are we really in Canada?" We were all coated in layers of privilege that had protected us from having to know that these things happen here, day in and day out – to Others.

The introduction of secret surveillance into a classroom at my university was a betrayal that happens in groups the world over, and here in Canada, where legal activities pose a threat to ruling powers. I knew this before the G20 Summit of 2010, but I know it in a whole different way now. The complacency that comes with believing in democracy, freedom of speech, and power to the people is a truly wondrous phenomenon. When that belief is shattered, as mine was that summer and thereafter, there is an internal shift. The awareness of being helpless under the gaze of law enforcement that actually has nothing to do with safety and everything to do with power, as you put it, is transformational. I would like to say, "There is no going back," and yet I have gone back. My fury is just under the surface, my conversations have changed, my analysis has changed, my work has changed, but the total immersion in activist thinking and activities that consumed me for the first year or more after the arrests has not continued. I can feel that wilful blindness creeping back. I have remained afraid and angry, but I have not remained fully animated – largely, I suspect, because I don't have to. Somehow, I believe, I have developed a two-chambered perspective: one that gets the reality and one that has regressed to complacency. My social location allows that; as long as I benefit from things as they are, I allow myself to be lulled into complacency. As long as my days are full of activities that make my life as good as it is, I can tell myself it's reasonable to claim, "I'm too busy." There are so many causes that ought to be championed under the current political and economic regime, one risks being overwhelmed by a sense of helplessness. Imperviousness is so much easier.

There is also the issue of fear for one's own material and social safety. I have experienced this in my own life before, as a woman and as a Jewish person, so it was not entirely new to me; but in the latter cases, I am very clear about which parts of my social identity put me at risk. Feeling unsafe in the aftermath of the G20 because of who I am, however, was utterly ambiguous for me – despite being palpable and very present. It is possible that some of my colleagues may have been fearful about getting involved. Some of them are more vulnerable than others because of their social identities or their status within the university. Nevertheless, my sense was that they were not *alarmed* about what the signs meant. Did they already know and I was late to the party? Did they not get it because it still had not touched them in a uniquely personal way? As for the leadership of the university, I suppose it's obvious that they were not going to bite the hand that feeds them. The government that funds institutions of higher education is the government on whose watch the G20 injustices had unfolded.

So the final question is: Why were radical activist graduate students and faculty from *outside* of social work so much readier to get involved in organizing a push-back than folks in social work? Only one social work student became actively involved in organizing our conference on the criminalization of dissent; not coincidentally, she had a long history of radical activism in the community. One social work faculty member who was very active in organizing and implementing the conference had been a dissident in her home country and is hypervigilant about signs of social injustice and political danger. A handful of other postgrad students and colleagues joined us explicitly out of a sense of solidarity and concern for me and for you. What I'm questioning here is: Why is it that the folks who are professionally (and genuinely) committed to social justice were not the ones who took up the cause – especially since the incursion had been under our own roof?

Perhaps the issue was too explicitly political. In this country the social work profession may see economic and social justice issues as lying within our domain, but not "political" issues. Can it be that we see economic and social justice issues as being unconnected to political ones, despite the mantra of "the personal is political"? This is unlike what happens in other parts of the world, like South Africa, South America, and India, for example, where social workers seem to be more a part of on-the-ground political struggles for social justice. Other chapters in this book tell stories that are shining examples of that kind of political solidarity. In Canada and the United States, however, we have worked very hard on burnishing our identities as professionals. "Professionalism" and "professionalization" are prevalent concerns, and they have to do with developing standards and ethical codes but also with staking out our territory, guarding our knowledge turf, and getting the respect from other professions that we believe we deserve. Professionalism presumes acceptance of principles and behaviours that are socially acceptable and responsible. However laudable, this seems to automatically preclude some of the aims and strategies of radical activism.

We North American social workers have also heavily favoured the clinical tradition of counselling, therapy, and casework for many decades now. Students who enter our Master of Social Work program often have little patience, at least early on, for all the talk about diversity, marginalization, power, and oppression that we expose them to. Most of them have difficulty seeing how social justice issues are relevant to therapeutic and psychological ones. In North America, the early history of social work – whether clinical or community oriented – is rooted in the concepts of adjustment and adaptation, so it's not so surprising, perhaps, that resisting the system is not a mainstream social work value for us. There are strands within social work worldwide that do explicitly expose the implication of social work as a profession in perpetuating social relationships of unequal power, but these are not yet considered "mainstream" voices. I suppose what I'm saying is that the culture of Canadian social work as a profession does not lend itself to collective political activism; it may, in fact, all but rule it out.

I think about all the young people who were surveilled, arrested, handcuffed, caged, labelled, abused, and harassed in connection with the G20 Summit. Many of you spent time in detention centres and prisons and/or on house arrest. Your lives were taken away from you for months and years. I don't know a single social worker to whom that happened, and I include myself, of course.

There's an old joke that goes something like this: "Well, that's enough about me. Let's talk about you.... What do *you* think of me?" What I'd like to ask you is what the perception is among activists of whether social workers can be allies in the many struggles for social justice.

Alex Writes

I think most activists in this country probably do not spend much time on the question of whether or not social workers are or can be allies to or a part of social justice movements – at least not what we might call "radical" activists. But I do know that activists who work as service providers or advocates do interact with social workers, and I also imagine that "social work" is a common consideration and career choice for more liberally minded people who may also recognize themselves as "activists."

I should mention that after all these years, having read both your books, and acquired my own university degree, I still cannot really identify what a "social worker" does. "Social work" is not something that I often consider outside of academic and state-agency frameworks, though I am well aware of the prevalent role that various forms of therapy occupy in clinical and private practice. But for various reasons, clinical and private practice social work do not register as central to the repertoire that belong to the field of social work understood as the work of bringing about social change and social justice. From a social justice perspective, especially a radical anti-capitalist, anti-colonial point of view, in the neo-liberal era, the notion of private practice social work registers as categorically antithetical to contemporary radical discourse.

When I talk to people who work as front-line service providers or to advocates who live and/or work in heavily marginalized communities or neighbourhoods, I hear that other than the explicitly negative associations of social workers as people working for government agencies that are part of the systemic and structural mechanisms by which the state monitors, regulates, and controls people's lives, radicals often have very little experience of dealing with "social workers" per se. Various community agencies and non-profits may employ people with social work backgrounds, but it seems to be rare that those individuals interface with the community or other agencies as professional social workers – again, that may be an incorrect assumption, but I think it reflects the lack of a presence for "social work" and "social workers" in activist visions of processes for radical social change. Professional social workers are understood, I believe, more often as *barriers* to social change and justice than as agents of it. I tend to think of professional social workers as being either part of agencies that take people's children away and kick people off of social assistance, or as academics, though I do recognize that clinical and "community" social work are tremendously broad subject fields. You have problematized the notion of professionalism and professionalization, saying that they "have to do with developing standards and ethical codes," going so far as to conclude that "the culture of Canadian social work as a profession does not lend itself to collective political activism." I agree with you. I think professionalism plays an important role in the capitalist system, which includes the normalization of state dominance and regularization of the authority of the system and its laws. The enforcement of a particular set of "standards and ethical codes" is very much a central part of the ways that modern (and "postmodern") systems of oppression operate, and so professionalism, I think, is often experienced as one of the ways that both whiteness and patriarchy operate in society, through the maintenance and regulation of authority. So any profession is inherently immediately suspect, and despite the self-description, as a professionalized field "social work" is likely to be rejected as carrying meaningful potential as an engine of social change. This in part is exacerbated by the fact that "social work" seems to rarely be directly connected or accountable to the communities its professionals (and academics) operate in. In many ways, this is anathema to the types of structures and methods "radicals" are trying to develop and support for the communities they live and work in.

In the case of professional social work operating through community agencies or non-profit organizations, where "social workers" can be seen to be working "on the ground," my perception is that there remains that lack of accountability, as the work tends to still be beholden to funding, either governmental, institutional, or from sources based on private-donor campaigns. Further, these workers are still operating in a professional capacity, rooted in their professional and academic cultures and identities, usually not as members of the communities they are operating in. And further still, funding access, mobility, and other issues create particular power dynamics between "social workers" and represented community members, while similar power dynamics operate within communities struggling against targeting and marginalization; this means that power and the alienating effects of professionalism (and other aspects of the work of "social work") play a large role in determining which community members have access to both directional input and services themselves.

The other way that I conceive of "social work" is as an academic discipline – which is obviously connected to the problem and processes of professionalization and professionalism. I have tended to imagine academic social work as a relatively liberal academic discipline – it has never struck me as a field that is especially radical in its criticalness or openness, and definitely not in terms of praxis. And not because it couldn't be; there are obviously very radical, if not revolutionary conceptions of what "social work" is and could be, and there must be examples of radical social work praxis, too. Knowing I was working on this section of the chapter, a friend suggested that I read Chambon, Irving, and Epstein's *Reading Foucault for Social Work* (1999). In reading that I found that almost all of my concerns and impressions – the problematics of professionalism, community accountability, liberalism versus radicalism, social change versus social maintenance – are mostly things that have been addressed more than a decade ago within academic social work. But for some reasons, as you have pointed out, people involved in and engaged with radical community organizing and radical activism are not the people who are tending to end up as students in Canadian Social Work programs. And so part of the question is, why is that?

When I make the distinction between liberalism and radicalism, what I intend is to distinguish between approaches that seek to fundamentally alter the root causes of systemic and structural oppressions, that seek to build new models of community social relationships, and to build anti-capitalist, anti-colonial alternative economic and political structures. One of the ways we would describe this project of resistance and empowerment is as decolonization. By liberalism I mean a conception of social justice rooted in philanthropic benevolence and a charitable model of social change – an approach that is predisposed to coaching and counselling assimilation and accommodation, preparing people for success in a colonial capitalist system, rather than empowering people and their communities to make their own genuinely autonomous decisions about visions, directions, and processes.

If the question is simply whether or not activists think that "social workers" can be allies, neither of the above arguments pertaining to academic or professional social work in any way precludes "social workers" as individuals from acting as and being understood as allies to or participants in social struggle. From a radical perspective though, there are deeply structural and systemic reasons why it seems to be intrinsically unlikely that this will happen; from a radical perspective, I think "social work" appears to be inherently steered toward maintaining dominant culture and social "order." In fact, I think that its rootedness in classical liberal values – a philanthropic/charity-based model for "social justice" – serves as a structural release-valve mechanism that oppressive systems keep in place to maintain the commitment to "benevolence" that undergirds the population's submission to modern and postmodern exertions of power, a release valve for the pressures built up through the experience of the oppressive nature of capitalist relationships to the state, the land, community, and to each other. That is to say, liberalism has always functioned as one of capitalism's structural mechanisms by which "the masses" are managed to prevent revolt and escalated dissent, and to maintain social "buy-in" and support for the authority of the state. While critical theory like that expressed by Chambon, Irving, and Epstein (1999) may be a more radical liberalism, even that does not transgress the function of "social work" vis-à-vis "order." They remain theories of accommodating oppression and assimilating to the colonial-capitalist system, and they do not transgress the role of professionalism by employing their systemic authority to advocate or enable genuine empowerment and autonomy, let alone organized resistance.

But perhaps the better question is not about what so-called activists think about "social workers," but about what people who are the objects of "social work" – those objectified by it – think: Do they see so-called social workers as allies? Again, in my experience, friends and allies who interact with "social workers," whether as imprisoned people, as parents living in poverty, or as community organizers, tend toward experiences of "social workers" as agents of an oppressive state, though they may not be broadly representative.

While unable to totally escape the nature of the role of "social work" as part of the systemic mechanisms of assimilation and legitimization, there is still the possibility for "social workers" to function as buffers for communities and individuals, to mitigate, offset, and delay some of the impacts of the state's oppressions, and also to work to help build structures of genuine empowerment, autonomy, and resistance.

So to hone my question, what has "social work" done with radical critiques to enable individual "social workers" (and "social work" in theory) to function as allies to people in communities that are otherwise targeted by the state, and what happened to/with these elements in the response to the targeting of social justice movement events on campus? Because, to answer your question, I do not think that activists or community radicals view "social work(ers)" (broadly speaking) as allies of movements of resistance, movements for social justice. Of course, though, individuals who are "social workers" often are or perform the role of allies, but this is rarely experienced as inherently being a part of their identity as "social workers."

Deena Writes

I find this analysis helpful, although I have to confess that it makes me profoundly uncomfortable. That discomfort is important, as it signals a disruption of that which has hitherto been far too comfortable.

Your comment that you still "cannot really identify what a 'social worker' does" gets to the heart of a never-ending identity crisis within our field. It's something that we wonder and argue about among ourselves all the time. It's a strange field insofar as it is hybridized on several levels. Our roots in North America are very much in the soil of philanthropy and benevolence. There have been isolated historical instances of social workers living in the communities they work alongside; some of these were pre-professionalization, though some have been more recent. The role of the social worker engaged in community development and community outreach work has elicited some serious hand-wringing, soul-searching, and theorizing about the nature of the activist/professional as inevitable outsider. It's one reason that approaches to this work now emphasize consultation, collaboration, and empowerment rather than the older model of charismatic leadership. Anti-oppressive practice and critical social work have shaken up traditional ways of thinking about professional social work in terms of epistemological underpinnings and the role of the profession in the larger enterprise of social control of marginalized groups. The child welfare and mental health sectors have taken a particularly hard hit in this regard. And yet, concurrent with this critical perspective in many (but by no means all) social work education programs, the practices that signal our implication in social control continue. (There's that bi-cameral perspective again.) You ask why.

I would venture to say that critical social work is much stronger on theory than it is on methods of practice, almost by definition. To adhere to any particular method or model necessarily decontextualizes the practice and at the same time relegates it to the domain of "professional" or "expert" knowledge. I can tell you that it makes teaching practice from a critical perspective very challenging. Professionalism demands clarity of purpose, practice, and outcomes. Students and practitioners in regulated organizations crave these certainties, often so do service users, but critical social work challenges this stance aggressively. In the universities, at the same time that many of us (by no means all of us) struggle to establish a critical approach, we find ourselves inundated by an increasingly outcome-oriented ethos both as an approach to education in the academy and to practise in the profession. In other words, it is an uphill battle for a radical perspective to gain ground.

The aspect of your analysis that is most unsettling is the assessment of the limits to any claim to radicalism within an essentially liberal enterprise. You are saying that even if we all adopted a critical social work stance, we cannot escape the constraints of our embeddedness in the structures of neo-liberal capitalism. Unless we're willing to pursue decolonizing practices as our Indigenous colleagues are doing, then our profile as catalysts for social change and social justice must remain shadowy, even non-existent. I have no doubt that individual Canadian social workers put themselves on the line (literally and figuratively) daily, but as a collective, as a profession and its gatekeepers, I don't believe we will be the ones to create a world that is socially just.

This conversation has been an important one for me. It has given me an opportunity to explore some issues about myself and my professional world that have been haunting me. As usual, our conversation has raised more questions than it has answered, but I always tell my students that this is the only way to keep learning and moving forward. Your perspective from outside the professionalized domain of social work, as someone who is always (even from inside the prison) involved in working for radical social change, has given me some helpful ways to think about the questions that inspired this chapter. Welcome out. Welcome home.

Notes

1 About two-thirds of the way through the writing, Alex completed the mandatory part of his sentence (he had been denied parole earlier), and he is currently unincarcerated.
2 Editor's note: In essence, "cis-gendered" (or "cis-sexual") refers to any person who does not identify as transgender.

Reference

Chambon, A., Irving, A., & Epstein, L. (Eds). (1999). *Reading Foucault for social work*. New York: Columbia University Press.

CHAPTER 2

Challenging State Aggression against Indigenous Australians

John Tomlinson

In September 1973 a 7-year-old Aboriginal girl, Nola, was collected from her white foster parents in Darwin and returned to her family who lived on a remote Northern Territory outstation. For years her Indigenous parents had unsuccessfully sought her return. I was the social worker who handed the young girl to her father and was subsequently suspended from the public service. My suspension resulted in the first strike ever by social workers in Australia. I will describe Nola's return to her family and reflect upon the initial aftermath of Nola's reunion with her community and the impact it had on social workers and others involved. In the latter part of this chapter, I will discuss the relevance of Nola's return to the ongoing struggle of Indigenous Australians to retain custody of their children and look at some wider social justice policy issues.

▶ SETTING THE SCENE

After working as a social worker in the Department of Social Security in Brisbane for six months, in 1965 I transferred to the Welfare Branch[1] of the Commonwealth Department of the Interior in Darwin. The population of the city at the time was about 20,000, many of whom were public servants or armed services personnel. Significant sections of the population had Greek, Asian, continental European, or Aboriginal origins, and many families combined some or all such origins. People of total Aboriginal descent[2] lived mainly on Bagot Reserve opposite the air force base or on the fringes of the town. About a kilometre down the road from Bagot Reserve, the conservative Aboriginal Inland Mission ran a series of cottages in which a foster couple would care for children of part-Aboriginal descent (Cummings, 1990). It was run along lines not dissimilar to the Kalin Compound of the 1930s described by Xavier Herbert in his 1975 semi-biographical novel, *Poor Fellow My Country*. Children of part-Aboriginal descent were separated from their mothers by police or Welfare Branch officers and taken to Kalin Compound to be raised as whites in large dormitories – their Aboriginal mothers were not allowed into the Compound. Speaking Aboriginal languages was forbidden. Some mothers managed to keep in touch by talking to their children through the back fence.

The full extent of government and institutional policies of removing children of partial Aboriginal descent from their Aboriginal communities became known in the 1990s as the "stolen generations." The century-long policy of removing children of part-Aboriginal descent was finally revealed by the National Inquiry into the Separation of Aboriginal and Torres Strait Islander Children from Their Families in the 1997 report entitled *Bringing Them Home*. But this is getting ahead of the story.

In 1965 the federal Liberal coalition government was firmly committed to the policy of assimilation. Assimilation was defined at the 1961 meeting of federal and state ministers in charge of Aboriginal affairs as follows:

> The policy of assimilation means in the view of all Australian governments that all Aborigines and part-Aborigines are expected eventually to attain the same manner of living as other Australians and to live as members of a single Australian community, enjoying the same rights and privileges, accepting the same responsibilities, observing the same customs and influenced by the same beliefs, hopes and loyalties as other Australians. (Cited in Pittock, 1969, pp. 12–13)

The definition was changed in 1965 in response to pressure, "so that now the policy officially seeks (rather than means) that all persons of Aboriginal descent will choose to attain (*rather than are expected eventually to attain*) a *similar* (rather than the same) manner and standard of living. The words 'observing the same customs' are omitted, and so too is reference to their 'being influenced by the same beliefs'" (Pittock, 1969, p. 13; original emphasis).

After twenty-three years of unbroken rule by the conservative Liberal coalition, the Whitlam Labor government was elected in December 1972. Whitlam had campaigned using the slogan "It's Time," and not the least of the foreshadowed changes were in the area of Aboriginal affairs and social welfare more generally. Gordon Bryant, who for years had been an executive member of the Federal Council of Aboriginal Advancement, was made minister for Aboriginal affairs. The incoming government spoke about introducing Aboriginal land rights and replacing the policy of assimilation with one of integration and self-determination. It was considered that under such policies Indigenous Australians would be free to choose the aspects of other cultures they wished to adopt and those of their own culture they wished to retain.

In Darwin in 1965 I found the government's policy of assimilating Aborigines was dramatically on display in the five stages of galvanized iron Kingstrand housing on Bagot Reserve. The first stage was a tin shed with a dirt floor and external fireplace, gradually evolving to a concrete floor, then a concrete floor with a floor covering. The advanced houses had internal stoves and cupboards to store food and clothing, floor-to-ceiling interior walls, beds and mattresses, and even toilets. The superintendent of the Reserve was supposed to assess the level of understanding of European sophistication incoming Indigenous families had "achieved" and assign them accordingly to one of the stages. Families would progress through the various stages. The actual process of assigning people to a house was much more haphazard than that. There was an added contradiction in that families were encouraged to eat in a communal dining hall.

During the 1960s the long-serving director of welfare, whose brother-in-law was a federal minister, closely supervised the minutiae of life on Aboriginal settlements.

I had come to Darwin fully believing that an individual (neo-Freudian or psychodynamic) casework approach was the most useful approach. In 1968 I returned to work at the Department of Social Security in Brisbane, knowing there was little that individual casework had to offer Indigenous people in the Territory. The three years I spent in Darwin showed me that the focus of social work should be directed toward working with the community to solve the issues they identified. The senior people in the Welfare Branch rejected such an approach. After returning to Brisbane I undertook an honours degree in Anthropology and Sociology and a research master's degree in Social Work that involved working with the financially impoverished Aboriginal and Torres Strait Islander community of South Brisbane.

I transferred back to the Welfare Branch in May 1973 after it had been moved to the newly established Department of Aboriginal Affairs. An energetic Canberra public servant had been installed as director of welfare. It appeared that exciting times lay ahead.

▶ The Story of Nola[3]

Nola was born in September 1966 at an outstation on the Cadell River, 50 kilometres from the Aboriginal settlement at Maningrida in Arnhem Land. She had arrived some weeks prematurely and was taken by her mother, Nellie, to Maningrida hospital and then flown to Darwin hospital. Initially Nola suffered intermittent bouts of ill health, and she spent her first eight months either at a government-run children's home or at the hospital, depending on her state of health.

The hospital's senior social worker made several requests for the Welfare Branch to locate an Aboriginal family with whom Nola could be fostered. The Branch at the time would only place children of Aboriginal descent with close relatives and often would refuse to pay foster allowance or would pay a lesser amount than they would pay a white foster family. The justification provided to me at the time was that it was common for Aboriginal families to take in children of relatives and in any case it cost less to raise an Aboriginal child in an Aboriginal family than in a white one. There was no active attempt to recruit Aboriginal families into the foster program and the Branch found no Aboriginal family for Nola.

The hospital's senior social worker wanted Nola out of the government-run home because she feared that Nola was not receiving sufficient individual attention and could become institutionalized and so she recruited a white foster family, Mr and Mrs Brown. It was several months before anyone from the Welfare Branch called on the Browns to see how they were managing with Nola. On 4 July 1967 the hospital's senior social worker wrote to the director of the Welfare Branch as follows: "It is again stressed that the need for long-term plans for Nola is imperative, so that when she is sufficiently robust to return to Maningrida, adequate arrangements are available for her care. The possibility of arranging for her to be cared for at Maningrida by another Aboriginal woman could perhaps be kept in mind, depending on her own mother's ability to care for her" (Northern Territory Government Archives, Darwin, File No. AW363).

Nola's father Jack had initially agreed to the temporary fostering of Nola, but in early 1968 when she was about eighteen months old Jack considered she should be well enough to come home and demanded that Nola be returned to her family. The superintendent of Maningrida, John Hunter, urged Nola's return. But reserve superintendents, while being the Welfare Branch's senior personnel on the spot, were under the control of the Branch's director. During the 1960s and early 1970s the director of the Welfare Branch ignored superintendents' views unless they concurred with his own.

In July 1968, on the second visit by an officer from the Welfare Branch, the Browns were advised that Nola would shortly be returning to Maningrida. Mr Brown approached the acting director of the Branch, Ted Evans, who instructed that Nola was not to be returned to her family until a full review was carried out. There was nothing on file to indicate the need for a review. The senior officer at Maningrida had urged Nola's return. A review was not carried out. The welfare officer who had been visiting the Browns was told she would not need to visit so often. She had made only two visits to the foster child in thirteen months. For several years, following Ted Evans's direction, the only contact the Browns had with the Branch was the receiving of the fostering payment.

In 1969 Nola's brother Jack John was born. He too did not thrive and was brought to Darwin, where he stayed until early 1973. The nursing sister and Superintendent Hunter reported that, on his return to his family, Jack John progressed satisfactorily and suggested that if Nola was to be returned it should be as soon as possible.

In May 1973 I had been promoted to a class 2, acting 3 social work position in charge of welfare services in the top half of the Northern Territory. In June of that year Elizabeth Lovett, the class 1 social worker who had been working with Jack John and Nola, brought their files to my attention. I put plans in place to ensure that Nola had some contact with her 12-year-old brother Leo, who was brought in from Maningrida. When Elizabeth Lovett informed Mr Brown that Leo was coming to town so that Nola could have contact with members of her family, he said he did not think that was a good idea, as Nola had "no time for the Aboriginal race." Despite such advice the visit went ahead.

Mr Brown feared that despite his earlier success in convincing Ted Evans to stop Nola's return to her family, the situation had changed and Nola might really be going home. He therefore contacted Gordon Bryant, the minister for Aboriginal affairs. The minister's secretary asked me to meet with the minister in Alice Springs. The director of welfare told me to stay in Darwin, and he went to Alice Springs in my stead to discuss the case with the minister. Gordon Bryant ordered that Nola should not be removed from the Browns but that Jack should be assisted through the Aboriginal Legal Aid Service to initiate an action in the Supreme Court against the Welfare Branch to regain custody of Nola.

I discussed the options open to us with several social workers (but not Miss Lovett because she had to work closely with the Browns). It was agreed that in face of any public consternation I was to be the "fall guy" who acted alone. I met and discussed the case with Bill Ryan, the director of Aboriginal Legal Aid, and with one of Aboriginal Legal Aid's lawyers. We were looking to reunite Nola with her natural family and for a way to do it that would distance the minister and the director from any direct responsibility for the return of Nola. In addition, Bill Ryan was the son of a Gurindji mother and a white father. Methodist missionaries on Croker Island had brought him up and as a result he was strongly opposed to Aboriginal children being raised in non-Aboriginal families. I had known Bill before he become director of Aboriginal Legal Aid when he had worked with the Welfare Branch as a welfare officer.

Weighing on my mind was the obvious public service and political pull the white foster family had already displayed. There had also been a couple of court cases in the previous decade where Northern Territory Aboriginal parents had not been able to regain custody of their child after a relatively short period of separation (for details, see Tomlinson 1978). Another major influence was the considerable number of Aboriginal children who had been removed from their Aboriginal communities on one pretext or another, being brought up in a white environment. We were determined that this would not happen to Nola.

My commitment to challenging European views about what was in Aboriginal people's best interests began in 1963, when as an undergraduate student I had spent a month visiting several Aboriginal communities in North Queensland at the suggestion of an Aboriginal leader associated with the Federal Council of Aboriginal Advancement (Taffe, 2005). I sat with community leaders and discussed the issues that troubled them most. The taking of children, low wages, poor rations, white police and superintendents' refusal to listen to them, and the racial discrimination they encountered from other Australians topped the list. By the time I returned to the Northern Territory I had worked full-time for two years on a community work project with the Indigenous community of South Brisbane and was committed to work with the Aboriginal community on the issues that troubled them. I was then and am now indebted to the many patient Indigenous people who made a considerable effort to teach me to understand events from their perspective. Recovering children from the white system was a major priority, and we hoped that Nola would be the first of many to return home.

A plane ticket was organized to bring Jack in from Maningrida supposedly so he could initiate lodging his Supreme Court action against the Welfare Branch. There was no doubt in the minds of those associated with the plan that Nola and Jack would return to Maningrida in an airplane chartered by Aboriginal Legal Aid Services, because we trusted Bill Ryan to carry through on the plan.

Elizabeth Lovett collected Nola from the Browns' house and informed Mr Brown that Nola would be seeing her father. When Jack, Leo, and Nola turned up at the agreed meeting spot, I was meeting Jack for the first time. Jack said to me, "I have my daughter back. Now I will take her to Maningrida." At this point I should have declared that his statement formally terminated the fostering arrangement and that Nola was back in the custody of her parents who were her legal guardians. (Prior to this point in time, this declaration would not have effected Nola's return to her family because the director of the Welfare Branch would not have let it happen and there would have been no way of getting Nola back to her community.) I don't know why I did not seize that opportunity. I suppose it was confusion about involving Elizabeth and the desire to stick strictly to the agreed plan. So I told Elizabeth I would take Nola back to the Browns, and the plan unfolded as we had agreed it would.

I took Jack, Nola, and Leo to rendezvous with Bill Ryan and then filled in a couple of hours to give Bill – along with Jack, Leo, and Nola – time to be on his way to Maningrida en route to Cadell River (Nola's home community). Later I went to the Browns' house and told Mr Brown I had left Nola at Bagot Reserve and subsequently could not find her. I left a note at the director's house saying something similar.

Everything was pretty quiet for the next 13 days, and it appeared we had been successful. By 13 September, Superintendent of Maningrida John Hunter had advised the Welfare Branch's head office that Nola had taken to Maningrida "like a duck to water." Crown Law advised (according to a file note) that it would not be possible for the Welfare Branch to have Nola returned to Darwin "in view of the fact that the custody of Nola apparently lay with her mother and natural father" (Northern Territory Government Archives, Darwin, File No. AW 363).

▶ THE PRESS

After the fortnight's lull all hell broke loose. The story broke on the front page of *The Australian* under the banner "Aboriginal Girl Abducted from Foster Parents."[4] In the stories that followed, Nola was supposed to have been raped, married to an old man, stabbed with a spear, and all of this was supposed to have occurred at the hands of her own people. None of these allegations was true.

Around the world, many journalists wrote of Nola and her return to Cadell River. Most accounts were lurid regurgitations of the original line run in *The Australian*. American and Dutch people sent the minister money to buy her back, believing that Nola's family only wanted her back so that they could sell her. The libellous statements printed by the media would have been inconceivable had they been made describing whites, because they would have sued for libel.

By far the most comprehensive and accurate journalistic account of Nola's removal from her European foster home was written by Gerri Willesee and published on 12 November 1973 in a most remarkable place, *Woman's Day* (pp. 2–5 and p. 13). Willesee, a month after Nola's return, had spent a fortnight living in Nola's community at Cadell River and had also spoken with her European foster parents in Darwin. Willesee described the outstation as a hive of activity, with art and craft work, hunting, fishing, cultural ceremonies, and a thirty-hectare fruit and vegetable garden. She wrote: "Despite Press reports to the contrary, there is no communication problem between Nola and her family. Nola is slowly learning Burera (her Aboriginal language) and her brothers all speak English as well as she does" (p. 5).

Willesee makes the point that "the loss of Nola has been made worse for the Browns by their belief in many completely untrue stories about Aboriginal people and customs" (p. 13).

▶ THE AFTERMATH

On 5 October 1973 five public service charges (institutional charges outside of the civil and criminal justice systems) were laid against me, and I was suspended from duty. The charges related to refusing the directions of the minister and misleading the director of the Welfare Branch. On 8 November 1973 I was reinstated but demoted to a class 1 social work salary. On 2 January 1974, following the Welfare Branch's refusal to reinstate me to my original position, the Welfare Branch social workers, with the exception of Elizabeth Lovett and one other, staged the first social work strike in Australia. It lasted three weeks. (Elizabeth felt that I had erred in not giving the Browns an opportunity to say goodbye to Nola.) The striking social workers had several other demands, namely, replacing the grocery voucher system of welfare relief with a cheque system, codifying the basis on which determinations of granting or refusing welfare assistance were made, employing more social workers, introducing fifty new Aboriginal welfare officers to work alongside the social workers, and giving foster payments to Aboriginal families who were looking after children other than their own at the same rate of payment as other foster parents. In the short term, none of these demands were met.

Minister for Aboriginal Affairs Gordon Bryant instructed his departmental head in October 1973 that in future "there should be no placement of Aboriginal children with European foster parents except in an emergency and then only for short periods" (Northern Territory Government Archives, Darwin, Telex ABAUS85262 to ABAUS AA62471 on 22/10/73). (Although this was one of the demands of the strikers, this instruction was not fully implemented.) This minister also issued the Aboriginal Legal Aid Service with the instruction that henceforth "it must confine itself to its role of legal assistance to Aboriginal people and general subjects such as land rights." Bryant's instruction limiting Aboriginal Legal Aid's power to support political and social initiatives, which had been set down as part of the Service's original charter, interfered with Indigenous Australians' capacity to become truly self-determining.

That Bryant, who had for so many years championed unpopular Aboriginal causes, argued that an Aboriginal girl should stay in the custody of a white foster family when her natural parents were legally entitled to have her returned, presents a bit of an enigma. He was under attack from many public service and parliamentary opponents and was soon to lose his portfolio. He became minister for the Australian Capital Territory in late 1973.

After Bill Ryan announced he had been involved in transporting Nola home, several white Aboriginal Legal Aid Service board members launched an attack on him and the directions the Aboriginal Legal Aid Service had recently taken. Ken White (2005), an experienced journalist who worked in Darwin at the time, in a chapter entitled "The Abduction of Nola Brown," details some of the activities of the two white lawyers working for Aboriginal Legal Aid at the time. He suggests that after witnessing the ferocity of local white opinion about the return of Nola, the lawyers joined in the criticism of Bill Ryan. Some of the whites associated with Aboriginal Legal Aid called a meeting of the governing council when Bill Ryan was out of town. The governing council decided to replace him with a more compliant director who would be less likely to upset the wider community.

Following the uproar in the press about Nola's return to her own community, most states of Australia undertook detailed reviews of all the Aboriginal children in foster care. This was only the start of the process, and it took determined vigilance by Aboriginal child care agencies and other Aboriginal individuals and agencies to keep the various state-run children's departments from slipping back into running a white fostering system for Aboriginal children. Ken White (2005, p. 70) notes that even after Gordon Bryant's instruction that Aboriginal children should only be fostered with Aboriginal families the Adoption Section of the Welfare Branch in the Northern Territory interpreted the instruction to apply only to children of total Aboriginal descent.

Nola returned to her traditional country, and from reports I received over the years she has been happy to be with her family. She eventually married and had children, none of whom needed to be looked after by the state.

▶ It's All in the Past, People Say

It is important to ask whether what happened to Nola was something that happened only in the Northern Territory in the 1960s and 1970s or whether it occurs elsewhere and to this day.

There are two parts to this question and the *Bringing Them Home* report clearly shows that the removal of Aboriginal children from Aboriginal communities, particularly those of partial-Aboriginal descent, occurred in many parts of Australia throughout the twentieth century and most probably before that. The 2002 film *Rabbit-Proof Fence* dramatically recounts such removals in Western Australia while dealing with the senior administrators of the removal policy in a most sympathetic manner.

Given the widespread nature of the policy of such removals, one has to ask what it was that drove whites to remove Aboriginal children from their communities. The motivations driving these removals were no doubt varied: sometimes it was missionary zeal and sometimes a desire to "save" the children from the impoverished living conditions their parents were forced to endure following their displacement from traditional land. At other times white fathers had disappeared and Aboriginal mothers had died or become incapacitated. There was a clear government policy to remove Aboriginal people from their land to make way for white settlers. It was believed that eventually Aboriginal people would die out and that removing children of partial-Aboriginal descent would remove one obstacle to the extinction of an Aboriginal presence.

The second part of the question is: Could it happen in the second decade of the twenty-first century? The short answer is that Aboriginal children are being fostered in white homes now because of the failure of governments to attract sufficient Indigenous families into the foster care programs and to adequately fund them. As fostering costs rise, governments are becoming more interested in allowing foster families to adopt children. Welfare workers in New South Wales are removing Aboriginal children from their homes in numbers far greater than during the Stolen Generations, and the recruitment of Aboriginal staff has done nothing to stem the tide. In 2008 Overington reported that 4,000 Aboriginal children were in state care in NSW, compared with about 1,000 Aboriginal children in foster homes, institutions, and missions in 1969. She went on to add that children are being removed at ten times the rate of white children – and the primary reason for removal is not abuse, but neglect (Overington, 2008, p. 1).

In addition, half the children in custodial institutions in Australia are of Indigenous descent. Aborigines constitute only 3% of the Australian population: "Figures from the Australian Institute of Health and Welfare show the national rate of Aboriginal juvenile incarceration has risen to a startling rate of 31 times the non-indigenous rate, up from 27 times in 2008" (Robinson, 2013). Social Justice Commissioner Mick Gooda puts the rise in the number of young Indigenous people being in prison and juvenile detention down to overpolicing of Aboriginal kids and harsh sentencing by country magistrates. I would argue that widespread racism directed toward Aborigines has to be recognized as a major contributor to a situation where, for example, 70% of the juvenile prisoners in Western Australia and nearly all juveniles in Northern Territory prisons are Aboriginal (Robinson, 2013).

Social workers are employed in the child welfare, court, and corrections system, and they are implementing policies that are resulting in increasing numbers of Aboriginal children being taken out of Indigenous communities. This is happening because social workers are not questioning the directions of their superior officers. They are unmindful of the importance of the Nuremberg Judgment, which stated that following orders does not absolve one from responsibility for one's actions. They should be working alongside Indigenous leaders to maintain children in their own communities. Social workers are citizens who should not divert their eyes from what their country is doing to Indigenous Australians. There are many government policy failures involving Indigenous Australians in the first two decades of the twenty-first century (see below), which Australian social workers should attempt to address.

I go along with the suggestion, often attributed to Thomas Jefferson, that "when injustice becomes law, resistance becomes duty." However, there are limits as to what an individual or a group of social workers can do. The need to maintain the capacity to continue working in the profession means that being criminalized has to be avoided. But this does not justify connivance or silence. Speaking out and refusing to obey directions may mean your promotional prospects are greatly diminished, but your dignity is enhanced, and you will be able to face yourself in the mirror the next morning.

▶ Challenges Facing Indigenous Australians

Indigenous Australians have some similar difficulties to other poor Australians in obtaining adequate health, disability, educational, and other services. The present government admits that there is a seventeen-year gap in life expectancy between Indigenous and other Australians. For example, Australia is the only developed country in the world not to have eradicated trachoma, a disease almost exclusively confined to the Indigenous population.

Australia did, in 2013, start to introduce a national disability program. By its nature it has commenced in the cities, so people living in rural and remote regions will be the last to see the benefits flowing from this program. Aborigines, in particular, but also other rural and remote dwellers, have more disabilities and poorer health than city dwellers (Tomlinson, 2003).

Shortly before the 2007 election, the Conservative government launched an "Intervention" into 73 Aboriginal communities in the Northern Territory, ostensibly to safeguard Aboriginal children from sexual abuse or neglect and to protect Aboriginal women from being assaulted. The police and the army were sent into remote Aboriginal communities. The government suspended the Racial Discrimination Act in order to quarantine half the social security payments made to Indigenous people. The amount quarantined was placed on a "Basics" card that could only be used for approved purposes at certain stores. Compulsory town leases and health checks were also imposed (Altman & Hinkson, 2007).

The Labor Party came to power in 2007 promising to continue the Intervention for a year before reviewing it. A committee was set up, headed by Aboriginal leader Peter Yu, that recommended winding back most of the compulsory aspects of the Intervention except where it could be proven that Indigenous people were incapable of handling money. Labor ignored the report; rather, Labor has moved toward providing incentives for the use of the Basics card while allowing people to request they not be required to have a Basics card. At the same time, this government has expanded the parts of the Northern Territory and elsewhere in Australia where Aboriginal and other ethnic groups are cajoled into a paternalistic administration of their social security. It has reinstated the Racial Discrimination Act and so cannot specify any particular ethnic group that is forced to participate. What it does instead is select geographical areas where particular ethnic groups predominate and legislates to force all residents of those areas to participate in its paternalistic form of social security.

Some Aboriginal people have supported the introduction of the Basics card but many are critical (Concerned Australians, 2010). Between 2007 and 2011, I wrote seven articles opposing aspects of the Intervention for the e-journal *On Line Opinion*.[5] In these articles I pointed to the long history of colonial intervention allegedly aiming to save Aborigines, particularly children, from their community when in fact governments and others were pursuing other ends.

Many have asked why governments from the 1970s with their billion-dollar budgets dedicated to Indigenous affairs have not been able to lift Aborigines out of poverty. Altman and Hinkson (2010) suggests that despite the assertions of this and previous governments that they are implementing evidence-based policy, they are actually imposing ideologically driven policies that link Indigenous violence to economic marginalization, inadequacies in Aboriginal culture, and "passive welfare." Altman and Hinkson further assert that right-wing think tanks, such as the Centre for Independent Studies, are closely linked to senior public servants driving the Intervention (pp. 266–267).

The Northern Territory government report, which the Conservative government claimed had inspired the Intervention, was released on 15 June 2007. The 500 pages of legislation, which supported the Intervention, were introduced on 7 August, passed without amendment, and given Royal Assent 10 days later. It would not be possible to draft 500 pages of legislation in that time frame. Altman and Hinkson are correct: there is a powerful group of neo-conservatives in the public service and on both sides of politics, in the media, and in right-wing think tanks, working hand in glove. These racist forces are driving both the government and the opposition.

It is the task of all anti-racists, including social workers, to confront and expose them if Indigenous Australians are to receive anything approaching social justice.

Notes

I wish to thank Penny Harrington for her extensive editorial assistance and continuing encouragement.

1 This Branch had several name changes after 1973 but throughout this chapter it is referred to by its original name.
2 Since the 1980s people of Aboriginal descent who identify as Aboriginal and who are accepted by their community as being of Aboriginal descent are considered to be

Aboriginal. The terms "total Aboriginal descent" and "part-Aboriginal" are used here to denote a distinction that was widely maintained in the Northern Territory in the 1970s.
3 Many people of Aboriginal descent do not use the Aboriginal name of those who have died. As some of the people referred to in this story have passed away, the Aboriginal names of people of total Aboriginal descent are not mentioned here.
4 The author was Jim Bowditch, who had lost the editorship of *NT News* to Murdoch's News Limited in 1972. As part of the sweetener, Bowditch was appointed a News Limited stringer for *The Australian* in Darwin and paid for any stories the newspaper accepted. His wife was of part-Aboriginal descent.
5 The articles dealing with the Intervention are categorized by the journal as relating to "Indigenous affairs."

References

Altman, J., & Hinkson, M. (Eds.). (2007). *Coercive reconciliation: Stabilise, normalise, exit Aboriginal Australia*. North Carlton: Arena.

Altman, J., & Hinkson, M. (Eds.). (2010). *Culture crisis: Anthropology and politics in Aboriginal Australia*. Sydney: University of New South Wales.

Bowditch, J. (1973, 20 Sept.). Tribe takes girl, 7, from family to be child bride. *The Australian*, p. 1.

Concerned Australians. (2010). *This is what we said: Australian Aborigines give their views on the Northern Territory intervention*. East Melbourne: Concerned Australians.

Cummings, B. (1990). *Take this child: From Kahlin Compound to the Retta Dixon Children's Home*. Canberra: Aboriginal Studies Press.

Herbert, X. (1975). *Poor fellow my country*. Sydney: Collins.

National Inquiry into the Separation of Aboriginal and Torres Strait Islander Children from Their Families. (1997). *Bringing them home*. Canberra: Commonwealth of Australia.

On Line Opinion. Tomlinson author. Retrieved 28 May 2015 from http://www.onlineopinion.com.au/author.asp?id=1984

Overington, C. (2008, 24 Nov.). Aboriginal foster generation exceeds Stolen Generations. *The Australian*. Retrieved 28 May 2015 from http://www.theaustralian.com.au/news/nation/more-aboriginal-children-in-carestory-e6frg6nf-1111118120107

Pittock, B. (1969). *Towards a multi-racial society*. Sydney: Quakers.

Robinson, N. (2013, 5 Jan.). Black sentences soar as juvenile jails become a "storing house." *The Australian*. Retrieved 28 May 2015 from http://www.theaustralian.com.au/national-affairs/indigenous/black-sentences-soar-as-juvenile-jails-become-a-storing-house/story-fn9hm1pm-1226547889340

Taffe, S. (2005). *Black and white together FCAATSI: The Federal Council for the Advancement of Aborigines and Torres Strait Islanders, 1958–1973*. St Lucia: University of Queensland.

Tomlinson, J. (1978). *Is Band-Aid social work enough?* Darwin: Wobbly Press.

Tomlinson, J. (2003). Income insecurity: The basic income alternative. Retrieved 28 May 2015 from http://www.basicincome.qut.edu.au/interest/e-books.jsp

White, K. (2005). *True stories of the top end*. Briar Hill: Indra.

Willesee, G. (1973, 12 Nov.). Nola – Black, beautiful and happy – Is home with her own people. *Woman's Day*, pp. 2–5, 13.

CHAPTER 3

Politicizing Welfare and Humanizing Politics

Social Workers Opposing Apartheid South Africa's Policies

Thérèse Sacco and Jeanette Schmid

In the early 1990s justice-cherishing South Africans and international comrades overcame apartheid South Africa's ideological and repressive state machinery. Concerned Social Workers (CSW), a group of South African social workers, made its contribution to this struggle for democracy. Our story, set in the mid-1980s and spanning states of emergency for five years, speaks to the possibilities of collective action when confronting a powerful, brutal, and unjust system. As social workers we envision a world that hears and responds to the cries of poor and dispossessed people and wish to leave a legacy on which future generations of social workers can build.

We share this account to encourage social workers to (re-)connect with essential social work values and take courage in collectively acting against injustice, both locally and globally. In doing so for this collection of narratives we hope to contribute to an international interchange of ideas, recognizing that global solidarity is vital in fostering social justice. As narrators of this account, we both have become aware that such a revisiting of the violence we witnessed, experienced, and opposed leaves a new mark on us – even though as white social workers we benefited and continue to derive advantage from the mechanisms of apartheid. We recognize that not all can engage in the retelling of the opposition to oppression and repression. This chapter presents our particular focus of events. It includes information gleaned from records we have of this period as well as some recollections of several CSW members.

Concerned Social Workers was established to identify just and Indigenous social work practice under apartheid. To enable the reader to appreciate this context, we briefly describe the roots of oppression in South Africa and depict the nature of apartheid repression in the 1980s. We highlight how children and youth, in particular, were scarred and damaged by injustice. We remember the challenges of practising social work under apartheid and how we creatively found ways to take social action in opposing it. We recall the personal cost to dedicated action and the motives for our commitment. In the end we take a step back and make conceptual sense of our activism so that it is meaningful for social work today.

▶ A CONTEXT OF OPPRESSION

Members of Concerned Social Workers came together at the height of apartheid in the mid-1980s to examine the place of social work in an overtly oppressive and repressive society. From the previous British colonial dispensation, the apartheid state had inherited racially based laws and practices that circumscribed, controlled, and dominated life in South Africa. In 1909 the British Parliament had transferred power to a white minority, effectively excluding South Africa's black majority from governance and decision making. Legal measures provided for white settlers to occupy 87% of land, black South Africans being restricted to the remaining 13% (Native Land Act of 1913). The Colour Bar Act of 1926 was central to job reservation, allocating jobs based on race, and excluding black South Africans from skilled and unskilled jobs: particular categories of employment were reserved for whites only. Later legislation, the Native Land and Trust Act of 1936 (further segregating rural land for the use of white settlers), and the Native Urban Areas Act of 1923 and amended in 1937 (that kept apart urban land and restricted the right of black South Africans to own land in the towns) preceded apartheid's formalized legislation by many years.[1]

As of 1948, when the National Party came to power, racial separation, inequality, and oppression became more deeply entrenched through the promulgation of laws that governed every aspect of people's lives along racial lines. These laws dictated where, with whom, and how people were to live, be educated, work, and marry. Whites had privileged access to opportunities and resources for farming, mining, living spaces, education, employment, and state medical and welfare services. Blacks[2] were, as a consequence, further impoverished, disenfranchised, and regulated.

In addition to ensuring unequal development through the discriminatory allocation of state resources, apartheid South Africa maintained its repressive control through centralized and complex security machinery, including both military and police forces. These organs of security reported to the State Security Council, chaired by the state president (Lawyers Committee for Human Rights, 1986, p. 15). Repression was, as of the 1950s, further embedded in an intricate series of laws: Internal security legislation allowed wide powers of detention without trial as well as the banning of people, organizations, gatherings, and publications (Human Rights Commission, 1990, p. 406). Public safety laws permitted declarations of states of emergency, invoked in 1960 and 1985, and from 1986 to 1989 continuously and uninterruptedly (Coleman, 1998, p. 14). Under a state of emergency every member of the police, railways police, prisons, and army was empowered to detain people without trial; detainees had no right to visitors or a lawyer, nor were they entitled to receive letters or any reading material other than the Bible;[3] no member of the force could be brought to account, by civil suit or criminal charge, for unlawful actions in carrying out emergency laws; it was a crime to reveal the identity of any detainee without prior disclosure by the minister of law and order; the commissioner of police was authorized to impose blanket censorship on press coverage of the state of emergency; the minister of law and order was empowered to ban organizations, individuals, or publications that were "calculated to endanger the security of the State or the maintenance of public order." Courts were denied jurisdiction to set aside any order or rule issued under emergency regulations (Truth and Reconciliation Commission, 1998a, p. 469).

This legislative landscape provided significant scope for abuse by security forces. As resistance to apartheid intensified in the 1980s and a state of emergency was proclaimed in 1985, the police retaliated with increased force and brutality (Lawyers Committee for Human Rights, 1986, p. 17). The military was expected to assist in containing internal disorder. This allowed the military unprecedented influence over internal affairs (pp. 17–18). More than 32,000 South African Defence Force troops were deployed in 96 black townships (Coleman, 1998, p. 11), and thousands of people were detained without trial, including children. Organizations were banned; people were placed under house arrest, made to disappear, and assassinated.

Children witnessed state violence in their communities and in their homes. They were not spared as targets: they were killed, injured, and detained. During 1985 alone, 201 children were killed by police. Nineteen of these victims were under 10 years old (Lawyers Committee for Human Rights, 1986, p. 31). The South African Truth and Reconciliation Commission found that the majority of killings reported to the Commission were young males between the ages of 13 and 24 years (1998b, p. 259).

Children who escaped death did not necessarily escape injury. They were wounded, for example, when security forces used live ammunition to disperse crowds. Children became victims in places where they should have felt safe, such as in their schools and at funerals (Lawyers Committee for Human Rights, 1986, p. 36). Injured children were further traumatized as they faced risks of arrest when seeking medical treatment (p. 42).

The Human Rights Committee conservatively estimated that 80,000 people were detained between 1960 and 1990, the majority being detained from 1985 to 1990 (Coleman 1988, pp. 14–15). Sixty percent of these detainees were younger than 25 years of age, including 25% who were younger than 18. Severe torture and assaults were routinely inflicted on political detainees, and children were no exception (Lawyers Committee for Human Rights, 1986, p. 101). Detention did not only impact directly on the persons held, but also had psychological and material consequences on their families as well. For example, many mothers lost their jobs as they searched for their detained children – the whereabouts of detainees not being publicly disclosed – and families incurred medical bills. Even after release from detention children were harassed by police attempts to force them to become informers, or to interrogate them further in schools and communities (Sacco, 1988, p. 93). This impacted families, as parents were powerless to protect and care for their children. Many young people were not permitted to return to school after detention. Children thus directly, frequently, and repeatedly experienced state violence.

Despite the state terror inflicted on the majority of South Africans, whites generally lived in a haze of collective and collusive amnesia. It seemed also that social workers largely ignored the oppression and discrimination experienced by most South Africans.

▶ IMPLICATIONS OF APARTHEID FOR SOCIAL WORK PRACTICE

As detailed in the welfare submission to the Truth and Reconciliation Commission (Greater Johannesburg Welfare Social Service and Development Forum, 1999), social workers and their activities were shaped by apartheid policies. Social workers were trained in racially segregated institutions. Salaries differed according to race. Such inequity was accepted as the norm and may have been invisible to many white social workers. Even in agencies that served all racial groups, social services were formally organized and subsidized along racial lines. This meant that social work resources, such as personnel and services, were directed primarily toward whites:

blacks being significantly underserviced. This mirrored broader patterns of resource allocation, for example, in health and education. Welfare organizations almost entirely supported apartheid policies. Not doing so would have meant losing their registration as a welfare agency as well as state subsidy, which for most agencies formed the core of their income. Social workers also had limited choices within this apartheid framework, with significant consequences. For example, black social workers were forced to work within their own racially defined communities. Social workers were expected to implement disparities in allocating grants and pensions. Many of our children's homes housed offspring from mixed unions, as it was illegal for parents of mixed descent to live as a family. Cross-racial adoptions were not permitted. Even where social workers were troubled by the inherent discrimination of apartheid policies, challenging apartheid practices placed individual workers at risk of police harassment, detention, and ultimately being excluded from practising as social workers.

A minority of social workers came to believe that they could not operate ethically in the face of such injustice. We became aware that silence was synonymous with support. Resistance became our duty in the face of such injustice. Our response came at a time when there was a groundswell of opposition to apartheid: various professional groupings began interrogating their role within apartheid South Africa. In Johannesburg a group of local professional social workers, with close links to the School of Social Work at the University of the Witwatersrand, organized ourselves as Concerned Social Workers. It must be noted that we were not the only social workers taking a progressive stance, but were among the first to oppose apartheid publicly.

In the early 1980s some social workers in Johannesburg gathered as a loose discussion group to examine social work practice under an oppressive regime. Although we shared the goal of opposing apartheid and lived with the hope that this system would be dismantled, our initial focus was on identifying alternative ways of doing social work that were respectful, empowering, and appropriate in the South African context.

During the state of emergency in July 1985 we were galvanized into direct action. Six hundred children (some as young as 9 years) were detained in Soweto, a township outside of Johannesburg. At this time there was neither response from child protection organizations nor the public, and so we felt compelled to act. Without much consideration we named ourselves Concerned Social Workers. As social workers committed to strengthening child and family welfare, we believed we needed to speak out against the repression, criminalization, and traumatization of children. This was due to the immediate impact on children, their families, and communities. We also realized that such brutalization would have extensive implications for future society. CSW members represented diverse ethnic and racial backgrounds, cultures, ages, and religious beliefs. Indeed, it was a conscious decision to ensure that our group was diverse and reflective of various populations. As a group we did not decide on a formal program of action; this organically emerged and developed over time. At first, we spoke out against harm being perpetrated against children and young people. We felt professionally obligated to take a stand and communicate that we could no longer directly or inadvertently support repressive state actions. Although Concerned Social Workers was not an affiliate of the United Democratic Front (UDF), an alliance of anti-apartheid groupings, we were aligned with its vision and values. These included establishing a democratic society that honours social justice, equality, and equitable resource distribution.

As we developed from a discussion group into a formal organization, the mandate we set ourselves became clearer. We saw ourselves first and foremost as a professional social work organization, and our motivation continued to be to develop a coherent model of just social work practice. We decided that it was important to, in the language of the time, "conscientize" the members of our profession. This concept derives from Paulo Freire (1981). "Conscientization" is the process whereby one becomes aware of oppressive societal forces that shape lived reality and as a consequence takes action. We aimed at translating our emerging theoretical insights into practice, research, and social action. Through this praxis it became important for us to demonstrate solidarity with victims of apartheid and partner in the struggle to end apartheid.

This meant that we engaged with a number of different sectors of the anti-apartheid movement, involving ourselves in policy work, advocating for the rights of children and adults, providing counselling and support services to those affected by apartheid, and enhancing the organizational and service skills of embryonic NGOs. In this narrative we focus on CSW's response to state violence against South African children and youth as this illustrates strategies utilized to expand the legal space to challenge a highly repressive and brutal state system.

All our actions were undertaken on a voluntary basis. This meant that activities were carried out in members' own time, after working hours, and that no one was obliged to engage in any activity that was uncomfortable for them. The unjust laws and practices were so inhuman that to be alive necessitated our commitment to the resistance movement. Some of us intentionally took jobs that gave enough political space and time to engage wholeheartedly in social activism; for example, the University of the Witwatersrand was known to value academic freedom highly.

▶ Mobilizing Social Workers

The first CSW civic action in 1985 was a media release protesting the violence against children. Within two weeks thereafter Concerned Social Workers organized a well-attended "Children under Repression" conference. This conference put state abuse of children on the public agenda. It underscored for the social work community that one could not in good conscience or as a competent professional remain impervious to the sociopolitical context. Rather, social workers must advance child and family protection and unite as social agents for change. Conference participants realized that the issues raised needed to be communicated internationally, the resolutions being sent to embassies and to a United Nations committee. Further strategic actions included focusing on the impact of violence on children rather than formally opposing the apartheid state, as such expression was illegal. We engaged the support of a range of high-profile individuals to provide protection, legitimacy, and attention to the cause. Holding the event at the University of the Witwatersrand minimized the chance of the state shutting down the conference, because this university had an international reputation for academic excellence, and police action against this university would have provoked an international outcry.

Concerned Social Workers produced a newsletter titled *In Touch* – mailed to more than 200 individuals and organizations in Johannesburg – with the aim of educating, conscientizing,[i] mobilizing, and organizing social workers. This newsletter featured work with children under repression, and articulated social work theory and practice within the political arena. Issue number 2 (November 1987) caught the state's attention and was deemed an undesirable publication and banned for distribution. The reasons for this banning were not detailed in the government gazette. This issue of In Touch did, however, present a profile of a social worker who had been banned and challenged proposed new welfare policy that aimed to further entrench apartheid inequality, and finally, it explicitly committed Concerned Social Workers to a non-racial democracy.

▶ Engaging in Partnerships

Concerned Social Workers saw the engagement in partnerships and alliances as a critical strategy in opposing repression. Below we recount our involvement in the Free the Children's Alliance, the Detainees' Parents' Support Committee, and the Detainee Counselling Service.

A year after the first conference, Concerned Social Workers formed the Free the Children's Alliance with 34 organizations, such as women's, religious, civic, and professional organizations, and academics. Again, the language used was cautious: even though efforts concentrated on stopping the apartheid government from detaining children, the campaign framed itself as working toward creating the conditions needed to promote children's general well-being. Involvement with this broad-based alliance was purposeful because it was more difficult for the government to discredit a grouping that included both progressive and liberal organizations. Also, as a single-issue campaign, the protest against the detention of children was powerful. International anti-apartheid organizations as well as transnational organizations specifically concerned with the detention and abuse of children provided an international voice. The alliance kept up constant pressure on the state through media briefings, press releases, and public meetings. One example is a public meeting organized by the alliance on National Detainees Day, 12 October 1987. We invited VIPs from various sectors of Johannesburg's society to the event that featured publicly signing postcards addressed to the minister of law and order petitioning for the release of our children. This event was filmed and internationally televised. Subsequently, on 29 April 1988, the alliance held a public Children's Commission on the impact of repression on our children. Ambassadors from various countries and representatives of international organizations were consistently invited as witnesses to these events. Their presence provided a limited degree of security, making it politically more awkward for security police to disrupt the event. Additionally, the alliance designed and produced "Free the Children" T-shirts, badges, and car-bumper stickers, as well as information leaflets for wide distribution. This allowed the alliance to create awareness in non-confrontational and accessible ways. We made public appearances on television and were interviewed on radio. For example, when in London on 16 and 17 June 1987, Thérèse was interviewed about the detention and repression of children in South Africa on BBC TV Breakfast News; BBC Africa News, London; Black London; and a teenage London program. These interviews coincided with commemorations of young people who died on 16 June 1976 in the streets of Soweto during uprisings against Afrikaans as the language of education and the system of Bantu Education. (The latter was established to ensure that blacks were prepared only for low-paying, menial jobs.) Concerned Social Workers (again represented by Thérèse) was also part of a delegation to the United States on 25–26 June 1987 to "Free South Africa's Children: A Symposium on Children in Detention." This congressional hearing was organized by the Lawyers' Committee for Civil Rights under Law in Washington, DC. The US Senate passed a resolution that called for the immediate release of all children detained under apartheid South Africa's state of emergency regulations.

Since it was comprised of social workers, Concerned Social Workers felt it was important not only to play an advocacy role in the alliance, but also to provide direct services to children and families. In this way we were able to develop a praxis that included exploring new possibilities for creative experiences even while living under a repressive state. For example, we brought children together for International Children's Days (days of safety and fun) and produced a booklet supporting traumatized children. Such support services also brought attention to the circumstances South African children faced.

Our commitment to social justice was also realized through CSW's partnership with the Detainees' Parents' Support Committee (DPSC). Our work with DPSC, as with all our coalitions, necessitated acting with courage, creativity, ingenuity, and craftiness. To illustrate: DPSC convened monthly "tea parties" with parents of detained children to monitor the extent of detentions, offer legal advice, and create support groups. The tea party format was a strategic choice, as meetings of more than three people were illegal under security legislation. Concerned Social Workers took on two distinct roles at these tea parties. First, we brought sandwiches and poured tea. This reinforced the tea party appearance of these events: however, it also created opportunities for us to host parents who were often very vulnerable and to nurture them in tangible, caring ways. Second, we took parents' statements (these being used as advocacy tools) and facilitated group discussions and peer support. Security forces typically stationed themselves outside meeting venues. At one of our tea parties at a church in Alexandra Township, northeast Johannesburg, military forces pointed rifles at us through the windows. We managed to hold tea parties every month for two and a half years. When the DPSC was banned in February 1988, activists regrouped under the name of Detainee Education and Welfare (DEW). We continued serving detainees. This work was risky and frightening: Dr David Webster was assassinated on 1 May 1989. He was a beloved friend, an anthropologist at the University of the Witwatersrand, and central to the detainee movement. We had organized these tea parties with him. In 1997, in an interview with journalist Jaques Pauw, Ferdi Barnard admitted to assassinating David. The reason he gave was: "It was all that tea parties and shit" (Pauw, 1997).

In another initiative, Concerned Social Workers was part of a coalition of progressive professional organizations. All member organizations were appalled at the physical and mental effects of pervasive repression and formed the Detainee Counselling Service (DCS) in Johannesburg. Social workers were part of managing the clinic and selecting and training counsellors. Of particular value in this training was social work's sensitivity to looking at people-in-context and on building resilience. So as not to jeopardize the safety of those using our services, case notes were not kept. A pamphlet "Detention – Torture to the Mind" on the effects of detention and dimensions of trauma, produced in accessible English, was given to each ex-detainee. Not only adults, but also children and youth were counselled.

Concerned Social Workers participated in a delegation of coalition members that met with the then minister of health and population development, Dr W.A. van Niekerk. We impressed upon him the deleterious health effects of detentions and restrictions on released detainees and political prisoners (Sacco 1989, 5).

CSW members were frequently also members of other political organizations. As such we participated in actions that met the goals of Concerned Social Workers but were not always part of the CSW mandate. For example, some of us offered our homes as places of safety to children and young activists, while others participated in broader campaigns, for instance, the Campaign Against Political Imprisonment.

▶ Reasons to Celebrate

Concerned Social Workers was part of a bigger movement that overturned apartheid. By 1990 there were no children in political detention. Positions promoted by the Free the Children's Alliance are reflected in the post-apartheid South Africa's Constitution (Republic of South Africa, 1996, pp. 13–14). Specifically, Article 28(1)(g) states that every child has the right "not to be detained, except as a measure of last resort, in which case, in addition to the rights a child enjoys under sections 12 and 35, the child may be detained only for the shortest appropriate period of time, and has the right to be kept separately from detained persons over the age of 18 years; and, treated in a manner, and kept in conditions, that take account of the child's age." Regrettably, children continue to be imprisoned on criminal charges, despite continued challenges to this practice and the proposal of alternative policies.

▶ CREATING EXTRALEGAL SPACE FOR SOCIAL WORK ACTION

In 2012 we designed a qualitative study. We wanted to document some of the work Concerned Social Workers had undertaken during a highly repressive time in South Africa, encourage young social workers to harness the power of collective action, and contribute to shaping professional identities. We reported the findings elsewhere (Schmid & Sacco, 2012). However, some of the insights we gained from that piece of research contribute to this narrative in naming the costs of our involvement and motives for our activism. We used a snowball method to reach former CSW members. We contacted 30 members, and 14 social workers responded. Members who participated reflected the diversity of the organization in age, culture, religion, and ethnicity. We asked that they fill out a questionnaire of open-ended questions exploring their memories of Concerned Social Workers and reflecting on the ways in which their CSW experiences may have impacted their professional identity. Some recollections regarding the costs of their involvement and their motives for their activism are presented below.

Costs of Involvement

Opposing the ideological fabric of apartheid put people in jeopardy. Our participation in Concerned Social Workers meant sacrifices regarding family life, friendships, intimacy, and the pursuit of further education and personal interests. We all lived with fear, uncertainty, and concern for our personal safety and that of our families. Everyone could count on being under surveillance by security forces. The consequences of CSW's social activism touched members differently.

In some instances differences depended upon our racial background: Some white members were increasingly socially isolated within their neighbourhoods and social circles; black members spoke of their community becoming more involved in working together to protect their children. Many of our members could not live a full life: their communities were intimidated; they witnessed cruelty and torture and lived by curfews. People were followed by police and sometimes by soldiers in *hippos* (armoured personnel vehicles). Some members were seized and detained, as were family members and friends. At least six members were detained without trial and/or charged for political actions. Both authors were detained without trial. The thing about detentions is that reasons were never given. People were detained for interrogation, torture, removal from society, to break people and organizations, and to wreak havoc in families, communities, and neighbourhoods. One member, who was detained for a six-month period, recounts being particularly distressed by the screams of detained children, and her offers of supporting the children were turned down by the prison psychiatrist. Offices were vandalized, homes were broken into, and cars damaged. As stated by one member, "We never knew the truth of where people were, what was happening to them: 60 days, 90 days and 100 days detention without trial. So many people lost jobs and lost their standing because of their commitment to social justice."

The security police worked closely with the South African Council and Associated Workers, a statutory body requiring compulsory registration by practising social workers. One CSW member recalled: "I gave a talk at the 'Free the Children' Alliance Children's Commission in 1988 which got me into trouble with the Security Police." The minister of law and order, Mr Adriaan Vlok, publicly denied the allegations in this talk. Complaints were lodged with the above-mentioned Council, and two of our members were charged with unprofessional conduct. As noted by another CSW member, "Through harassing me, the Security Police were trying to make an example of me and stop others from speaking out."

Anti-apartheid organizations knew that security police regularly planted undercover agents in our midst. Security police used this common knowledge and started rumours about people being spies for the apartheid state. Their intention was to break people and organizations. A CSW member moved to Cape Town and was a founding member of a similar grouping there. This organization, the member recollected, was "virtually destroyed after I had been accused of being a spy, and there was a split between people who supported me in this crisis and those who did not. The Security Police knew exactly who to target – the new guy to Cape Town."

Motives for Activism

Former CSW members who participated in our study shared their reasons for being involved in CSW's anti-apartheid activism. Looking at responses we perceive political, professional, and personal motives.

Political intentions were spurred on by the socio-political reality of the time. One participant wrote, "The mass detention of children & youth as well as the escalating state repression during the mid-1980s made it imperative that social workers actively engage with the socio-political reality of the time." Another member said, "I was concerned about the detention of children during the State of Emergency and other injustices of the Apartheid regime, as well as my detention." State repression was such that social work seemed hopeless. One CSW member stated, "Initially I just went along to listen – times were so bleak and there was so little space to speak out. It helped me place in context my sense of the injustice." A social work student welcomed the opportunity to take social action, "I was a social work student at the University of the Witwatersrand and CSW provided me with a platform to participate in the struggle against apartheid … as well as offer tangible and concrete ways of expressing my beliefs – through the campaigns, conferences and work we did." The formation of the United Democratic Front gave impetus to a social work student who remembered, "It was the politics at the time. I was supporting UDF, and CSW was a natural organization to join as a social work student."

These political reasons were resonant with professional intentions. Professional values, our humanity and spirituality, and the desire to take collective action as social workers were at the core of our opposition to apartheid's unjust and repressive policies and practices. In the words of some CSW members:

"There was a need for social workers to take a stand and to be actively involved in the struggle for democracy and social justice."

"Justice and Peace."

"CSW shook many people out of complacency and it enabled a joining together of older and younger social workers with political conscience."

"It was imperative to usher in a developmental, just and equitable social welfare system."

"As a student social worker in CSW, I learned Social Work could be a vehicle, the means to living out my activism. So just like Liberation Theology was fundamentally about the integration of faith and life, and therefore, the fight and struggle to overcome injustice and inequality, so Social Work enabled me to 'professionally' bring about equality and justice in South Africa and fight racism to restore the dignity of ALL South Africans."

In addition, social workers wanted to belong to a social work association not bound by race. We were enraged at the expulsion of colleagues from registration with the statutory body South African Council for Social and Associated Workers. A participant said, "I wanted to break free from the racially based associations." While another declared, "It also was Maxine's expulsion from the social workers professional body."

Political and professional reasons were accompanied by personal imperatives. Personal motives included wishes to share spaces with social workers with a similar vision and dreams for all South Africans. A CSW member verbalized, "For me CSW provided me with a base where I felt incredibly comfortable, especially in sharing my socio-political views with like-minded folk." Another one replied, "There was a tremendous need for progressive social workers to gather together and work for justice, to keep alive decency, awareness and information, to support one another, and to be witnesses for truth."

Despite the harassment and intimidation, CSW members spoke about the enduring friendships and close bonds that formed. This is a valuable and precious unintended consequence of collectively participating in a movement that fosters justice.

> "There was a lot of sharing and loving of each other: We supported each other, we respected each other, and we assisted each other."
> "I started appreciating our bonds: those bonds have held for all time."
> "I think of all the years that we have known each other and these days I simply love being with people with whom I have long-term relations. There is something enduring about that as the years pass."

▶ Opposing Apartheid Policies: Making Conceptual Sense

The events that we have recounted happened 30 years ago. The question this raises is why have we looked back: what are the reasons for opening old wounds in the telling? Like all other discourses, social work is on a journey of building knowledge and developing insights, concepts, and wisdom. So that these are not lost in this narrative, we would like to stand back and take a look at what makes conceptual sense. What ideas do we need to capture so that this remembering becomes part of an intellectual flow that is rooted in lived experiences and knowledge gained from our guts, sadness, and longing for a better global community?

First, we explore social work perspectives that were available to us at that time and that helped frame our activism conceptually. These perspectives embrace particular ideological positions, values, and imperatives for practice. We also identify current social work perspectives that reflect the positions we took, but had not been articulated yet. Second, we grappled with concepts relating to people's experiences of trauma and came up with contextually tuned ideas. This conceptual development took place with alliance partners who also were clinicians sensitive to the impact of political oppression and repression on health. Finally, we name strategies that assisted us in expanding legal spaces to practise competent social work informed by core social work values.

Conceptually Framing Our Activism

Our engagement with Concerned Social Workers was located within the radical social work tradition of activism (Bailey & Brake, 1975). This tradition takes an expressly structural approach to understanding the root challenges, issues, and problems of marginalized and poor people. As social workers we could locate the difficulties experienced by the majority of South Africans in the racist, apartheid ideology that facilitated and embedded white power and privilege. The notion of praxis – the iterative process of questioning theory in the light of practice and vice versa – was inspired by liberation movements in South America and drew from Paulo Freire's work (1981) regarding conscientization: enabling people to explore structural factors determining their lived realities. However, we expanded this structural analysis by, first, constantly stepping outside of our experiences and back in again (Statham, 1978, p. 13). Second, we were aware of the feminist position that the personal is the political. We sought, through regular reflective forums, to raise consciousness in ourselves of injustice, prejudice, discrimination, and oppression, and though it was not termed as such, for those of us that were white, understanding "whiteness." Third, as a group we developed insights about the flow of power and our social location. It became clear to us that social activism was an essential part of practice. Further, we adopted strengths perspectives (Saleebey, 2009), although they were not yet available to us. Additionally, while being aware of our particular expertise as social workers, we never attempted to speak for those affected by state repression. Rather, we recognized the importance of facilitating peer support, as well as becoming allies.

With retrospective lenses we see that the CSW work was both anti-discriminatory (Thompson, 2006) and anti-oppressive practice (Clifford & Burke, 2009). As progressive social work literature developed and became available to us in South Africa, we drew on anti-racist social work (Dominelli, 1988) and anti-sexist perspectives (Langan & Day, 1992). Although we did not have the language of critical social work, as this was only popularized in the 1990s, we were living a critically reflexive practice (Adams, Dominelli, & Payne, 2009). Critical social work centres on analyzing and transforming power in all its manifestations in society and social work practice, drawing together concepts from Marxist social work, radical social work, structural social work, feminist social work, and anti-racist social work, as well as anti-oppressive and anti-discriminatory social work

(Healy, 2005, qtd. in Ferguson, 2008, p. 103). Our work in Concerned Social Workers is consistent with the four key elements of a critical social science paradigm: macro-social structures shape social relations at every level of social life; the world is divided between those who have and those who do not have, and the interests of these groups are opposed and irreconcilable; the oppressed are complicit in their oppression; and the emphasis is on empowering.

We engaged in applying our insights directly to practice and as such did not concentrate on formalizing our approach. However, much of our analysis was articulated in the foundational contribution by Leila Patel (1992) to the restructuring of post-apartheid South African social welfare as a developmental social welfare system. The fact that our analysis, which predated later theoretical developments, is not internationally recognized is consistent with Shashok's conclusion (as qtd. by Badenhorst, 2010, p. 36) that globally, the peer review process favours "the north over the south and the west over the east."

Developing Trauma Theory and Practice

Internationally, theory regarding the effects of political violence was being developed and described as Post Traumatic Stress Disorder in the same period that we were constructing theory to address South African realities. Locally, we learned to normalize feelings and responses to horrific events. We did not "psychologize" the fear, anxiety, or distress of survivors and name their experiences "paranoid": Their need for safety was taken seriously and measures to ensure this were sought each time this issue was raised. South African professionals (including members of Concerned Social Workers) coined the term "continuous stress syndrome." It is ironical to talk about a syndrome when one actually wanted to avoid using a pathology-oriented descriptor. The intent however was to acknowledge that ex-detainees and those who were under house arrest lived in perilous circumstances, never knowing when and how their safety would again be compromised. Concepts recognizing the trauma of house arrest were also developed, acknowledging that the particular form of house arrest in the 1980s, which required people to be their own jailers, was extremely stressful. In addition, house arrest and being required to report to police stations opened people up to possible assassination en route.

Developing Strategies to Expand Legal Space

In addition to developing Indigenous theory and practice, Concerned Social Workers aimed to challenge apartheid through legal means. While individual members participated in illegal activities, Concerned Social Workers, alongside other anti-apartheid organizations, consciously developed strategies to expand the legal space for protest.

One strategy involved reconstructing the language used by the state in its legislation and policies. This is seen in the examples above of having "tea parties" rather than meetings and "freeing children" rather than ending detention. We also developed unconventional ways of gathering. For example, we would ferry relatives of persons on death row to visits in minibuses. This enabled mutual support and information sharing while travelling.

Other strategies used to minimize state repercussions included developing alliances with a broad range of organizations, providing direct services that were difficult for the state to criminalize, using churches and "legitimate" public spaces as venues, and having open meetings, rather than clandestine, underground meetings. Limiting state repercussions was also achieved by involving high-profile persons, particularly persons with international standing, in conferences and events. This also had the goal of increasing the public legitimacy of our actions. Having widespread public support made it more difficult for the state to criminalize our actions. At the same time, steps were taken to protect members by, for example, not keeping membership lists or excluding identifying information on case notes. Creating Concerned Social Workers as a professional body was a further strategy: the organization did not simply protest against apartheid, but grounded its challenges in professional expertise. As social workers, recognized by society as serving those who are most vulnerable and registered by a statutory body, we also were tolerated to act as a conscience to society.

A further strategy to expand legal space was situating ourselves within a broad coalition of legal organizations, interests converging around an explicitly political objective (Dluhy & with the assistance of Stanford Kravitz, 1990, p. 10).

▶ Lessons Learned

Having recounted our story of resisting apartheid South Africa's policies, particularly regarding children, we would like to identify some enduring lessons about the nature and practice of social work.

We have had a lived experience of social work's power as a profession. We learned that we could stand by our truth even in the face of fear and that this created meaning – for us and for service users. We saw that social workers have the capacity to be forces of change and transformation. Our social work values of social justice, human rights, compassion, and activist service remain inspirational and sustaining. We learned to locate our practice within the political arena and to simultaneously maintain care and compassion at the individual level. In this way, we politicized welfare and humanized politics. It became evident that collective action, both as a profession and as a global community, is powerful in bearing witness and actively challenging injustice.

Our experience 30 years ago has shaped us as social workers, strengthening our values and sharpening our theory and practice. Working in solidarity also has provided a lifelong community of support. It remains essential for social workers, as an expression of our professional identity, to oppose injustice in all contexts.

Notes

1. We use labels regarding race reservedly, as these are constructions of ideology and language rather than all-encompassing descriptors of various groups of people. We resort to these labels because apartheid was centred on particular constructions of race, this impacting on every area of life.
2. In the context of the South African struggle for liberation, "black" denotes all people who were oppressed and discriminated against. This included people of Asian and mixed race descent as well as African Indigenous peoples.
3. Police power was such that some detainees were deprived of minimal liberties such as the statutory provision of Bibles.
4. This is the process of raising consciousness of the ways in which structural dynamics impact people's everyday experiences (Freire, 1981).

References

Adams, R., Dominelli, D., & Payne, M. (Eds.). (2009). *Critical practice in social work*. (2nd ed.). Basingstoke: Palgrave Macmillan.

Badenhorst, C. (2010). *Productive writing: Becoming a prolific academic writer*. Pretoria: Van Schaik.

Bailey, R., & Brake, M. (Eds.). (1975). *Radical social work*. London: Edward Arnold.

Clifford, D., & Burke, B. (2009). *Anti-oppressive ethics and values in social work*. Basingstoke: Palgrave Macmillan.

Coleman, M. (1998). *A crime against humanity*. Cape Town: David Philip.

Dluhy, M.J., & Kravitz, S. (1990). *Building coalitions in the human services*. Newbury Park, CA: Sage.

Dominelli, L. (1988). *Anti-racist social work*. London: Macmillan.

Ferguson, I. (2008). *Reclaiming social work: Challenging neo-liberalism and promoting social justice*. Los Angeles: Sage.

Freire, P. (1981). *Education for critical consciousness*. New York: Continuum.

Greater Johannesburg Welfare Social Service and Development Forum. (1999). Submissions from the welfare sector to the Truth and Reconciliation Commission. Unpublished manuscript. Johannesburg.
Human Rights Commission. (1990). Violence in detention. In B. McKendrick and W. Hoffmann (Eds.), *People and violence in South Africa* (pp. 405–435). Cape Town: Oxford University Press.
Langan, M., & Day, L. (1992). *Women, oppression and social work*. London: Routledge.
Lawyers Committee for Human Rights. (1986). *The war against children: South Africa's youngest victims*. New York: Lawyers Committee for Human Rights.
Patel, L. (1992). *Restructuring social welfare: Options for South Africa*. Johannesburg: Ravan Press.
Pauw, J. (1997). *The night Ferdi Barnard told me he killed*. http://mg.co.za/article/1997-11-21-the-night-ferdi-barnard-told-me-he-killed
Republic of South Africa. (1996). *Constitution of South Africa. Act 108 of 1996*. Pretoria: Government Printers.
Sacco, T.M. (1988). Free South Africa's children: The effects of detention on children and their families. *Human Rights Quarterly, 10*(1), 91–95.
Sacco, T.M. (1989). Detentions: Minister of health admits health hazards. *In Touch: Newsletter of Concerned Social Workers,* 1, 5.
Saleebey, D. (2009). *The strengths perspective in social work practice*. (5th ed.). Boston: Allyn and Bacon.
Schmid, J., & Sacco, T.M. (2012). A story of resistance: "Concerned Social Workers." *Social Work Researcher – Practitioner, 24*(3), 291–308.
Statham, D. (1978). *Radicals in social work*. London: Routledge Kegan and Paul.
Thompson, N. (2006). *Anti-discriminatory practice*. (4th ed.). Basingstoke: Palgrave Macmillan.
Truth and Reconciliation Commission. (1998a). *Truth and Reconciliation Commission of South Africa Report*. Vol. 1. Cape Town: CTP Book Printers.
Truth and Reconciliation Commission. (1998b). *Truth and Reconciliation Commission of South Africa Report*. Vol. 4. Cape Town: CTP Book Printers.
Union of South Africa. Native Land Act (Act No. 27 of 1913).
Union of South Africa. Native Land and Trust Act (Act No. 18 of 1936).
Union of South Africa. Native Urban Areas Act (Act No. 21 of 1923) as amended in 1937.
Union of South Africa. The Colour Bar Act (Act No. 25 of 1926).

CHAPTER 4

Social Workers, Resistance, and Martial Law in the Philippines

A View from Below

Mary Lou L. Alcid

> *The transition from legal to underground worker was seamless. I worked and lived with peasants in Eastern Visayas. I was shocked by their state of impoverishment. We ate twice a day, subsisting on sweet potatoes. Rice and salt were precious commodities. There was no electricity. The repressive conditions in the countryside raised consciousness, mine included. All I thought about was the imperative of joining the people's movement against repression, even if it cost me my life.*
>
> Lita, personal communication, 4 May 2013

Lita is one of hundreds of social workers who joined the national democratic movement during martial law in the Philippines – from its imposition on 23 September 1972 until its formal lifting on 17 January 1981 and the ouster of President Ferdinand E. Marcos in February 1986. Her story is typical of her generation of progressive social workers in the 1970s. It underscores how prevailing socio-economic and political realities shape social workers' consciousness as well as their professional and personal choices.

Martial law radicalized many social work students and professionals who, upon individual and collective reflection, realized that to be a social worker is to be on the side of the poor and marginalized, working alongside them in the struggle for freedom, democracy, and justice. It is about the transformative character of social work – that is, engaging client systems in processes and relationships directed toward changing social structures that reproduce and perpetuate poverty, inequality, and oppression.

This chapter is part of ongoing research on that generation of courageous social workers. It is based mainly but not solely on the narratives of nine women social workers, including the author. Except for one, all obtained their Bachelor of Science in Social Work degree in the academic year 1975–76 from the then Institute of Social Work and Community Development, University of the Philippines in Diliman, Quezon City. The graduation of the sole exception was delayed by two years because she dropped out to join the underground national democratic movement.

The main objective of this chapter is to show that while the Philippine Association of Social Workers Inc, supported and cooperated with the Marcos dictatorship in the 1970s (Yu, 2006, p. 259), there were social workers who took the opposite direction. They worked in various sites of struggle toward mainstreaming democratic ideals, processes, and social relations, either of the national democratic tradition, which was then considered radical, or the moderate social democratic one. By the ethos of that period, they were all considered subversives.

The chapter describes the socio-political conditions under martial law. It then examines the process of how the nine social workers became socially aware as students, and the way they reframed social work to serve the interests of the poor. The critical elements and processes of "subversive" social work are presented, as articulated by the social workers, and the attendant risks and challenges are discussed.

▶ THE SOCIO-POLITICAL CONTEXT UNDER MARTIAL LAW

Filipino sociologist Randy David (2012, p. 1) describes Philippine society in the early 1970s as politically unstable, marked by rising criminality, endless congressional investigations, restiveness in Mindanao, and the presence of a communist movement that easily recruited the youth. De Dios (1996, p. 144) adds it was a time of nationalist revival, of protests against US imperialism and its local partners. Student activism that emerged strongly in the 1960s in the Philippines and globally continued and intensified in the 1970s (Llanes, 2012, p. 7). Universities and colleges, especially publicly owned ones like the University of the Philippines, were sites of discontent and protests. The government used police force to disperse and quell rallies and demonstrations, leading to accusations of fascism. Eventually, it put the country under martial law through Proclamation No. 1081, dated 21 September 1972. Said Proclamation outlined purportedly verified information about a conspiracy by "lawless elements" to wage armed insurrection and rebellion against the government of the Republic of the Philippines to justify martial rule. But many knew it was Marcos's only option to extend his reign.

Martial law suspended all democratic rights and institutions. Curfew was imposed. Mass media entities that were perceived to be critical of Marcos were shut down. Oppositionist political leaders such as Senator Benigno Aquino, considered to be a rising star in politics and a direct threat to Marcos, were arrested and detained. All universities were closed and would reopen only after a month. Checkpoints were set up on the streets and at colleges and universities. Protest actions were banned.

In the countryside, militarization intensified, particularly in areas the government suspected of being sympathetic to the outlawed Communist Party of the Philippines and the New People's Army. Communities felt the effects of hamletting – that is, being placed under direct military control – and the creation of paramilitary units.

More than 50,000 people were arrested in the first three years of martial law (Amnesty International, 1981). Various forms of torture were also used on detainees. An Amnesty International mission in 1975 revealed that 71 out of 107 detainees it interviewed claimed to have been tortured. As a consequence of political repression, many progressive people's organizations had to go underground. The government used its resources to run after those it suspected of being subversive. Its military force of only 60,000 in 1972 increased to 300,000 in 1975. This excludes the 221,000 members of the paramilitary Civilian Home Defense Forces (de Dios, 1996).

Poverty worsened under martial law. Almario (2011) cites a World Bank study that revealed that the proportion of people living below the poverty line grew from 24% in 1974 to 50% in 1986. Inequality based on income and wealth increased. The upper 13% of the people increased their share in national income from 22% in 1980 to 46% in 1983. On the other hand, for the same period, the bottom 11% of the people saw a decrease in their share, from 17% to only 6% (from McDougal, in Almario, 2011). Foreign debt increased, from less than US$1 billion in 1966 to $28 billion in February 1986 (Padilla, 2004). This was the context in which nine young women came to grips with what social work means to us personally and professionally.

▶ THE RESEARCH STUDY

The data for this chapter were obtained from an ongoing study that began in the third quarter of 2012. The study seeks to determine why and how social workers challenged and resisted martial law. The initial design was national in scope. However, some of the known activist social workers in the 1970s who are based outside of Metro Manila, where the author is, while expressing interest in the study, did not have the time to write their personal narratives. For the purpose of writing this chapter, the author decided to focus on her college batch (cohort) at the University of the Philippines in Diliman.

The nine research participants were chosen because they became part of the anti-dictatorship movement in the Philippines as students and/or as professional social workers. Moreover, they have also managed to sustain their friendship and communication through the decades. Five wrote their own personal narratives based on the guide questions the author gave. Another four were interviewed by phone. In the case of one participant, this phone interview complements the autobiographical sketch she submitted to the college alumni association which has been uploaded on its website. The narrative of the ninth participant was based on an autobiographical sketch she contributed to the same alumni association.

The names of the women have been changed to protect their privacy except for those who have published accounts of their experiences.

Resistance is operationally defined as any act to challenge, undermine, and replace legal authority. Ewick and Silbey (2003, pp. 1336–1337) identify elements of resistance, namely, a consciousness that one is in a position of less power relative to another, a consciousness of opportunity which the less powerful use to their advantage, and the presence of claims regarding justice and fairness. Since resistance is a practical consequence of oppositional social and political consciousnesss, the study looked into the process of consciousness-raising or what Paulo Freire calls conscientization that the nine women went through and how this process led to a definition of the kind of social work education and practices that was needed by prevailing socio-political realities under martial law.

▶ REFRAMING SOCIAL WORK AS A FORM OF RESISTANCE

Personal Profile of the Nine Social Workers

The nine women social workers belonged to a batch of at least 45 Bachelor of Science in Social Work majors. The batch, all women except for two, was remarkable for its relatively big size, its diversity in terms of socio-economic variables, ideological persuasion, as well as year of admission to the University, and its performance in the 1976 social work licensure exam, where batch members took seven of the top ten positions. It was also caught in that historical juncture when martial law was declared, and students reconsidered the conventional definition of social work amid an oppressive regime. About 11 were either already activists since high school or became activists while in college. Five were known to have joined the underground national democratic movement after college.

Three of the nine social workers were from the province, and the rest from Metro Manila. All but two, Lita and Beng, were products of private Catholic schools. Their narratives revealed the influence of a middle-class family, Catholic education, and the concomitant charitable practices (e.g., visiting orphanages, teaching Catechism, engaging in community outreach activities) in orienting them to care for and be in solidarity with the poor and marginalized. Social responsibility was something they learned and practised early on. It is defined as a consciousness of "the nature of a person's relationship with others and with the larger social and political world" (Berman, 1997, p. 12). According to Maruyama (2002, p. 11), this consciousness is stimulated in situations when one is confronted with people's suffering, struggles, and oppression. Thus, it may be argued that social responsibility is the outcome of social awareness. Social responsibility, in turn, leads to compassionate actions that may range from the charitable to the more politically charged ones that include popular education, social mobilization, and organizing among the poor.

One participant, Vilma, identified Ananda Marga (Sanskrit for "Path of Bliss"), a global organization engaged in social services, meditation and yoga, and in community development, as a major influence on her development of social awareness and responsibility.

Five – Agnes, Carrie, Ana, Mary, and Vilma – were already involved in student activism in high school. They had access to and were members of campus organizations that were part of social movements. They helped organize students, peasants, public utility drivers, and urban poor communities then referred to as "squatters." They took part in mass actions like rallies and demonstrations and in sit-ins to generate public awareness and support for multi-sectoral issues and demands. Through the discussion groups they attended, they learned to connect the lived realities of the poor to systemic and structural bases such as feudalism, capitalism, and imperialism. These discussions taught them that charity was not the solution to people's impoverishment.

The women were between 16 and 17 years of age when they entered the University of the Philippines in 1970 (Seth), 1971 (Beng, Aida, and Agnes), 1972 (Ana, Carrie, Lita, and the author), and 1974 (Vilma, who was a transferee from a private university in the Visayas). Social work was not their first choice. The eight who started their college life at the University of the Philippines shifted to Social Work from other academic programs such as Associate Bachelor General, or in sociology, psychology, broadcast communications, economics, or nursing. Martial law was a factor in their decision to shift. Because of widespread poverty, inequality, and repression, they looked for a degree program that would give them the competencies to work directly with the poor and the marginalized. Carrie felt that sociology only sought to understand but not solve social problems. Aida, who enrolled in economics to know the causes of recurring oil price hikes, became dissatisfied with conventional quantitative economic analysis which dominated the discipline.

The women also wanted to distance themselves from serving the dictatorship. For example, the broadcast communications major did not see a future for herself in her chosen field because all media companies were government-controlled and she did not want to be a Marcos mouthpiece.

Ana captured the experience of the women in saying that the shift to social work "was a continuation of growing social awareness and understanding."

Community Exposures and Field Instruction as Pedagogical Tools

As students of social work in the early 1970s, the women were taught that social work was the enhancement of social functioning. The law regulating the practice of social work, which was enacted in 1965 (Republic Act No. 4373), defines social work as the "profession which is primarily concerned with organized social service activity aimed to facilitate and strengthen basic social relationships and the mutual adjustment between individuals and their social environment for the good of the individual and of society." A number of social work educators emphasized adjustment to, not the interrogation of the roots of Philippine impoverishment, and working with individuals and groups amid the status quo. The women felt the curriculum lacked the critical focus on working with communities and engaged their faculty in this regard. Under martial law, community organizing, particularly that which involved consciousness raising and mobilization, was often regarded by the government as subversive. Despite this, the women thought it was the more relevant and appropriate social work method given the circumstances.

Because of the liberal education at the University of the Philippines even under martial law, the nine women were exposed to the ideas of Karl Marx, Mao Tse Tung, Paolo Freire, Gustavo Gutierrez, and Saul Alinsky. Locally, they were inspired by the nationalist, anti-colonial and anti-imperialist ideas of Claro M. Recto, Teodoro Agoncillo, Renato Constantino, and Jose Maria Sison, a former University of the Philippines professor who led the re-establishment of the Communist Party of the Philippines in the late 1960s. Consequently, the women found the clinical emphasis and coping in social work limiting to the situation of the Filipino people. They also consciously endeavoured to think, speak, and write in Filipino, the national language, instead of English, which they viewed as the language of power and status. Lita, particularly, deliberately wrote all her term papers in Filipino in keeping with her patriotic philosophy.

The social work curriculum and pedagogy at the University of the Philippines increased social awareness and responsibility. Community immersion and the supervised field instruction courses provided social work students the opportunity to work with individuals, groups, and communities for a cumulative total of 1,000 hours. The latter is a legal provision of R.A. No. 4373. The women came face to face with poverty and the oppressive and exploitative character of the state in rural and urban areas. At least two faculty members who were involved with progressive non-governmental organizations and people's organizations linked the students with non-traditional social work settings for supervised field instruction, particularly those engaged in community organizing.

Agnes, an activist since high school, remembers being deeply affected by a field visit to an urban poor community where she met a mother who carried her dead 3-week-old baby wrapped in a native mat. The mother had no money for her baby's burial. For her field instruction, Agnes opted to work with Task Force Detainees, undertaking research, advocacy, and direct services to promote the rights and interests of political detainees and their families. She served people who had directly experienced military atrocities. She has not forgotten one client, a laundry woman who had had a hot clothes iron pressed against her leg by military personnel when she could not tell them the whereabouts of her child, a suspected subversive.

Seven of the nine women worked with urban poor communities in Quezon City for their field instruction on community organizing, a five-unit course. Seth, just back from an exchange program in Canada, thought her classroom courses did not prepare her enough for the glaring realities of poverty in the urban community she and one other classmate were assigned to. In her own words, "We lived (more like scratched a living), ate (there was hardly enough), breathed (stale air) and learned (a lot) complementing the theories that were taught in the classroom and prepared me for what I could expect when I graduate" (Papasin, 2012).

Beng's supervised field instruction in an urban poor community provided her with an opportunity to experience with the people what it was like to be socially excluded from mainstream development. Moreover, she had the chance to engage them in the action-reflection praxis of community organizing to address issues such as lack of potable water. She was elated to see a change in the mothers she worked with – "from feelings of helplessness and resignation towards hope and empowerment, and a resolve that only through organized and highly conscientized actions can meaningful social transformation take place" (Buenaventura, 2012). It was well worth the risks she took. She and her classmate incurred the ire of the pro-Marcos officials of the community who put them under surveillance. They played cat and mouse with the Metropolitan Command of the Philippine Constabulary and with the Military Intelligence Special Group that branded them as communists. Consequently, tactics sessions had to be done clandestinely.

Living and working in the community dispelled stereotypes of the urban poor as lazy, hopeless, and criminal. Seth marvelled at the dignity, respect, and ingenuity that marked the way the urban poor lived, and how they always dreamed, always hoped that one day they would be able to pull themselves out of poverty.

Social Work: From Enhancement of Social Functioning to Organizing People for Power

Precisely because of the repressive environment, the women's exposure to the actual conditions of the poor, living and working with them, and for some, involvement in the underground movement, in their work these women were attracted to and applied structural frameworks and tools of social analysis as opposed to psychodynamic and clinical ones. According to Carrie,

> We didn't agree with the way social work was being taught ... and the (individual) context in which it was taught. We challenged our professors about the need to deal with root causes and addressing issues at a community level rather than limiting social work only to an individual and family level. We expanded social work thinking to include community organizing and holding government accountable for the rights of people, ensuring that ordinary folks are empowered to participate in decisions that affected their lives. (Personal communication, 2013)

One militant faculty member, the late Flora Celi-Lansang, who was one of the first to be arrested and detained after martial law was imposed, had a profound and lasting influence on these women. Lansing taught courses on social welfare policies, programs and services, and social action. She inspired the women "to make a difference in the lives of poor people in urban and rural communities through organizing and mobilizing them in actions that transformed them into critical participants in development" (Buenaventura, 2012). Professor Lansang was a role model for the anti-oppressive kind of social work that the women came to learn and apply in their community work.

Accordingly, the women reframed the ideological basis of social work in response to existing realities. The popular call of the 1970s was "Serve the people." These women realized that in social work, serving the people required the pursuit of social justice and structural change. Social work, therefore, assumed an anti-dictatorship character as the women opted for grassroots organizing using democratic and participatory processes as opposed to the government's top-down and technocratic approach. It "became a means to engage the oppressed in organising, consciousness raising, and collective action towards building another society totally different from, and opposed to Marcos's *Bagong Lipunan* (New Society)" (Alcid, 2012, p. 1). As Ana explains, "Power to the people through community organizing was the way to true democracy. With the masses empowered and organized, a united front of people's organizations had the potential to overthrow the dictatorship and effect social change" (personal communication, 2013).

Although urban poor realities played a major role in the development of their social awareness as social work students, the women did acknowledge the fact that the majority of the poor were in rural areas. They also realized that the so-called rural development programs under martial law, including agrarian reform, only pushed the people deeper into debt and penury. At the Institute then there were already discussions on the role of social work education in rural development. The administration, faculty, and students were open to the idea of the Institute producing social workers who would work in rural areas. But, first, the curriculum had to be revised.

The revision of the Bachelor of Science in Social Work curriculum began as a project of the women in their social action class under Professor Lansang. It became a reality when the social work faculty accepted the proposed changes and obtained University approval. The curricular changes set the direction and content of the Bachelor of Science in Social Work program for the next decade. They included (1) the stress on rural development, (2) the addition of a course on rural social work practice, and (3) the streamlining of field instruction courses, from three to two. The first field instruction course was on working with individuals and groups and was given 5 units. The second field instruction course, now equivalent to 15 units and on block arrangement, focused on developing knowledge, skills, and the right attitudes in community organizing in the context of rural areas. By the late 1970s, the Institute had officially adopted participatory development with a rural thrust as its platform.

By the second semester of the academic year 1977–78, the Department of Social Work of the Institute deployed its first batch of 13 senior students to live in three rural villages in Southern Luzon. There the students engaged leaders from the ranks of peasants and fisherfolk in a participatory process of addressing issues and concerns such as river pollution, low farm income in the face of increasing costs, and malnutrition.

This kind of social work raised suspicions of subversion. Subversion, under martial law, operationally referred to all actions that were perceived by the government as challenging, undermining, and/or opposing it. Such actions included raising awareness of and organizing the poor and/or moving from urban centres to rural areas for immersion or employment. The military assumed that college students and/or professionals, already based in urban centres, would not decide to work in rural areas unless they were subversives with a hidden agenda. The military became more suspicious when the students or professionals came from the University of the Philippines which had developed the reputation of being the breeding ground of radical students and faculty. Thus, Institute officials often met with town mayors and military commanders to explain the presence of the faculty and students in rural communities, the participatory rural development model that they operationalized, and organizing work, and why it transformed once passive people into active and articulate stakeholders in their communities.

▶ OTHER SITES OF RESISTANCE TO MARTIAL LAW

There were two main arenas of resistance to martial law: above ground (open/legal) and underground (clandestine revolutionary movements). All of the women in the study were linked at various levels to either the legal or clandestine arms of the national or social democratic movements. While working above ground, a few of them did have links with the underground. Thus, above ground and underground work did not always run along separate parallel lines.

Social Workers in the Underground

Seth was the only one of the nine to drop out of college to join the underground movement. The repressive political environment forced her to do so. According to Seth,

> Fellow activists were being picked up, tortured, imprisoned. I had to go underground and was sheltered by numerous friends who took me to the mountains in Laguna. I was in the company of people who only have first names preceded by Ka, as in Kasama (i.e., comrade). My indoctrination in the Maoist-Leninist philosophy deepened. I had to leave my family and friends and the little comforts that I got used to. (Personal communication, 2012)

But she resurfaced and completed her remaining semester in 1978.

Seth was not alone, as two others (Lita and Vilma) also became full-time underground organizers after working with church-based organizations with links to the clandestine arm of the national democratic movement. Lita, who was then a 20-year-old new graduate, sought answers to questions like "Where can I best practise my profession? What do prevailing social conditions require from the profession?" As a student, she had joined mass actions and witnessed police brutality from the sidelines. After college, she was recruited to work in a community-based health program in one of the poorest provinces in Eastern Visayas. She was assigned to a village that was three hours away from the town centre. This village, she was to find out later, was among the areas influenced by the clandestine national democratic movement.

Lita learned the local language, shared the people's impoverishment, and witnessed repression. The people's love boosted her morale and inspired her to carry on. She remembers people engaging in basic claim-making actions for access to basic services which the government labelled "subversive." The repressive conditions raised her consciousness, making the decision to go underground easy, and the transition seamless. Personal security was not an issue. In the underground, she was able to use skills she learned in social work such as counselling and organizing.

Vilma decided to forego attendance in the college graduation rites and membership in honour societies in favour of proceeding immediately to community work. She worked with peasants, factory workers, urban poor, and the Indigenous peoples. Social work for her was not just a profession but also an embodiment of active citizenship, being part of a movement for change. The personal and professional were one and the same.

Among the social workers who joined the underground movement, one of the more prominent was Judy Taguiwalo, Ph.D., who obtained her Bachelor's degree in Social Work from the University of the Philippines in 1969. She was 18 years old when she became aware of the contradictions in society through her participation in discussion groups. When martial law was declared, she opted to go to the countryside. Integrating with peasant families, she came to grips in a concrete way with feudalism, imperialism, and military violence. She was arrested in 1973 and subjected to severe physical and mental torture. She was stripped, made to sit on a block of ice, and given the "water cure" – a torture method where water is poured through the nostrils until one feels as if one is drowning. She escaped in 1974 and went back to the underground movement (Taguiwalo, 2012a). In 1984, four months pregnant, she was arrested again, charged under two secret presidential decrees (PD Nos. 1834 and 1839) that made subversion, rebellion, sedition, and other related crimes capital offences, with penalties ranging from life imprisonment to death (Human Rights Online Philippines, 2012). She gave birth in prison. The Philippine Association for Social Workers Inc campaigned for her release on humanitarian grounds. Its executive secretary then was another progressive social worker, Evelyn Balais-Serrano. The said campaign was supported by the International Federation of Social Workers through Serrano's efforts. On 1 March 1986, shortly after the ouster of Marcos, Judy was released from detention.

Purificacion "Puri" Pedro, another social work alumna of the University of the Philippines (1968) is among the anti-dictatorship martyrs – perhaps the only social worker – whose names are inscribed in the Bantayog ng mga Bayani (Heroes' Memorial). According to the Bantayog website, she worked in the Catholic Church's social action programs. In a letter to her family, she acknowledged the difficulties and dangers of her work (Taguiwalo, 2012b). But she was at peace with herself, finding joy in her choice of profession where financial gain was not the primary consideration. She asked her family not to worry about her, assuring them that she was happy serving the poor and the oppressed.

In 1977, while visiting friends who had joined the New People's Army in a provincial area that she did not know was under military operation, Purificacion Pedro was shot in the shoulder and captured. The military kept watch during her hospital confinement. On the sixth day, Philippine Constabulary men forced their way into her room to interrogate her. After they left, family members found Puri, 29 years old, dead by strangulation in the hospital bathroom.

Social Workers above Ground

The academy was one arena of resistance to martial law. Four of these nine women joined the academy. Two went into teaching while the other two engaged in research and training. All but one stayed on at the Institute. The Institute with its espousal of bias for the poor and participatory development provided an enabling environment for popularizing progressive social work and fostering partnerships with sectoral people's organizations among the urban poor, peasants, and workers for action research and social movement building. One action research study that Carrie and the author were part of explored the perceptions of the people of San Juan, Batangas, with regard to the government-initiated establishment of a copper smelting plant in one of the villages. The research showed overwhelming opposition to the proposed project, mainly on ecological grounds. The provincial governor used the findings to successfully convince Marcos to transfer the plant elsewhere.

Another site of resistance were the non-governmental organizations that were established so that social workers would not have to work with the government and could autonomously develop their own programs and services. One of the first to be established was the Agency for Community Services that worked with small farmers. One of its founders is the current secretary of Social Welfare and Development, Corazon Juliano-Soliman. Two of the nine women, namely, Mary and Carrie, were part of this NGO.

The Agency for Community Services was followed by the Organization for Training, Research and Development Inc which the author and nine former students, all University of the Philippines Bachelor of Science in Social Work graduates, founded in 1979. The oldest among the Organization's founders was a former political detainee who was in his 30s and served as the de facto visionary. The Organization for Training, Research and Development engaged in community organizing, project development, and advocacy with Indigenous peoples and small fisherfolk. It encountered serious challenges, particularly in explaining its presence in upland communities to the military, and even experiencing occasional harassment and intimidation. After three years, two among the women founders felt that this kind of resistance was slow and limiting in terms of pursuing structural change in society and they opted to join the underground movement.

Three (Beng, Agnes, and Ana) of the nine women joined national government agencies such as the National Irrigation Administration. They sought to create spaces to pursue participatory development. At the National Irrigation Administration, Agnes developed a participatory approach to the management of irrigation systems at the national and local levels. This required investment in the education, capacity building, and organizing of farmers. With a supportive management, she was able to have irrigation systems operated and managed by farmers' associations. She was branded "subversive" by some of her colleagues. At the same time, the New People's Army was also suspicious of this move by government. Through this work, Agnes says she evolved from a grassroots orientation to one of institution building. By this, she refers to the importance of institutionalizing participatory and innovative practices.

Social Work under Martial Law

While established leaders of social welfare and social work supported martial law, there were young social work students and practitioners who engaged in organized efforts to resist, undermine, and challenge the legitimacy of the government, thereby contributing to the ouster of Marcos in February 1986. Pedro, Taguiwalo, and the nine women, all alumni of the University of the Philippines, are but a few representatives. Coming from mostly middle-class and Catholic backgrounds, they grew up during one of the most turbulent and repressive periods in Philippine history. Social awareness and responsibility as well as political involvement came as early as in high school for some, and intensified in college at the University of the Philippines. The school was a site for socialization into traditional social work but community immersion, the presence of progressive faculty members, and supervised field instruction in non-traditional settings provided spaces that these nine women utilized to engage each other and their faculty about how social work could be more responsive to the plight of the people under martial law. These young professionals, who were in search of their own identity and meaning in their personal and professional lives, found it in living with the poor and marginalized communities in rural and urban areas, using participatory and democratic processes, in consciousness-raising activities, and for some, in joining the revolutionary movement.

Martial law confronted these women with the challenge of defending the democratic rights of the communities they worked with in the face of state repression and violence. Faced with the challenges of the times, the social workers resorted to various forms of extralegal action even in the face of threats to their personal security. These forms of social action, subversive at that time, embodied many of the principles we lay claim to today: social justice, human rights, empowerment, liberation, and social change. Many of the kinds of work they undertook – popular education, organizing and mobilizing communities, enabling communities to link with and become part of a social movement to gain scale and power – are not illegal in many contemporary societies but were deliberately defined as such within the repressive Philippine state. In choosing to act as they did, these women social workers redefined the realm of legitimate action beyond the political-legal framework of the established order.

References

Alcid, Mary Lou. (2012, 23 Aug.). *Home grown and growing*. Retrieved 8 Jan. 2013 from http://cswcd.upd.edu.ph/?p=3275

Almario, M.F. (2011, 11 Feb.). *The dismal record of the Marcos regime.* Retrieved 5 Dec. 2012 from http://www.philstar.com/letters-editor/660957/dismal-record-marcos-regime

Amnesty International. (1981, 11–28 Nov.). *Report as cited in Martial Law Files: A history of resistance.* Retrieved 8 Jan. 2013 from http://martiallawfiles.net/

Bantayog ng mga Bayani. *Pedro, Purificacion A.* Retrieved 8 Jan. 2013 from http://www.bantayog.org/node/172

Berman, S. (1997). *Children's consciousness and the development of social responsibility.* Albany: State University of New York Press.

Buenaventura, E.M. (2012, 1 Oct.). *"Papa, look where I am now! Thank you, CSWCD!"* Retrieved 8 Jan. 2013 from http://cswcd.upd.edu.ph/?p=3393

David, R. (2012, 13 Sept.). *Marcos and martial law.* Retrieved 5 Dec. 2012 from http://opinion.inquirer.net/36606/marcos-and-martial-law

de Dios, A. (1996). Participation of women's groups in the anti-dictatorship struggle: Genesis of a movement. In Myrna S. Feliciano, Zeus Salaza, Romero V. Cruz, Carolyn Israel Sobritchea, Mary Grace Ampil Tirona, Sofia Logarta, Aurora Javate de Dios, Socorro L. Reyes, Luzviminda G. Tancangco, and Albinan Peczon-Fernandez, *Women's role in philippine history: Selected essays* (2nd ed.) (pp. 141–168). Quezon City: University of the Philippines and UP Center for Women's Studies.

Ewick, P., & Silbey, S. (2003). Narrating social structure: Stories of resistance to legal authority. *American Journal of Sociology, 108*(6), 1328–1372.

Llanes, F.C. (Ed.). (2012). *Tibak rising: Activism in the days of martial law.* Manila: Anvil.

Maruyama, E. (2002). *Identity and political consciousness: Community involvement of Mexican/Chicano youth.* Master's thesis, San Jose State University. Retrieved 5 June 2015 from http://scholarworks.sjsu.edu/etd_theses/2366/

Padilla, A. (2004). Taxpayers to pay Marcos debt until 2015. Retrieved 8 Jan. 2013 from http://www.bulatlat.com/news/4-33/4-33-marcosdebt.html

Papasin, S. (2012, 5 Sept.). *What I learned from the Institute.* Retrieved 8 Jan. 2013 from http://cswcd.upd.edu.ph/?p=3333

Taguiwalo, J. (2012a). Babaeng "Makibaka" sa Likod ng Rehas. In F.C. Llanes (Ed.), *Tibak rising: Activism in the days of martial law* (pp. 44–47). Manila: Anvil.

Taguiwalo, J. (2012b, 10 Apr.). *Hangarin at Pagsisikap para sa Tunay na Makataong Kaunlaran ni Puri Pedro.* Retrieved 8 Jan. 2013 from http://cswcd.upd.edu.ph/?cat=8&paged=6

Human Rights Online Philippines. (2012, 11 May). *Remember Judy Taguiwalo #remember ML @40.* Retrieved 10 Jan. 2013 from http://hronlineph.com/2012/05/11/remember-judy-taguiwalo-rememberml40/

Yu, N.G. (2006). Interrogating social work: Philippine social work and human rights under martial law. *International Journal of Social Welfare, 15*(3), 257–263.

CHAPTER 5

Medha Patkar's Environmental Activism and Professional Social Work in India

Mass Legitimacy and Myopic Structures

Manohar Pawar and Venkat Pulla

> *The first prime minister of India, Jawaharlal Nehru, called dams the "temples of modern India" in 1955. – Certainly this quote from him is still used and paraded even in primary schools, but he said something different three years later. He described big dams as "a disease of gigantism" that we must withdraw from as he realised that approach to water management was not going to work. But unfortunately the text books have the first quote not the second one.*
>
> Interview with Medha Patkar, 2004

This chapter aims to discuss the environmental activism of Medha Patkar – legitimized by the masses, restricted by the state, and mostly passively observed by the social work profession. Drawing on secondary data, we examine the nature and scope of Medha Patkar's environmental activism involving the mobilization of masses against challenges posed by the state in India, particularly through a range of *satyagraha*/social action methods employed to achieve social justice for poor and marginalized people threatened with displacement as a consequence of large-scale dam construction projects. The struggle centres on state interventions that obstruct the social action and question the legitimacy of the action that was undertaken with mass support, raising critical questions for the social work profession. We discuss the goals of the social movement, the satyagraha methods employed toward achieving them, and the responses of the state, and finally, we explore the implications for the social work profession.

▶ Brief Biography of Medha Patkar

Medha Patkar was born in Bombay/Mumbai, India, in 1954, and raised there. Her father, Vasant Khanolkar, was a lawyer working on behalf of industrial labour unions who took an active interest in India's struggle for independence. Her mother, Indu-ji, was involved in assisting women in difficult circumstances through a not-for-profit organization called Swadhaar (*Swa* in Sanskirt and Hindi means "self"; *adhaar* means support/reliance).

With a Bachelor of Science degree from Ruia College, Medha Patkar moved to the prestigious Tata Institute of Social Sciences (TISS) in 1974 and completed a master's degree in social work with specialization in community organization and development. Medha Patkar worked in non-governmental organizations for a few years before joining TISS as a faculty member and beginning work on a Ph.D. In this role, she visited the Narmada Valley Development Project/Plan, and in particular the Sardar Sarovar Project, to explore the issues of development and displacement and the resettlement and rehabilitation of displaced people.

Witnessing and understanding the upheaval and injustice caused to the innocent people including the *adivasis* (Indigenous peoples) living in the Narmada Valley, Medha Patkar immersed herself into fighting for their cause, forgoing her doctoral studies. Medha Patkar used the methods of community organization and social action to mobilize the communities and win the hearts of women, children, and men living in the Narmada Valley and beyond. By bringing together hundreds of local groups and organizations, Medha Patkar established and spearheaded one of the largest non-violent social movements in existence, both nationally and internationally, the Narmada Bachao Andolan (Save Narmada Movement) – to save and protect the Narmada River. Medha Patkar also helped create the National Alliance of People's Movements, a coalition of over 150 mass-based movements, and she is a coordinator of it.

Social workers in the West who are familiar with models of social planning, community organization, and social action will appreciate the integration of the three models in Medha Patkar's "campaign" that ran for a period of three decades. Social action and advocacy are the main strategies in Medha Patkar's work. A distinct element of her campaign is the use of satyagraha/social action methods, founded on the principle of non-violent resistance. These methods enabled her to develop the links from micro to macro levels and from macro to micro levels in the field. Her campaign was well connected at the grassroots levels with all affected communities and at the macro level with the three state governments of Gujarat, Maharashtra, and Madhya Pradesh, the central government of India, and with international non-government organizations and the World Bank. Her work espouses social justice and human rights, fundamental principles of social work. Medha Patkar has received a number of prestigious awards and these include the Right Livelihood Award (also known as the Alternative Nobel Prize) in 1992; the Goldman Environmental Prize in 1993; BBC's Green Ribbon Award for the Best International Political Campaigner; and the Human Rights Defender's Award from Amnesty International. Medha Patkar is an outstanding global citizen, yet rooted in the local. Her courage, conviction, integrity, and selfless sacrifice inspired the struggle of the people of the Narmada Valley against the threat of displacement and ecological destruction brought about by the construction of dams on the Narmada River.

▶ Dams and the Displacement of People in the Narmada Valley

The Narmada is the fifth-largest river located in central and western India, running over 13,000 kilometres through the states of Madhya Pradesh, Maharashtra, and Gujarat, joining the Arabian Sea. Along the valley of this river, several adivasi groups such as Bhil, Bhilala, Gond, and Korku live primarily in the forested land farther downstream from the riparian plains. Their survival depends upon the river water and the land, and the relationship they have with them (Baviskar, 1995; Paranjpe, 1991; Basu, 2010).

As part of the nation-building and economic development process following the independence of India, plans to build dams in the Narmada Valley were drawn up, and building work began in the early 1960s with the aim of providing irrigation and power to drought-prone regions and their surrounding areas. Due to disputes over project costs and benefits between Gujarat, Madhya Pradesh, and Maharashtra, the Narmada Water Disputes Tribunal was constituted in 1969. The Tribunal took about 10 years to resolve the matter, and the resolution resulted in a proposal to build 30 major dams, 135 medium-sized dams, 3,000 minor dams, and over 30,000 micro-harvesting (conservation) reservoirs. It was estimated that these dams will lead to direct displacement of 250,000 people living in the Narmada Valley and affect the livelihood of over one million people (Fisher, 1995; Sangvai, 2000; Bose, 2004).

The Narmada Valley Development Project/Plan (NVDP), and in particular the Sardar Sarovar Project (SSP) – the largest dam built on the Narmada

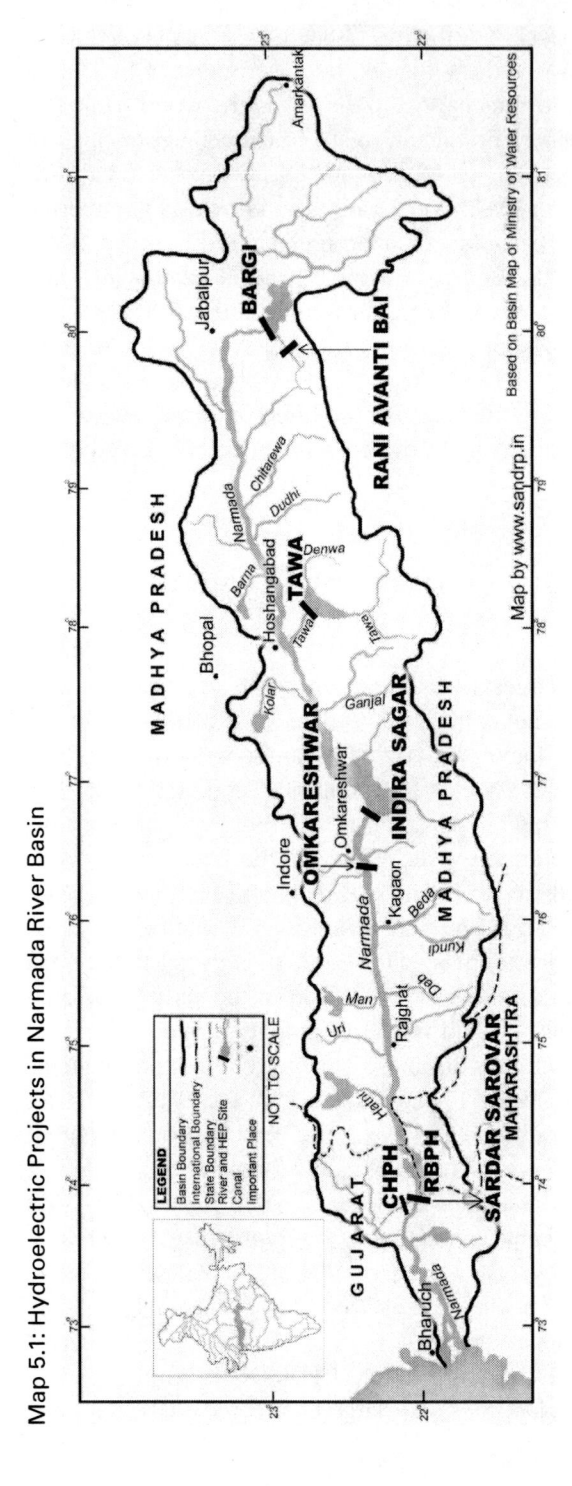

Map 5.1: Hydroelectric Projects in Narmada River Basin

Source: South Asia Network on Dams, Rivers and People (undated)

River which forms part of the NVDP – became controversial from the very beginning as questions were raised about the socio-economic and ecological benefits, the costs for the people most affected, and the long-term social and ecological impacts. Progress on the projects was weighed down by disputes over their impact and the process of implementation such as inadequate resettlement and rehabilitation measures. The core benefits of the projects, as outlined by proponents, primarily focused on economic development in the form of irrigation and hydroelectric power and drinking water, primarily focusing on economic development. The core arguments of the opponents focused on the massive social, ecological, and financial costs; displacement of adivasis without adequate resettlement support and consequent socio-cultural issues; and fundamental weaknesses in the sustainability of the development approach. The arguments of proponents (Patel, 1992; Pathak, 1991; Bose, 2004) and opponents (Singh, 1992; Bose, 2004; Jacques, 2006) are presented in Table 5.1.

Table 5.1: Supporting and Opposing Arguments on Narmada Valley Development Project

PROPONENT'S ARGUMENTS	OPPONENT'S ARGUMENTS
The irrigation of over 1.8 million hectares of land.	The flooding of the lands of 140,000 farmers for irrigation canals.
The provision of drinking water to 135 urban centres and 8,215 villages.	Disrupted livelihoods of thousands of farmers & fisher folk downstream.
The generation of over 200 megawatts (MW) of hydroelectric energy.	Most impact on indigenous peoples.
Flood protection for 210 villages as well as the major city of Bharuch.	Heavy ecological and financial burden on the region.
800 MW energy production for the state of Madhya Pradesh.	Loss of dense forests and the extinction of rare and endangered wildlife.
400 MW energy production for the state of Maharashtra.	Possible risk of tectonic instability and resulting earthquake activity. Increased danger of siltation, salinity & the loss of topsoil.
Potential irrigation gain for Rajsahstan's over 75,000 hectares of desert land.	Increased health risks from waterborne diseases.
	80% of Gujarat's irrigation and water budget is diverted to the project at the cost of other water conservation projects.
	Lack of transparency in project planning and implementation.
	Lack of public participation.
	In 100 years or so sediment will fill the reservoir turning the $10 billion dam into a useless waterfall.

The people most affected were Dalits, the "Untouchables" of the caste system, living in villages that would be submerged, and the adivasis of a region. A disproportionate number of those likely to be displaced were Indigenous people. Eight percent of India's populations are adivasis and 15% are Dalits, but an incredible 60% of those threatened with displacement by the Narmada dam projects were adivasis and Dalits. What the state failed to take into account were the costs associated with displacements affected by the devastating environmental impacts of building dams. In this context, Medha Patkar's activism led to the building of a massive social movement to challenge the prevailing development model and to protect the rights of the poor and marginalized people of the Narmada Valley.

▶ MEDHA PATKAR'S ENVIRONMENTAL ACTIVISM AND LEADERSHIP OF SOCIAL MOVEMENTS

Opposition to dams in local communities has gained prominence since the 1960s in India. At the beginning of the project in the Narmada region, residents of six villages were displaced to accommodate dam builders and officials. The residents protested but they were not adequately compensated (Singh, 1992, p. 31). There has been a lot of anecdotal evidence of inadequate and inappropriate resettlement in other similar projects. A general lack of awareness of information and rights, on the one hand, and official heavy-handedness and apathy, on the other, have contributed to significant personal trauma and injustices to displaced communities in several development projects despite the local people's protests, resistance, and opposition.

Medha Patkar's environmental activism and movement building came as a response to this challenge. Although it is not practical to discuss nearly 30 years of her social activism, we briefly present some of the critical, creative, and radical satyagraha methods successfully employed to build the Narmada Bachao Andolan (NBA), or Save Narmada Movement. Medha Patkar's environmental activism follows the Gandhian non-violent *satyagraha* and *asahakar* methods, which in Western terms may be understood as social action methods, though their meaning is much more powerful than "social action" as used in in Western literature. Satya means truth and *graha* means force. *Satyagraha* means accepting the force of the truth and *asahakar* means non-cooperation. According to Nehru, the first prime Minster of India, "Gandhi's non-violent form of 'satya graha' was 'accepted as a method, the congress has made that method its own, because of a belief in its effectiveness Gandhiji has placed it before the country not only as the right method but as the most effective one for our purpose.... It was not a coward's refuge from action, but a brave man's defiance of evil and national subjection'" (Nehru, 1958, cited from Sharp, 1980, p. 87). Further Sharp (1980) notes that "Gandhi operated on the basis of a view of power and avowedly based his newly developed approach to conflict – satyagraha ('the insistence on truth') – upon a theory of power: 'In politics its use is based upon the immutable maxim that government of the people is possible so long as they consent either consciously or unconsciously to be governed' (Gandhi, 1914)" (Nehru, 1958, in Sharp, 1980, pp. 87–88).

Medha Patkar's activism was very similar to the freedom struggle of India. If not for the leadership of Gandhi, the struggle for Indian independence would have been marked by violence. Medha Patkar's leadership of the Narmada Bachao Andolan followed the path of non-violence. Our arguments on the basis of historical comparison are summarized in Table 5.2.

Medha Patkar's work in Gujarat began with the Ahmedabad-based organization called Centre for Social Knowledge and Action – Ahmedabad, locally known as SETU. Here she was entrusted with the task of surveying the affected villages to ascertain whether people were informed about the impact of the Narmada Valley Development Project/Plan and aware of their rights as displaced people (Kishwar, 2006). As an action researcher, she visited Nandurbar District to conduct a survey of the affected communities. Her first impression of the adivasi communities was one of a lack of information and knowledge about the Sardar Sarovar Project and its impacts: "The first two days we walked through the Valley, we realized that people didn't even know about the projec.... When we moved through the villages, we realized that there was no information" (Patkar, 1995, pp. 157–158).

As the news of the dams began to filter into central and eastern parts of the country, Medha Patkar discovered that all construction activities for the Sardar Sarovar Project, which is the centrepiece of the Narmada Valley Development Project, had been suspended, including excavations and earthworks. The Project's halt came at the request of the Ministry of Environment, with the government of India acting on information that the project had not fulfilled basic environmental conditions and crucial studies and plans had not been completed (Crawford, undated). But the Sardar Sarovar Project regained international prominence when the World Bank approved a loan to build the dam at a later stage.

Table 5.2: Historical Comparison of Gandhi and Medha Patkar through Satyagraha

GANDHI	MEDHA PATKAR
Every Satyagrahi was asked to pledge to preach disaffection toward the government established by British law in India.	Every Satyagrahi had enough understanding and reign to determine the nature and scope of his or her actions. It was not merely carrying conviction this time.
The Satyagraha was seen as a strictly moral movement aimed at the overthrow of the government and was despite being legally seditious in terms of the Indian penal code.	By no means was it inevitable that NBA would remain non-violent, and there were strong indications that in the absence of Medha Patkar the Maoists and other militant groups would have carried away its achievements.
The withdrawal of support Gandhi said should be in proportion to their (Satyagrahi's) ability to preserve order in the social structure, without the assistance of the British ruler (Sharp, 1980, p. 87).	Evolving new force of satyagraha through "Jal samarpan" (ready to embrace death by drowning) offered by thousands of Satyagrahis during Medha Patkar's time are clearly indications of the power of non-violent social action.
Satyagraha of non-cooperation thus meant refusal of all of the so-called benefits that the government might lure or compensate for compliance. In Gandhi's time Great Britain defended its Indian commerce through repression for quite some time, until it saw the non-violent force of satyagraha and that the Gandhian social action was ready to "embrace death."	Silencing the armed revolts and evoking nationalism in Gandhi's time against the alien oppressor and keeping away from other militant non-state actors in Medha Patkar's time bear vivid similarities.
	Gandhi and Medha Patkar both were arrested several times, the difference being one was carrying satyagraha for freedom of the country (Gandhi) and the other was for carrying satyagraha for freedom for people to live in their native habitat without destruction.

Raising Awareness and Mass Mobilization

The first thing Medha Patkar did was to establish a dialogue between herself and the inhabitants of the Narmada Valley area. Listening to the people, Medha Patkar learned that the only information they had been given was that the dams would be built and people in the area would be displaced. Medha Patkar also found out that the residents had not seen any plans of the dam and rehabilitation nor had they been briefed by any representative, as was claimed by the local governments. She carefully listened to their questions and concerns about their rights as well as their outrage at the situation. After facilitating face-to-face dialogues between representatives of the national government and residents, she served as an advocate of the residents in meetings and presented these critiques to the local governments. She then delivered the government's responses and new information back to the people of the Narmada Valley. Listening to and gathering information from the government, and providing the people with relevant information was a key strategy. As she became deeply immersed in the Narmada struggle, she decided to leave her doctoral studies at the Tata Institute of Social Sciences. Like her parents, she chose the path of social activism but on a much larger scale.

Using group work and community organization methods, Medha Patkar enabled those affected by the Narmada Valley Development Project to examine their socio-economic environment and the deprivation they were experiencing, and she mobilized them for the cause. The social attitudes toward the Dalits and Indigenous populations and the oppression and discrimination constantly experienced by them became central issues in her campaign. These issues were crucial for mobilizing and uniting not only local-level organizations, people's groups, and ordinary people living in villages of the Narmada Valley, but also environmentalists, human rights activists, youth, other NGOs, academics, and leaders in different fields even beyond the Narmada Valley. The affected populations were marginalized in at least three ways: (1) by virtue of their identity within the caste system ascribed at birth, (2) by their remote rural location – far from opportunities offered by urban development, and then (3) by having practically little or no benefit from the projects. As their lands were submerged, they have nothing to look forward to except what is, more often than not, monetary compensation that will most certainly not last their lifetimes. In group and community meetings, Medha Patkar and her colleagues would confront people with these realities. The eerie silence that often accompanied these conversations would only be interrupted by such questions as "Do we want this to happen to our lives?" An emphatic "No" would often be the answer. The critical awareness of issues led to satyagraha in whichever way and whatever form it was required.

Organization of a 36-Day-Long March

Among the various non-cooperation activities of several local groups and organizations to protest against the Narmada Valley Development Project and the Sardar Sarovar Project, in particular (see Dwivedi, 1997), the 36-day march (in 1986) led by Medha Patkar and other workers proved to be the most critical. The protest action involved marching on foot (*padayatra*) across several villages from Madhya Pardesh to the site of the Sardar Sarovar Dam. In this march, people demonstrated the non-violence of satyagraha, with their hands folded and tied in front of themselves. As marchers arrived at the Gujarat state border and crossed, police reportedly acted with violent means of repression. According to Medha Patkar, the police were "caning the marchers and arresting them and tearing the clothes off women activists" (Patkar, 1995, p. 166). This long march united villagers, people's organizations, and local NGOs spread over the three states that the project involved. Medha Patkar described the march as "'a path symbolizing the long path of struggle (both immediate and long-term) that [they] really had" (p. 166). The meetings, discussions, and public demonstrations held in villages as the march progressed not only developed solidarity and a common goal and focus, but also raised awareness of the issue and mobilized people beyond the Narmada Valley.

Effective Slogans

Another very important part of this satyagraha campaign was the use of carefully chosen slogans that were formed in local languages by local people. Some of the slogans were as follows: "Vikas Chahiye Vinash Nahin" (We want development, not destruction); "Hamara Gaon Mein Hamara Raj" (Our village, our rule); "Dubenge Par Hatenge Nahin" (We will drown but not move); "Bandh Nahin Banega, Kohi Nahin Hatega" (The dam won't be made, nobody would move); and "Narmada ki Gahti Mein Ladai Jaari Hai, Chalo Utho, Chalo Utho Rokna Vinash Hain" (War is declared on the Narmada Valley, Rise up, Rise up, not doing so is destructive). Such slogans were culturally and contextually very powerful means of raising critical awareness and mobilizing people by engaging local people. Some of the slogans were also loaded with the ideology of self-governance/rule, self-assertion, and self-determination.

Progress of the Sardar Sarovar Project, 1984–1988

Despite such organized protests and resistance between 1984 and 1987, the loan deal with the World Bank was approved, financial clearance from the Indian government was received, and conditional environmental clearance was granted from the Ministry of Forests and Environment (Dwivedi, 1997, p. 9). The government of Gujarat also announced substantial modifications to a relief and rehabilitation package. In October 1998 the Gujarat government announced that the dam site, the project headquarters at Kevadia, and 12 adjacent villages were subject to the Official Secrets Act 1923. The Bharuch District (falling in the jurisdiction of the project) was also declared a "prohibited area" under section 144 of the Criminal Procedure Code (Dwivedi, 1997, p. 12). The construction of the dam began again in 1988.

THE FORMATION OF THE NARMADA BACHAO ANDOLAN (SAVE NARMADA MOVEMENT)

Against the backdrop of such developments and with the increasing government repression, Medha Patkar's relentless awareness and mass mobilization efforts, achieved by walking every day from village to village; from one group meeting to another, and through consultations with a range of NGOs, resulted in the formation of the Narmada Bachao Andolan (NBA) in 1989. The Save Narmada Movement became a unifying force for all individuals and organizations that opposed the Sardar Sarovar Project. The work of the NBA led by Medha Patkar represented empowering practice by building critical awareness with the use of group work and community organization, which are basic methods in social work. It changed the focus of the campaign from merely advocating for relief and rehabilitation of displaced communities to complete opposition to the Sardar Sarovar Project in the interest of sustainable development.

March/Dharana/Hunger Strike/Fasting

As the Sardar Sarovar Dam construction restarted with the World Bank's financial support and the issuance of a conditional government clearance, so did the efforts of the Save Narmada Movement. Protest activities continued including the obstruction of the construction of bridges across the Narmada River, the setting up of road blocks at strategic points, demonstrations and rallies, *gherao* (the "encirclement" of officials), and the uprooting of stone markers from the proposed submergence areas and dumping them outside the Vidhan Sabha or the state parliament building in Bhopal. Thousands of people and hundreds of NGOs joined the Movement, including about 100 NGOs from overseas. The campaign against the Sardar Sarovar Project and the whole Narmada Valley Development Project received tremendous support in India as well as from overseas. Recognizing that the withdrawal of financial support from the World Bank could stop the construction of the dam, the NBA began directing its efforts at the World Bank. To physically stop work on the dam and to pressure the government to comprehensively review the Sardar Sarovar Project, a month-long march known as Jan Vikas Sangharsh Yatra (Struggle March for People's Development) was undertaken in 1990 to 1991. The entire planned march would have covered the distance of 200 kilometres, but the marchers were stopped at the Madhya Pradesh-Gujarat border by the Gujarat government. Marchers camped at the border for one month. Seven marchers, including Medha Patkar, went on an indefinite hunger strike lasting 22 days. Medha Patkar was close to death by the end of this hunger strike. Unfortunately, while the government agreed to review and offer several concessions to people, events that followed clearly indicated that there were no positive outcomes for the NBA workers. Since the Gujarat government did not respond, people decided to boycott government activities in villages (Dwivedi, 1997). In 1993, Medha Patkar again went on a hunger strike to pressure the government to undertake a comprehensive review of the Sardar Sarovar Project. She was arrested on the 14th day of her hunger strike, even as the government promised to review the project. The hunger strike was called off. Once again a review was promised and nothing came through.

Drowning in the Rising Narmada River

Drowning in the rising Narmada River was another powerful protest method employed by the Narmada Bachao Andolan, led by Medha Patkar. Groups of Samarpit Dal were formed, that is, groups of people who prepared themselves to drown in the rising water in Manibeli, the first village to be submerged in Maharashtra. *Samarpit* means "giving voluntarily" and *dal* means a group – more akin to a battalion in social action terms. A Samarpit Dal is a large group of people who are ready to sacrifice their lives for a cause. When the government promise to review the project did not progress, the Save Narmada Movement decided to take up this ultimate form of protest. The government responded by declaring such areas as areas prohibited and initiating a statewide crackdown on NBA activists. As a consequence, the Samarpit Dal went underground. Their attempts to carry out their protest in the form of drowning were stopped by the government with more assurances that the Sardar Sarovar Project would be reviewed.

Status of the Sardar Sarovar Project, 1990–1993

Partly due to the pressure created by the Save Narmada Movement and its network of international agencies, the World Bank appointed an Independent Review Committee that found several flaws in the Sardar Sarovar Project and recommended that the World Bank withdraw from the project. Consequently, in 1993, the World Bank decided to withdraw its support from the Sardar Sarovar Project. Similarly, the Japanese government also withdrew all further funding for the dam. These decisions were an important victory for the Narmada Bachao Andolan. The victory was short-lived as the Gujarat government decided to raise money and fund the project itself. The NBA's protest by way of drowning in the river caused the Ministry of Water Resources, government of India, to appoint a Five-Member

Group tasked to examine all issues relating to the Sardar Sarovar Project, even in the face of opposition from the Gujarat government to the formation of such a group.

Litigation

Under the leadership of Medha Patkar, the Narmada Bachao Andolan filed a petition in the Supreme Court of India in 1994. It challenged the construction of the Sardar Sarovar Dam on "social, environmental, technical, economic and financial grounds" and argued that the project as conceived was "not in the national interest" (Dwivedi, 1997, p. 17). The petition led to a stay order on the construction (Basu, 2010). The NBA also had filed a petition in the National Human Rights Commission. Several parties to the petition filed affidavits as directed by the Supreme Court. Along with the litigation, protests and rallies were continued to pressure the authorities to release the report of the review by the Five-Member Group and to resist the Gujarat governments' proposal to raise the dam height from 80.3 metres to 110 metres. These strategies helped to release the report and put on pressure to block the proposed increase in the height of the dam. Several cases had been filed in different courts at the state levels as well as in the Supreme Court on different aspects of the Narmada Valley Development Project (see Friends of Narmada River, 2010). In addition, a public hearing was also conducted, but neither the affected state governments nor the central government presented their cases.

Other Strategies Used by the NBA

Along with the above-mentioned satyagraha methods, a range of other advocacy strategies such as letter writing, media briefs, international networking with NGOs committed to the environmental cause, public speeches to a variety of audiences both at national and international levels, documentary films, and electronic media were effectively used by the Narmada Bachao Andolan.

Current Status of the Sardar Sarovar Project and the Narmada Bachao Andolan

After seven years of legal deliberations, the Supreme Court of India decided in favour of the Sardar Sarovar Project. The judgments allowed immediate construction on the dam up to a height of 90 metres and authorized construction up to the originally planned height of 138 metres in 5-metre increments subject to receiving approval from the relief and rehabilitation arm of the Narmada Control Authority (Friends of River Narmada, 2010).

In the face of the myopic and short-sighted structures of the state, the Narmada Bachao Andolan continued to fight for the people's rights to land and, where appropriate, adequate relief and rehabilitation.

Since 1992, Medha Patkar's activism became much broader when she helped to form the National Alliance of People's Movements (NAPM), a network of more than 150 political organizations across India. She served as one of the national coordinators of the NAPM. Today, the NAPM has been playing a significant role in bringing important structural changes by developing a comprehensive National Development, Displacement, and Rehabilitation Policy and submitting a bill to the Indian Parliament. Consequently, the Right to Fair Compensation and Transparency in Land Acquisition, Rehabilitation and Resettlement Act, 2013 ("the Act") came into force in India on 1 January 2014. Medha Patkar, as one of the national coordinators of NAPM, not only leads the NBA but also spearheads a number of grassroots-level movements involving slum dwellers, farmers, Indigenous peoples, and women across India. In her satyagraha to support these movements, Medha Patkar is often arrested and detained in custody, but she remains relentless in her fight to defend the rights of the poor and the marginalized in India.

▶ THE CREATION OF SOCIAL MOVEMENTS AND PROFESSIONAL SOCIAL WORK

One wonders what motivated Medha Patkar to pursue these social causes – which was not what she had originally set out to do. It is helpful to look at Medha Patkar's life to find the answer. In 1984 Medha Patkar studied "social inequality amongst the tribal groups in northeastern Gujarat" for her Ph.D. at the Tata Institute of Social Sciences. She was confronted by important questions and went on to develop some answers to them. Her initial question was about the suitability of dominant paradigms and Western models of development for India and their long-term sustainability. There was already talk about the building of a dam and people were preparing to move. She started developing local residents' organizations following a simple locality development model of community organizing. Medha Patkar initially worked toward achieving the best compensation scenarios for the residents. Over the course of such work, she began to question the long-term sustainability of the government's approaches to water, to people, and to habitat.

This critical insight into the plight of the poor people and the deep discomfort she felt within paved the way for Medha Patkar's environmental activism. She went on to form the Narmada Bachao Andolan (Save Narmada Movement), the largest social movement in India and, quite possibly, the world. She created a successful, inspiring, and vibrant social movement that has, through social mobilization, created awareness of environmental and developmental dilemmas and issues, enhanced the accountability of government actions, and initiated important policy modifications and developments.

A leading magazine in India notes, "One of the largest and most successful environmental campaigns has been the Narmada Bachao Andolan that began with a wide developmental agenda, questioning the very rationale of large dam projects in India" (*India Today*, 2007). Her struggle and the movement still continue.

Medha Patkar's environmental activism may be discussed in terms of four dimensions as presented in Figure 5.1. Unbroken arrow lines in the figure indicate strong theoretical connections, whereas the broken ones show broken or weak connections. The four dimensions are (1) goals, (2) satyagraha methods, (3) the role of the state, and (4) the role of the social work profession and social workers, as Medha Patkar was a professional social worker.

Figure 5. 1: Medha Patkar's environmental activism: Goals, satyagraha methods, role of the state and the social work profession

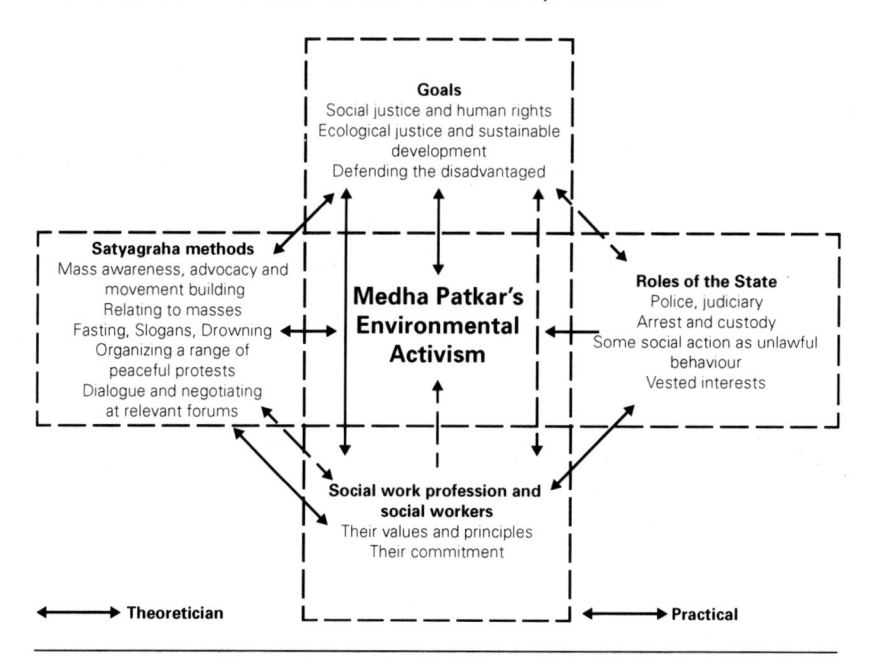

Goals
Social justice and human rights
Ecological justice and sustainable development
Defending the disadvantaged

Satyagraha methods
Mass awareness, advocacy and movement building
Relating to masses
Fasting, Slogans, Drowning
Organizing a range of peaceful protests
Dialogue and negotiating at relevant forums

Medha Patkar's Environmental Activism

Roles of the State
Police, judiciary
Arrest and custody
Some social action as unlawful behaviour
Vested interests

Social work profession and social workers
Their values and principles
Their commitment

←——→ Theoretician   ←——→ Practical

It is important to raise a simple question: What is the ideology and goal of Medha Patkar's environmental activism? It is difficult to clearly decipher the main ideology, motivation, or goal of her satyagraha/social activism. Drawing on her actions, speeches and letters, media commentary, and articles written on her work, it may be surmised that, initially, her goals were to secure adequate relief and rehabilitation for displaced people, seek social justice, and protect the rights of people affected by the Narmada Valley Development Project and the Sardar Sarovar Project, as well as to ensure that the natural and cultural sources of livelihood for marginalized and poor people were maintained. As her engagement progressed, her goals extended to ecological conservation and sustainable development as an alternative development model, in line with green politics and green ideology. Toward this, her work shifted to opposing the building of dams, stopping increases in the heights of dams so as to prevent submergence of more land and the displacement of more people, exposing the mismanagement of dam projects, raising awareness of the negative consequences of building big dams, and opposing foreign investment and market interventions that exploit people and create dependency. In Medha Patkar's words, "We are basically fighting this battle for an alternative economic and political perspective against the present development paradigm, which is being imposed on the people and the market" (from the film *A Threat to Living communities*, Global Oneness Project, 2006–2013).

Based on our analysis, the ideology and goals of Medha Patkar's environmental activism are informed by the principles of social justice, human rights, sustainable development, and defence of the disadvantaged. This is achieved through non-violent means in the form of satyagraha, which is the second dimension of our discussion.

As presented in an earlier section, Medha Patkar consistently used carefully chosen satyagraha methods. They were based on an ideology of non-violence, but the nature of each one of them was unique. Long marches by foot, days of hunger strikes, threats of drowning in the rising Narmada River, the use of effective slogans, litigation, and a range of other strategies raised critical awareness among people living in and beyond the Narmada Valley and created pressure on both state and central governments to re-examine their decisions, policies, and project implementation strategies.

Despite such laudable goals and non-violent methods, why did the state act or react the way it did? Medha Patkar created an unparalleled mass environmental movement (the NBA), negotiated with elected local politicians, participated and called for open debates, and engaged only in active non-violent strategies. The Narmada Bachao Andolan is unique as Medha Patkar creatively and clearly connected grassroots level realities with state, national, and international level structures, linking the micro to the macro. She was not opposing the "state" as much as she was fighting on behalf of the poor who were not "free" in any real sense of that term. She took on a pro-poor stance that pitted her against state forces. Although governments articulate similar goals and values, with references made to social justice and human rights, in practice the link between the articulated values and the commitment to such goals appeared broken (see broken line in Figure 7.1). Otherwise, government agencies should not have resorted to legal sanctions prohibiting people's participation, and punishing them with caning, arrests, and detentions. Such state actions continue to occur. How can the state explicitly demonstrate their commitment to social justice and human rights? Medha Patkar wrote to the prime minister of India about the critical role of the state in ensuring and safeguarding the rights and lives of the very people in whose name it was carrying out massive development projects. She argued that the state was not acting as a neutral arbiter between competing interests nor was the state protecting the oppressed minorities from manipulation and exploitation. After nearly three decades of people's struggle, the state appeared amenable to the Narmada Bachao Andolan's pressure and enacted the New Act of 2013 (referred to above) that requires transparency with regard to the issue of land acquisition and relief and rehabilitation. Now, the state should use its power to implement the Act rather than using it to oppress certain groups.

Finally, where does the profession of social work stand in relation to environmental activism and social movement building? Its codes of ethics articulate a commitment to social justice, human rights, and sustainable development (see, e.g., Pawar, 2000; Australian Association of Social Workers, 2010; National Association of Social Workers, 2008). One item of the global social work agenda relates to the goal of sustainable development. Satyagraha/social action methods go well with the principles and techniques of sustainable development, and it plays a significant role in implementing some of the state's policies. Despite such strong theoretical commitments, social work goals, social action methods, and Medha Patkar's activism, in practice, social work as a profession seems to have contributed very little to this movement formally and informally (except at the individual level). Has the profession of social work in India contributed to the Narmada Bachao Andolan? If yes, in what ways? For that matter, have the international social work bodies such as the International Association of Schools of Social Work or the International Federation of Social Workers recognized and contributed to this movement? A professional social worker building the largest movement in the world is an extraordinary achievement for the profession. But how much recognition has been given to the work of Medha Patkar in social work literature? While we cannot say to what extent Medha Patkar might attribute her activism to her professional social work training, what is certain is that the social movement she has created has significant implications for social work both nationally and internationally in terms of education, training, practice, research, awareness-raising, and social mobilization.

Medha Patkar's activism and social movement work point to gaps in social work thinking. Medha Patkar's base in professional social work and her passion did not conform to the traditionally embedded role of social work in the welfare state. Her work paves the way for new workers entering the field of social work. Given the shrinking role of social work in the neo-liberal economy and market, it is important to revive and revisit the critical role that social workers can play in facilitating community organization and development. If we are to become effective community advocates, we must not withdraw from the political dimensions of our professional role. At the front line, where social policy intersects with people's lives, social workers need to disengage from being gatekeepers in the welfare marketplace and re-establish social work as the voice of human rights activism and resistance to oppression.

Modern social work theoretically includes curriculum on social action and social change. However, social workers increasingly enter the workforce and function as agents of social control rather than creative improvers of the welfare regime. For example, reform through (public interest) litigation has always been an important element that the social work profession is familiar with, and it receives several mentions in our training in social work schools through the subjects of law and social work, but seldom have we seen litigation as an opportunity to strengthen our practice and expertise or give more consideration to it as an avenue to work and empower oppressed people. Medha Patkar's approach clearly indicates the capacity to respond effectively in several ways to client and community-determined need, in that social workers' commitment to the pursuit of social justice and human rights become unavoidable.

Medha Patkar's environmental activism confronts us with the question of the nature and role of social work in the contemporary unequal world. It illustrates the role that social workers can play in facilitating development and working for capacity building, and the freedoms and achievements of people. To what extent is social work's community advocacy role reflected in contemporary practice? How can social workers be actively involved in political processes rather than simply serving as gatekeepers in the welfare marketplace? The challenge for the social work profession in general is to find ways of supporting anti-oppressive practice regardless of where the worker is located. Medha Patkar's environmental activism represents a model of practice embodying human rights activism and resistance to oppression, principles that resonate with critical conceptions of social work. Her approach clearly demonstrates principles of human rights and empowerment, commitment to social justice, citizenship rights, self-determination, collective action, recognition of diversity, and participatory democracy. But our question for the future is: Do our conceptions of social work encompass social action that challenges oppressive practices sanctioned by the state in the way Medha Patkar's environmental activism does? It can be argued that such forms of practice would be integral to social work if the profession is to remain true to its espoused values of human rights and social justice. It appears, however, that Medha Patkar's work remains largely ignored in social work.

▶ CONCLUSION

This chapter is about Medha Patkar, her activism, and the creation of a social movement, the Narmada Bachao Andolan. Medha Patkar became a torchbearer for the rights and lives of vulnerable people through *sayagraha* on behalf of the poor. Over the past 30 years the struggle against dam projects that threaten the right to life and livelihood for the people of India's Narmada Valley has grown into one of the world's largest non-violent social movements. Activist Medha Patkar has been at the centre of these struggles and their champion.

Medha Patkar's social movement is symbolized by the Narmada River. The NBA reflects the depth, the purity, and the current of the Narmada River. It is an ancient Hindu belief that the Narmada River sprang from the body of the god Shiva, and in sanctity the Narmada ranks second only to the Ganges. The NBA's nearly 30-year-journey has been a struggle like the Narmada water running through 13,000 kilometres of rugged terrain. Despite such rugged terrain, water keeps running rather with more speed; so is the NBA of Medha Patkar. The state-led obstructions to and denial of the Movement and people of Narmada Valley symbolize the dam built on the Narmada River to stop the flow of the water. With the current of the water, the dam will burst if water is not allowed to flow further downstream. Similarly, the state will burst if the will of the people is not allowed to flow. Medha Patkar's social movement, the struggle of the people, and the state's response offer a good number of lessons. We hope this chapter inspires readers to learn more about Medha Patkar's Narmada Bachao Andolan and examine how her social activism can be reflected in social work practice. We conclude this chapter by introducing a poem that apparently was inspired by the NBA, from a site of an individual blogger (Amit, 2009):

A poem inspired by the Narmada Bachao Andolan

आपने कहा देश की समृद्धि की लिए
मेरा गाँव डुबाया गया
मेरे डूबे खेतों के आधार पर
बिजली का उत्पादन किया गया
पर जिन्हें वोह बिजली मिली
उन्होंने उसके लिए क्या खोया?

For the prosperity of the nation
My village was flooded
My flooded fields provided the basis
For you to generate electricity
But the people using that electricity
What did they lose?

आपके वादे के बलबूते पर
आप कहें हम जमीन छोड़ दें
पर तब हम क्या करें
जब आप अपना वादा तोड़ दें?

Based on your promises
You say we should give up the land
But what do we do then
when you break your promise?

जिस देश की विकास की आप बात करते हैं
उस देश का अटूट हिस्सा हूँ मैं
बिसरे लोगों और टूटे वादों का
अनकहा किस्सा हूँ मैं.

The country whose development you talk about
I am an integral part of it
The forgotten people and the broken promises
I am their untold story.

Source: http://emptywoods.blogspot.com.au/2009/05/poem-inspired-by-narmada-bachao-andolan.html

References

Amit. (2009). Part of the poem, translated from Hindi into English, inspired by the Narmada Bachao Andolan, 22 May. Retrieved 11 Mar. 2013 from http://empty-woods.blogspot.com.au

Australian Association of Social Workers. (2010). *Code of ethics*. Canberra: Australian Association of Social Workers.

Basu, Pratyusha. (2010). Scale, place, and social movements: Strategies of resistance along India's Narmada River. *Revista NERA*, 13(16), 96–113.

Baviskar, Amita. (1995). *In the belly of the river: Tribal conflicts over development in the Narmada Valley*. Delhi: Oxford University Press.

Bose, Pablo S. (2004). Critics and experts, activists and academics: Intellectuals in the fight for social and ecological justice in the Narmada Valley, India. *International Review of Social History, 49*, 133–157.

Crawford, Aaron. (Undated). *Medha Patkar*. Retrieved 4 Apr. 2013 from www.womeninworldhistory.com/imow-Patkar.pdf

Dwivedi, Ranjit. (1997). *People's movements in environmental politics: A critical analysis of the Narmada Bachao Andolan in India*. Working Paper Series No. 242. The Hague: Institute of Social Studies.

Fisher, William F. (Ed.). (1995). *Toward sustainable development: Struggling over India's Narmada River.* New York: M.E. Sharpe.

Friends of River Narmada. 2010. *The Supreme Court ruling.* Retrieved 12 Mar. 2013 from http://www.narmada.org/sardar-sarovar/sc.ruling/

Jacques, Leslie. (2006). *Medha Patkar, India's unsinkable anti-dam activist.* Retrieved 8 Mar. 2013 from http://nchro.org/index.php?option=com_content&view=article&id=4091:medha-patkar-indias-unsinkable-anti-dam-activist&catid=15:women&Itemid=25

Kishwar, M. P. (2006). Twenty years on the banks of the Narmada. *Indian Express (Friday April 21).* Retrieved 1 June 2015 from http://archive.indianexpress.com/news/twenty-years-on-the-banks-of-the-narmada/2887/

National Alliance of People's Movements. (2013). *Land rights campaign and related documents.* Retrieved 13 Mar. 2013 from http://napm-india.org/node/326

National Association of Social Workers. (2008). *NASW Code of ethics.* Retrieved 25 Sept. 2012 from http://www.socialworkers.org/pubs/code/code.asp

Nehru, Jawaharlal. (1958). *Toward freedom: The autobiography of Jawaharlal Nehru.* Retrieved 12 Mar. 2013 from http://openlibrary.org/books/OL24222255M/Toward_freedom

Patel, C.C. 1992. Surging ahead: The Sardar Sarovar Project, hope of millions. *Harvard International Review, 15,* 24–27.

Paranjpe, Vijay. (1991). The cultural ethos. *Loyakan Bulletin, 9*(3/4), 21–31.

Pathak, Mahesh. (Ed.). (1991). *Sardar Sarovar Project: A promise for plenty.* New Delhi: Oxford University Press & IBH Publishing.

Patkar, Medha. (1995). The struggle for participation and justice: A historical narrative. In William F. Fisher (Ed.), *Towards sustainable development? Struggling over India's Narmada River* (pp. 157–78). London: M.E. Sharpe.

Patkar, Medha. (2004). *Interview with Medha Patkar.* Retrieved 12 Mar. 2013 from http://www.zcommunications.org/interview-with-medha-patkar-by-site-administrator

Pawar, Manohar. (2000). Australian and Indian social work codes of ethics. *Australian Journal of Professional and Applied Ethics, 2*(2), 72–85.

Sangvai, Sanjay. (2000). *The river and life: People's struggle in the Narmada Valley.* Calcutta: Earthcare Books.

Sharp, Gene. (1980). *The politics of non-violent action,* Part 1: *Power and struggle.* Boston: Porter Sergean.

Singh, M. (1992). *Displacement by Sardar Sarovar and Tehri: A comparative study of two dams.* New Delhi: Multiple Action Research Group.

South Asia Network on Dams, Rivers and People. (Undated). *Hydro electric projects in Narmada River Basin.* Retrieved 1 Apr. 2013 from http://www.sandrp.in/basin_maps/Hydropower_Projects_in_Narmada_Basin.pdf

CHAPTER 6

Challenging the Authority of the State and Reclaiming Citizenship

A Case on Eviction and Deportation of Pavement Dwellers in Bombay, India

Purnima George and Ferzana Chaze

In this chapter we tell the story of a case of mass eviction and deportation[1] of pavement (sidewalk) dwellers by the Municipal Corporation of the City of Bombay[2] and the innovative and daring response of the College of Social Work, Nirmala Niketan (under the leadership Dr Armaity Desai), to those events. The evictions that took place in 1981 were perceived by social activists as a gross violation of the fundamental rights guaranteed to all citizens by the constitution of India. The response of the College of Social Work was influenced by the principles of radical community organizing that emphasize the basic humanity, equality, and justice due to all people (Gil, 1998). The orientation of radical community organizing applies a political-economic perspective to its analysis of social issues and focuses on power dynamics between communities and the larger societal forces with which communities interact (Bailey & Brake, 1975). People's problems are regarded as being the result not of their own failings but of the fundamental operations of capitalistic and market forces (Galper, 1980). The aim of such organizing is to promote fundamental structural and institutional change through the redistribution of resources and power at community and societal levels (Gorz, 1977).

Purnima George, the first author of this chapter, was a faculty member of the College of Social Work at that point in time, and she also played the role of coordinator of the Ad Hoc Committee (AHC) formed by the College to respond to this issue. As the AHC coordinator she was involved in the planning and implementation of the entire strategy of action planned by the Committee. This chapter is based on her recollections of the same, and stems from her resolve to document the rich and unique history of activism by a college of social work. As a social work student of the same institute in the 1990s, the second author, Ferzana Chaze, was at a distance from direct action in relation to the pavement dwellers' issues, but she has benefited from its legacy in terms of rich classroom examples of social activism and the goodwill of the College in the pavement and slum communities she has worked with. Through dialogue the authors reflect on the extralegal actions undertaken all those years ago in response to the pavement dwellers' issue and on the role of such action within the social work profession then and in current times.

We begin the story with an introduction to the pavement dwellers and to the massive government eviction and deportation of pavement dwellers that took place in July 1981. We will follow with a narration of the response of the College of Social Work (faculty, staff, and students) and the Ad Hoc Committee to the mass eviction of pavement dwellers. We will then break from the conventional format and showcase our reflections as an interview between the two authors.

▶ Pavement Dwellers

In the 1980s Bombay was a financial and commercial centre of India. It was known for its manufacturing sector, discovery of offshore oil, national and international trade networks, financial services, and many public sector units and educational institutions. Existing alongside this prosperity were glaring inequalities specifically related to housing in the city. Out of 9.9 million people living in Bombay in 1981 (Demographia, 2001), approximately 2.28 million were living in slums (Singh, 2006). The estimated number of individuals living on pavements at the time ranged from between 100,000 and 300,000 (People's Union of Civil Liberties [hereafter PUCL], 1983; Mahtani, 1985). While there was some provision for subsidized grain and fuel, water, and sanitation for some slum dwellers, even these meagre entitlements to them as citizens were denied to persons living on pavements, making them the most vulnerable among the urban poor in Bombay. Pavement dwellers in the 1980s, as today, were persons and families that had made their homes on the sidewalks of the city. They lived in shanties or in makeshift structures at the side of the roads, as they were unable to afford the rent payable for any other kind of housing in Bombay (Ramachandran, 1972). The meagre incomes they earned through part-time, contractual, unorganized labour offered them little opportunity to afford any standard of housing, even that of a home in a slum. They were often found in the heart of the city close to free/cheap cooked food or public water sources (Ramachandran 1972) and where they did not have to spend on transportation for they could not afford to travel to work (Mahtani, 1985). Pavement dwellers predominantly worked as unskilled labourers (domestic workers, labourers, vendors, coolies) or were employed in petty businesses (Tata Institute of Social Sciences in Society for Promotion of Area Resource Centres [hereafter SPARC] & Society for Participatory Research in Asia [hereafter PRIA], 1985). Many pavement dwellers had households and lived on the same pavement for many years. The findings of one study (SPARC & PRIA, 1985) challenged prevailing myths that these pavement dwellers were new migrants to the city; for 13.5% of the 6,054 households interviewed, the head of the household was born in Bombay, and among migrant households, almost 60% had migrated more than ten years earlier.

Considered by the government to be encroachers on public land, pavement dwellers were denied all amenities, including resettlement, rehousing, or rehabilitation programs that were offered by the state or municipal governments to slum dwellers (SPARC & PRIA, 1985). Because pavement dwellers were seen as encroachers, the state refused to recognize their status as citizens, and it was this conceptualization of pavement dwellers as non-citizens that allowed the municipal government to ultimately evict thousands of pavement dwellers and demolish their structures/makeshift homes in a raid in 1981 (Mohapatra, 2004). The city justified its action at the time by stating that "pavements were meant for pedestrians to walk and not for people to stay on" (Desai, 1991, p. 174). This statement is representative of the government's disrespect and flagrant disregard of issues that force the poor to live on the pavements in the first place. Other arguments offered to justify demolitions included the following: Bombay was getting overpopulated on account of migration from rural areas; there was excessive migration to central and southern Bombay leading to overcrowding; there was no land available to provide housing for everyone; and it was financially impossible to house the poor (Gonsalves, in Hosbet, n.d.). These arguments highlight ways in which the government used the discourses of blame, threat, and scarce resources to absolve itself from doing anything about the issue (Mullaly, 2002), and negated the rights of pavement dwellers as citizens (Ife, 2005). In doing so, the government neglected to interrogate and address the root causes of migration from rural areas and reasons that led some people to live on pavements.

A critical analysis of the root causes of migration reveals a number of socio-economic and political factors operating in rural areas that were forcing villagers to move to the city in order to survive. Most of them migrated to escape starvation and death due to poverty in the villages (Lokshahi Hakk Sanghatana Bombay, 1991). Intense poverty in rural areas as a result of the concentration of assets within a few households and the increasing unemployment and underemployment of men, women, and children as agricultural labourers had made it difficult for agricultural labourers to survive in rural areas (Lokshahi Hakk Sanghatana Bombay, 1991). Frequent droughts in Maharashtra from 1970 to 1973 impacted the ability of agricultural labourers in rural areas to earn their livelihood and pushed many of them to cities (Subramanian, 1975). A steady loss of employment by traditional village craftsmen (Desai, 1991) and the lack of industrialization in rural areas also pushed people out of their villages (Sebastian, 1991). The rural poor had thus been reduced to the most vulnerable condition and were immigrating to Bombay.

Lacking the resources to afford any conventional housing or to have a hut in a slum area, these people most often put up temporary structures close to their places of work. They lived in subhuman conditions on the pavements, without electricity or running water or sanitation facilities. However, they remained "invisible" (SPARC & PRIA, 1985) citizens who enjoyed no rights except for the right to vote (Mohapatra, 2004). There were no housing policies and programs (other than some amenities for slum dwellers) for slum and pavement dwellers, and hence there was no public sector investment allocated for housing the poor. The decision to demolish the dwellings and subsequently deport pavement dwellers was based on government claims of scarcity of land. Yet several sources claimed that there were between 1,000 and 3,000 hectares of vacant land available for accommodating the poor who were living in slums and on pavements (Gonsalves in Hosbet, n.d.; PUCL, 1983; Sebastian, 1991). In fact, Desai (1991) asserts that "there was enough vacant land to house four times the number of pavement dwellers already there" (p. 171); however, there was lack of political will on the part of the government to go against the interests of the elite of the city (Desai, 1991; Gonsalves in Hosbet, n.d.; Sebastian, 1991).

▶ THE CRITICAL INCIDENT

On 23 July 1981, on a day of heavy rains, the state government undertook massive eviction and deportation of pavement dwellers residing on an arterial road of the city in the central part of Bombay. The government based its action on the strength of the legislation called Bombay Municipal Corporation (BMC) Act of 1888, section 61(D), that empowered the BMC to remove "obstructions" in streets and other public places. The eviction was carried out without any prior notice to the pavement dwellers, and in order to stop any resistance there was the presence of a large police force. The demolition squad broke 1,700 huts/structures (Mahtani, 1985) and confiscated and dumped all the belongings of pavement dwellers into trucks that were brought in for that purpose. Additionally, pavement dwellers (including children) who were present at the scene were asked to give the name of the village they originally hailed from and, based on their response, were forced to get into buses kept ready for various rural destinations and deported out of the city. The deportees were dropped off at the outskirts of Bombay and were made to leave the city in buses destined for their villages. At the outposts a heavy police presence ensured that the dwellers did not get back into the city.

This eviction evoked a public outcry against the government for to a number of reasons. The eviction was unprecedented as this was the first time that people were deported. The eviction was carried out on a day when it was raining heavily, and there was no consideration given to disrupting the lives of people who, in any case, were the worst affected during the monsoon. Also, the dwellers had no hope of retrieving their belongings that they had lost as they were dumped into trucks without any identification of the owner. This meant that the dwellers had to start their lives again completely from scratch. There was no attention paid to the sick, elderly, or pregnant women while undertaking demolitions or deportation. A document reporting on the incident states that "families were separated, young children and old people died and a woman even delivered a child in one of the busses" (PUCL, 1983, p. 3). Above all, the deportation separated family members – parents and children who got deported to different destinations had no means of reuniting.

It was highly likely that the government would try to replicate the eviction and deportation with pavement dwellers in other parts of Bombay, potentially leading to an escalated scale of disruption among thousands of families.

The state government justified its act of eviction and deportation with the rationale that since pavement dwellers are basically migrants they needed to go back to the villages from which they had come. Also, as they had illegally encroached on public land, evictions were necessary. Alternate explanations for the government's actions have, however, been suggested. According to Desai (1991), the demolitions were carried out to keep the city clean and make it attractive for tourists who were likely to visit the country for the Asian Games that were going to take place in 1982. Additionally, the government was interested in reducing travel time by reducing obstructions on roads and therefore resorted to this mechanism. More importantly, the newly elected ruling party and the chief minister of the state wanted to impress the electorate that it had the power to take stringent action when necessary (p. 171).

In the days following the demolition, fear, tension, and anxiety gripped the city, specifically among pavement dwellers from other parts of Bombay who were anticipating further similar action to affect them at any time. There was a lot of anger at the government's actions among grassroots/ civil liberties groups and radical social movements, and there was a sense of urgency that the state government needed to be stopped from repeating such an act. These groups started deliberating on what could be done to prevent further similar government action.

▶ REFRAMING THE ISSUE AND DELIBERATING AN APPROPRIATE SOCIAL WORK RESPONSE

We (faculty members, staff members of field action projects, and students) at the College of Social Work were equally disturbed with the demolitions and felt that it was an issue of social injustice and oppression against the most marginalized people (Alinsky, 1971; Freire, 1970); a case of denial of rights to pavement dwellers as citizens (Ife, 2005); and therefore, a violation of fundamental rights granted to every citizen of the country under the constitution of India. The government's actions challenged foundational social work values of social justice, equity, dignity, and the worth of human beings (International Federation of Social Workers [hereafter, IFSW], 2013). Some of us worked closely with slum dwellers as part of our community work and felt the impending threat of demolition and disruption of these slum communities that, like the pavement dwellings, were situated on government land. This meant intensifying work with our slum communities, on the one hand, and simultaneously taking a stance to initiate some intervention with the pavement dweller communities despite the fact that we had no experience working with the latter groups. For us, the critical common factor that bound both groups (slum and pavement dwellers) was the actual or perceived threat of eviction and deportation that amounted to the negation of these persons' rights as citizens. We also felt impelled as social workers to be responsive to the emergent issues of that time and needed to define the contribution that social work could make in addressing newer and emerging social issues. As educators, we felt it was our responsibility to model for our students what social-change-oriented practice looked like within the prevailing context.

The faculty members of the College of Social Work held townhall meetings to gather the opinions of students and staff members of field action projects and to brainstorm on what action could be initiated. After interesting and challenging discussions there was an agreement to move forward and develop an action plan. We recognized that as an educational institution it was beyond the mandate of the College to get involved in social action that challenged the government and that our action could jeopardize the grant that our college received from the government. After much deliberation it was proposed that an Ad Hoc Committee (AHC) be set up and that this committee be positioned at an arm's length from the College, with voluntary representation from faculty members, students, and interested organizations. As a faculty member of the College with an interest in community practice and issues of urban communities, Purnima was asked to take up the role of coordinator of this Ad Hoc Committee, in which capacity she was responsible for developing an action plan and coordinating the implementation of the action plan by the AHC members.

Chalking Out a Plan

One of the first tasks that the Ad Hoc Committee undertook was reaching out to all placement agencies of the College, inviting them to join with the Ad Hoc Committee in taking action on the issue. Interested members were invited to attend the AHC meeting at the College of Social Work. At that meeting, besides students, faculty, and staff members there were representatives from 23 organizations (including religious organizations, grassroots organizations, and student movement groups) present. Despite their diverse perspectives, the organizations were willing to be a part of the Ad Hoc Committee and work on the issue. The Ad Hoc Committee thus became an alliance of individuals and organizations concerned about the eviction and deportation of pavement dwellers determined to show resistance to the action taken by the government. The membership to the Ad Hoc Committee continued to increase in the following days as news of the work spread. The Ad Hoc Committee also started building networks with other groups in the city that were taking action, and a strategic partnership was developed with a group of progressive lawyers. This partnership is discussed further along in this chapter.

At the first meeting, a proposed draft action plan was presented to the Ad Hoc Committee. The action plan was multi-pronged, encompassing a variety of "modes of intervention" ranging from "collaborative, campaign and contest" (Specht, 1969, p. 375) and tactics ranging including "joint action, education, violation of normative behavior and violation of legal norms" (Specht, 1969, p. 378). Collaborative strategies of intervention are used in a situation where there is a high possibility of agreement between the parties engaged in conflict. The agreement is reached by engaging in cooperative and educational tactics to influence the opponents. In contrast, campaign and contest strategies are used in situations where there is a high possibility of conflicting parties not reaching any agreement; in this situation the agitating group uses various tactics that breach legal and acceptable practices in that society. The AHC plan included grassroots mobilization, research on pavement dwellers, public education regarding pavement dwellers, direct action, and networking with other groups in the city who were also planning some form of action.

The first component of the plan aimed at *grassroots mobilization* of slum and pavement communities. The demolitions had created a lot of fear, insecurity, and anxiety among pavement dwellers in other parts of the city. However, it was strategically important for pavement and slum dwellers to show their resistance to the government's action and not to be perceived as docile victims awaiting their turn. The Ad Hoc Committee also found it to be a strategic moment for building solidarity between slum and pavement dwellers. Such an alliance had never been attempted before in the history of Bombay. Despite enjoying a relatively better status than pavement dwellers, slum dwellers were still considered as encroachers by the state. In bringing them together we were building a broader base of opposition (Shragge, 2003) or counterpower of people (Alinsky, 1971) against the state. This work was carried out by tapping into the grassroots contacts of AHC members who were already working in slum communities. With pavement communities, this work was initiated by identifying pavement communities in and around central Bombay facing the maximum threat of eviction and starting to work in those communities with the help of AHC members.

The second component of the action plan aimed at *conducting research* that could serve to compile a profile of pavement dwellers. Through our own observations of pavement communities we knew that the government's justifications for deporting pavement dwellers were baseless. We wanted to use empirical evidence to debunk stereotypes related to pavement dwellers' transient and unemployed status. As an educational institution the College of Social Work was uniquely positioned to undertake this research, having the necessary infrastructure and the resources of a Research Unit to carry out the study. We also thought that the College's standing as an educational institution would lend the research greater credibility, hence this component of the plan was undertaken by the College directly. Although most of the responsibility for this research was taken by the Research Unit of the College, the responsibility for data collection was shared by students and staff members of field action projects. The aim of the study was to profile the socio-economic conditions of the pavement dwellers and document their reasons for migration to Bombay. Additionally the survey asked the pavement dwellers about their minimum expectations if they were relocated. The sample included 329 pavement dwellers from 18 different pavement communities spread over Bombay (Mahtani, 1985).

The third component of the plan was about *creating public education and awareness* on the realities of the lives of pavement dwellers. This was a conscious strategy to counter the negative stereotypes propagated by the government regarding pavement dwellers. Our aim was to create favourable public opinion, specifically in the middle class that often expressed its stance through letters to editors of newspapers. As a part of this strategy it was decided to write letters to editors of newspapers and mount poster campaigns at spots most visited by middle-class people, namely, suburban train stations and train compartments. Posters were stuck on railway station walls and in train compartments illegally, without official permission from the railway authorities as we considered it highly unlikely that we would have obtained such permission. Most of the posters were prepared by students and staff members, while maintaining a continuous flow of letters to editors was the responsibility of staff and faculty members.

The Ad Hoc Committee also provided support for a *legal action* that was being planned by a group of well-known progressive lawyers called the Lawyers Collective. The College of Social Work shared its interim research results with the Lawyers Collective as requested so that the findings could be used to support legal action in favour of the pavement dwellers (Mahtani, 1985). The study provided a socio-economic profile of the pavement dwellers (that included details of temporary low-skilled jobs and the paltry wages pavement dwellers made) and reasons for migration to the city, and it also documented the willingness of the pavement dwellers to live elsewhere if they were provided with alternate housing (Mahtani, 1985). Members of the Lawyers Collective voiced a need to disseminate the research findings and influence the opinion of the larger community of lawyers and judges who were engaged with the case at the Supreme Court. This led to organizing a joint conference by the College of Social Work and the Lawyers Collective for the Bar Association of India in 1982. At the conference, Purnima George presented the preliminary findings of the research on behalf of the College to lawyers and judges from all over India, and this interim research report by the College became landmark evidence in arguing the case for pavement dwellers at the Supreme Court of India; the final research report was published by the College of Social Work in 1985 (Mahtani, 1985).

The last component of the action plan was to undertake *direct action* that demonstrated people's power (Alinsky, 1971) and send a strong message to the government. The direct action comprised a protest march that culminated in taking over the city's racecourse for two hours. The idea to take over the racecourse temporarily emerged while deliberating what kind of action would make the government and the public sit up and take notice of the protests against the demolitions. It was proposed by one of the members of the Ad Hoc Committee who belonged to a radical student movement group. The idea appealed to all members, as taking over the racecourse was a very symbolic challenge to the land use pattern favoured by the government. Through its past actions the government had demonstrated its intention to dedicate land in Bombay for the construction of high-rise apartments or buildings for multinational companies, which in turn could be sold at exorbitantly high prices. The land was not meant for the middle- and lower-income groups though they had as much right to the land as other citizens of the country. In the heart of Bombay, where land is at a premium and where thousands of people live without adequate housing, there existed (and still exists) a racecourse occupying 225 acres of prime land that caters to but a microscopic segment of the population – the extremely rich who can afford to indulge in horse racing as entertainment.

Taking over the racecourse also had the additional appeal of providing an opportunity to showcase the people's strength, and it was in line with what we were teaching in our classrooms in relation to planning tactics in mass actions that go outside of the experience of the opponent (Alinsky, 1971, p. 127). While India has a long history of resistance, there had never been a precedent of taking over government-owned space, and we were anticipating that the unexpected nature of this resistance would contribute to its success. To make sure it remained unexpected, however, the plan to take over the racecourse was kept under tight wraps. Only the Ad Hoc Committee knew of the complete plan concerning the direct action, and only one or two members knew of the finer details related to the planned unlawful entry into the racecourse grounds.

Organizing this march and having the maximum impact was very critical for the Ad Hoc Committee. Members responsible for the march spent endless hours meticulously planning all aspects of the march. The protest march was scheduled on a working day during the late afternoon hours to attract maximum public attention. The march was to begin from an important landmark junction (a confluence of six major roads) for all traffic moving into and out of central Bombay. This location was also close to the site of an earlier demolition. From this junction the march was to proceed to an arterial bridge that linked central and south Bombay. In other words, the march was intended to impact central and south Bombay traffic.

As per the plan, the march began in the afternoon at the intended location and proceeded to the bridge. The march was attended by slum and pavement dwellers with whom the Ad Hoc Committee had been working, member organizations of the Ad Hoc Committee, and students and faculty members of the College of Social Work. It is estimated that a couple of thousand people participated in the march. Shortly after, in a bold and unexpected move for everyone including the marchers, the members of the Ad Hoc Committee led the protesters into the nearby racecourse through an opening in the fence that had been created by an AHC member the night prior to the march. When the fence leading to the racecourse was opened, the crowd poured into the grounds. The protesters carried sticks and tarps and put up temporary structures resembling huts on the racecourse. By this symbolic gesture we communicated to the government that if it did not consider the rights of citizens to live on pavements to survive, the masses were capable of constructing huts and living anywhere, even on the racecourse.

The sheer numbers of the protesters appeared to have immobilized the racecourse authorities and the police, and no action was taken against the protesters for trespassing and organizing a "sit-in" on the property. The takeover of the racecourse became a prime time news item, and both the evening and the next morning's editions of the news covered the event, including interviews with members of the Ad Hoc Committee. The action had boosted the morale of slum dwellers and, most importantly, of pavement dwellers. The success achieved by the action demonstrated the counterpower of people (Alinsky, 1971). In the next section we discuss the direct action that took place and reflect on the ethical dilemmas of social workers involved in extralegal activities.

▶ A Critical Reflection on the Action

Ferzana Chaze (FC): Let's talk a bit about the achievements of the Ad Hoc Committee. I know that the College benefited as a social work educational institution through the actions of the action plan. The response of the College provided a live field of work for students to learn community organization through actually participating in action. The research project had provided insights into the issues faced by pavement communities and pointed to many areas for future social work intervention. Student social workers had an opportunity to participate in data collection and analysis. Even a decade later the goodwill that was created by the College among the slum and pavement communities was a fertile ground for further intervention. Apart from this huge contribution to social work knowledge and practice what other important gains were made? Could you elaborate on the achievements of the project in relation to its main objectives, which included advocating for the rights of pavement dwellers as citizens?

Purnima George (PG): The protest march was successful in that it created a positive impact all over the city among various radical groups and other groups that were also responding to the issue. And actually, after the takeover of the racecourse, the morale of the Ad Hoc Committee and the pavement and slum dwellers was greatly boosted. It was the first time in the history of social work in India that social workers had taken such a leading role in this kind of radical community organizing. This greatly enhanced our credibility with the pavement and slum communities, and with other social and progressive organizations of our time. In recognition of what we were doing, the group of public interest litigation lawyers requested that we collaborate with them and support their legal action. Our collaboration with lawyers revealed the important contribution social work could make to the issue, not only through sharing the findings of our research but also through sharing the perspectives and experiences gained from our grassroots work with slum and pavement dwellers at the joint conference we organized. The Honourable Chief Justice of India, Justice Krishna Iyer, who was one of the judges on the pavement-dwellers' case, was present at that conference. In fact, it was a milestone for all of us at the College to share our critical perspectives and the rich experience of our work with slum and pavement dwellers, with lawyers and judges who had so far heard mainly the popular discourses/stereotypes. Challenging those discourses through documented facts and real stories was influential in shaping their stance on the issue. For the first time ever, the social work profession in Bombay worked closely and intensively with the legal system in getting justice. The case received a judgment in favour of pavement dwellers that acknowledged their fundamental right as citizens of the country.

FC: Illegally occupying the racecourse was quite a deviation from professional social work's traditional responses to social injustices in India at that time. What was the committee thinking of and why did they decide on a plan that was so alien to what one would expect a coalition led by professional social workers to take up?

PG: As organizers we considered two critical points while developing our direct action. First, how do we resist and protest against the injustice that has been already done? Second, what counter-response is the demand for justice likely to evoke from the government? With regard to the first point, we wanted to strongly voice our protest and prevent the government from repeating similar action in the future. This was particularly important as the government seemed firm in its decision to "clean up" the other areas of the city as well. As social workers we were standing in alliance with the most oppressed sections of our society whose dignity and worth had been stolen and whose rights as citizens violated. A peaceful protest would not have pitched our response at the level at which the government had acted.

Second, in demanding the recognition of pavement dwellers as citizens and recognition of their right to live in Bombay as any other citizens of the country, we were redefining the existing relationship between the state and pavement dwellers and also challenging the existing pattern of distribution of resources by the state that totally excluded pavement dwellers. We knew that this demand was not going to be acceptable to the state, and therefore we had to use much stronger tactics of breaking legal norms to bring pressure on the state. Social action, protest, and the breach of legal norms are also thought to be more effective for marginalized groups that are totally dismissed by the decision makers and therefore have very limited access to them (Hoefer, 2000; Rubin & Rubin, 2001). The history of the Indian Independence movement and the Civil Rights movement in the United States are great examples of such strategies. Under these circumstances, we had to go beyond the legal norms in order for a fundamental change to occur. Through this action we as social workers were merely operationalizing the vision of social change we espouse, and we were practising our core values of social justice and equity which, unfortunately, seems "alien" in current times.

FC: What were some of the ethical dilemmas that the Ad Hoc Committee had to grapple with in deciding upon action that could have legal consequences or even cause potential harm to the participants? How did you address these?

PG: Unfortunately there are no ethical codes of conduct or guidelines around involvement of community members especially children in protests and demonstrations. According to Mendes (2002) the existing social work code of ethics provides little or no guidance to social workers engaged in community action campaigns (p. 157). The biggest ethical dilemma we perceived was related to maintaining the secrecy of our plan on taking over the racecourse. As the coordinator of the Ad Hoc Committee, and being a part of this secret plan of the takeover of the racecourse, I was aware that there was every possibility of police action. However, we could not share this information as, if it leaked out, there was a danger of potential sabotage and police action even before we engaged in any direct action. This would have defeated the whole purpose of what we meant to convey to the government.

However, I would like to say that it is we, the middle class, who have always held the fear of violating the law. For us it becomes an issue of insecurity as we wonder how this is going to impact our work, our class background, and our family. These are our fears, which we put in the form of ethics. But let us not forget that the ethic of a radical social worker is also about standing with the community and being its ally (Bailey & Brake, 1975). Do we ever pause and question whether what the government does is ethical? Is not the violation of fundamental rights unethical? So, how can ethics be one-sided and how should social workers who engage in such organizing deal with a system that has committed gross unethical practices? I challenge the very categorization of what is legal and what is considered to be illegal. After all, the discourse about what is legal or illegal is socially constructed by the privileged who are interested in maintaining the status quo. For those pavement dwellers who participated in taking over the racecourse, their actions were no more illegal than their everyday reality. The action provided an opportunity to voice their feelings about the gross misuse of vast tracts of land for the pleasure of the elite when they were not allowed to live on a street exposed to the vagaries of the weather and other dangers to health. They feared being deported and losing whatever little they had in Bombay that allowed them to survive and whatever they had to do in order to protect their survival was ethical enough.

I would like to share some famous ideas on the ethics of means and ends presented by Alinsky (1971) that have inspired me in my work over the years. I have always recalled his discussion whenever I have engaged in social action at other times (George, 2006). According to Alinsky (1971), "The judgment of the ethics of means is dependent upon the political position of those sitting in judgment.... [The] judgment must be made in the context of the times in which the action occurred and not from any other chronological vantage point.... The morality of a means depends upon whether the means is being employed at a time of imminent defeat or imminent victory" (pp. 26–34). Viewed in this context, our action of taking over the racecourse was ethical and justified.

The participating pavement dwellers were not given information about the racecourse takeover earlier as it was imperative to maintain utmost secrecy. It was left to them to make that decision when they were entering the racecourse. Generally, based on their life experiences, pavement dwellers often know the consequences of breaking legal norms. It was assumed that based on this wisdom they would be able to make a decision to participate or not. It was also decided that in case of police action the organizers at the racecourse would insist on mass arrest and would get themselves arrested along with pavement dwellers. In insisting on mass arrest the AHC organizers were adopting a tactic that would ensure an early release of people. Also, with the organizers remaining in custody with slum and pavement dwellers, the chances of police atrocities on them could be kept in check. Typically the police in India are more wary of dealing with an educated and vocal middle class that has the ability to influence politicians (and in turn the police), or respond with legal action, than they are in dealing with marginalized populations.

The Ad Hoc Committee had established certain safeguards for members who were participating in the direct action. All organizers, including students who were participating in the protest march, were given the choice of deciding the nature and extent of their engagement in the direct action. They were told that they could withdraw their participation at any time they felt uneasy or threatened. Hence, a few of us who decided not to participate in the takeover of the racecourse were given the responsibility of remaining vigilant about police movement on the bridge and informing others of any such movement, contacting the College of Social Work and other network members (from public pay phones as there were no cell phones at that time) in case of any emergency, and communicating with the media and the press. We had to give this option to all AHC members as the Committee was only a coalition with very diverse membership ranging from faith-based organizations to radical student movements, which also included social work students. Taking over the racecourse did not fit well with the mandates of some members. This compelled us to share the information with the AHC members.

FC: What also are your feelings in retrospect about deciding on a course of action without the participation of the pavement dwellers themselves?

PG: In retrospect, more than 30 years after the action, I realize that we could have done some things differently. This realization is based on the scholarship on critical, poststructural, and anti-oppression perspectives and their application to social work practice (Dominelli, 1998; Fook, 2002; Foucault, 1991; Healy, 2000; Kristeva, 1981) that has evolved since the incident. As we understood it then, social advocates took action on "behalf of" the oppressed – probably as "professional experts." The Ad Hoc Committee was comprised of members who were not affected by the issue. All of us, with the possible exception of some of our project staff, came from backgrounds that included secure incomes and housing. A majority had never experienced the insecurities, uncertainties, and marginalization experienced by pavement dwellers. Looking back, I see the lack of representation of pavement dwellers on the Ad Hoc Committee as a significant limitation. In not seeking their representation we reproduced the very power relations we were encouraging them to challenge.

I wonder whether there was any possibility of having some representation when the grassroots mobilization began in pavement communities, and how this representation might have influenced our actions. I also wonder whether the Ad Hoc Committee could have been more accountable to its community members by way of sharing its decisions and plan of action. Would a more egalitarian relationship and engagement of pavement dwellers in decision making have led to different outcomes, and if so, what would they have been? Besides merely focusing on change, should our work not have focused on process and seen the process itself as an outcome? Our work of redefining and re-establishing fundamental rights could have focused on a grassroots, community-based process (Ferguson & Lavalette, 2005; Ife, 2010; Bailey & Brake, 1975). Such efforts could have established a model of social advocacy that entails a "work with" rather than "work on behalf of" approach.

FC: What do you see as some of the key implications for contemporary social work practice in India and North America that emerge from this action plan three decades ago?

PG: Currently, we live in a world that is under siege by neo-liberalism and where neo-liberal policies have taken control of the social service sector through funding restrictions, increased surveillance, and expectations of efficiency. This context poses challenges to the radical organizing or subversive social action of the type we engaged in. The vision of societal change seems elusive in current times, and few social workers are willing to engage in theories and methods of radical practice or subversive social action. However, the history of resistance has demonstrated that the existence of the most severe forms of oppression provides the most fertile soil for any resistance and transformation. The current context requires subversive strategies that synergize social movements and open space for working across and through differences toward building a "broad opposition movement" (Shragge, 2003), a "counterpower" of people (Alinsky, 1971) that can challenge the global neo-liberal capitalist agenda. The development of collaborative community-based research, field education, and training projects that link faculty, students, practitioners, and community members may be one means of initiating and promoting such a movement from the corridors of educational institutions.

Notes

1 While the term "deportation" usually refers to expulsion of a person from a country, in this chapter we use it with reference to the expulsion of the pavement dwellers from the city of Bombay. This use of the term is consistent with public documents that record the event.
2 Bombay was renamed Mumbai in 1996. As this chapter is largely a documentation of history, the name Bombay is used throughout the chapter rather than the new name of the city, Mumbai.

References

Alinsky, S. (1971). *Rules for radicals: A pragmatic primer for realistic radicals.* New York: Random House.
Bailey, R., & Brake, M. (1975). *Radical social work.* London: Edward Arnold.
Bombay Municipal Corporation Act. (1988). Bombay: Government of Maharashtra Publication.
Demographia. (2001). *Mumbai Municipality & Suburban Population from 1981.* Retrieved 2 Dec. 2014 from http://www.demographia.com/db-Mumbai 1981 .htm
Desai, M. (1991). Operation clean-up. In A.R. Desai (Ed.), *Expanding government lawlessness and organized struggles* (pp. 170–173). Bombay: Popular Prakashan.
Dominelli, L. (1998). Anti-oppressive practice in context. In R. Adams, L. Dominelli, & M. Payne (Eds.), *Social work: Themes, issues and critical debates* (2nd ed.) (pp. 3–19). Hampshire, NY: Palgrave Macmillan.
Ferguson, I., & Lavalette, M. (2005). Another world is possible: Social work and the struggle for social justice. In I. Ferguson, M. Lavalette, & E. Whitmore (Eds.), *Globalization, global justice and social work* (pp. 207–223). London: Routledge.
Fook, J. (2002). Power. In *Social work: Critical theory and practice* (pp. 45–55). London: Sage.
Foucault, M. (1991). *Discipline and punish: The birth of the prison.* Translated by A. Sheridan. London: Penguin.
Freire, P. (1970). *Pedagogy of the oppressed.* New York: Continuum.
Galper, J. (1980). *Social work practice: A radical perspective.* Englewood Cliffs, NJ: Prentice-Hall.
George, P. (2006). Social action with pavement dwellers in India. In B. Lee & S. Todd (Eds.), *A casebook of community practice: Problems and strategies* (pp. 192–201). Mississauga, ON: CommonAct Press.
Gil, D. (1998). *Confronting injustice and oppression: Concepts and strategies for social workers.* New York: Columbia University Press.

Gorz, A. (1977). *Strategy for labor.* Boston: Beacon Press.

Healy, K. (2000). *Social work practices: Contemporary perspectives on change.* London: Sage.

Hoefer, R. (2000). Human services interest groups in four states: Lessons for effective advocacy. *Journal of Community Practice, 7*(4), 77–94.

Hosbet, S. (n.d.). *Forced evictions: An "Indian People's Tribunal" enquiry into the brutal demolitions of pavement and slum dwellers homes.* Bombay: Committee for the Right to Housing.

Ife, J. (2005). Human rights and critical social work. In S. Hick, J. Fook, & R. Pozzuto (Eds.), *Social work: A critical turn* (pp. 57–66). Toronto: Thompson Educational.

Ife, J. (2010). *Human rights from below: Achieving rights through community development.* Melbourne: Cambridge University Press.

International Federation of Social Workers (IFSW). (2013). *Statement of ethical principles.* Retrieved 2 Dec. 2014 from http://ifsw.org/policies/statement-of-ethical-principles/

Kristeva, J. (1981). Women's time. Translated by A. Jardine & H. Blake. *Signs, 7,* 13–35.

Lokshahi Hakk Sanghatana Bombay. (1991). Slum: Workers Colony – Report of the fact-finding committee on slums. In A.R. Desai (Ed.), *Expanding government lawlessness and organized struggles* (pp. 154–169). Bombay: Popular Prakashan.

Mahtani, R. (1985). *A profile of pavement dwellers in Bombay.* Bombay: Research Unit, College of Social Work.

Mendes, P. (2002). Social workers and the ethical dilemma of community action campaigns: Lessons from the Australian State of Victoria. *Community Development Journal, 37*(2), 157–166.

Mohapatra, B.N. (2004). A view from the subalterns: The pavement dwellers of Mumbai. In R. Tandon & R. Mohanty (Eds.), *Does civil society matter? Governance in contemporary India* (pp. 285–314). New Delhi: Sage.

Mullaly, R. (2002). *Challenging oppression: A critical social work approach.* Don Mills, ON: Oxford University Press.

People's Union for Civil Liberties (PUCL). (1983). *The shunned and the shunted – the slum and pavement dwellers of Bombay.* Retrieved Dec. 2014 from http://www.unipune.ac.in/snc/cssh/HumanRights/08%20STATE%20AND%20HOUSING/02.pdf

Ramachandran, P. (1975). *Pavement dwellers in Bombay city.* Bombay: Registrar, Tata Institute of Social Science.

Rubin, H. J., & Rubin, I.S. (2001). Community organizing and development. (3rd ed.). Toronto: Allyn and Bacon.

Sebastian, P. (1991). Who lives in slums? In A.R. Desai (Ed.), *Expanding government lawlessness and organized struggles* (pp. 175–178). Bombay: Popular Prakashan.

Shragge, E. (2003). *Activism and social change: Lessons for community & local organizing.* Toronto: University of Toronto Press.

Singh, D.P. (2006). Slum population in Mumbai. Part I. Published in IIPS Mumbai, ENVIS Center (Mar. 2006). Retrieved 2 Dec. 2014 from http://www.iipsenvis.nic.in/newsletters/vol3no1/Slum_Poplation_InMumbai.htm

Society for Promotion of Area Resource Centres (SPARC) & Society for Participatory Research in Asia (PRIA). (1985). We, the invisible – A census of pavement dwellers. SPARC & PRIA. Retrieved 2 Dec. 2014 from http://pria.org/publication/We,%20The%20Invisible%20a%20Census%20of%20Pavement%20Dwellers.pdf

Specht, H. (1969). Disruptive tactics. In R.M. Kramer and H. Specht (Eds.), *Readings in community organization practice* (pp. 372–386). Englewood Cliffs, NJ: Prentice-Hall.

Subramanian, V. (1975). *Parched earth: The Maharashtra drought, 1970–73*. India: Orient Longman.

CHAPTER 7

Non-violent Resistance

The Landless Rural Workers Movement of Brazil

Wilder Robles

This chapter examines the Movimento dos Trabalhadores Rurais Sem Terra (MST), or Landless Rural Workers Movement, and non-violent resistance in Brazil. Unlike in contemporary Colombia or El Salvador, this Brazilian landless peasant movement has slowly but firmly advanced democratic change without resorting to open armed insurrection. The MST has carried out massive occupations of uncultivated private and public lands, and this has been effective in contesting and transforming Brazil's unjust agrarian structure. The movement has succeeded in placing land reform at the centre of the debate regarding democracy, development, and social justice in Brazil and beyond. More importantly, the MST links micro-politics to macro-politics to advance large-scale collective mobilization that goes beyond political and economic reformism.

This chapter argues that the MST's strategy of non-violence[1] was shaped by the country's political context and a progressive Catholic Christian ideology. This movement has relied on the active and committed participation of its members, and operated with decentralized grassroots structures that stress self-reliance, solidarity, and empowerment. The MST has also benefited from extensive national and international solidarity networks to advance its struggle. This chapter's conclusions are threefold: First, the political system in Brazil is biased in favour of the affluent and powerful. As such, the poor and powerless are forced to engage in activities that are considered to be extralegal or illegal (i.e., collective protest) in order to reassert their basic rights. Second, non-violent popular struggles, within specific political contexts, are conducive to effective and transformative forms of democratic citizenship. They tend to stir people's consciousness regarding injustices in the public and private spheres of human life; they are also effective conduits for promoting dialogue, tolerance, and understanding. All of these are essential elements for cultivating a culture of peace, which, in turn, is fundamental for devising transformative visions of progressive social change (Holmes, 2004). Third, in the present context of Latin America, non-violent popular struggles are valuable alternatives to counter the forces of structural poverty, oppression, and exploitation that have continued to prevail in this region. Because of complex and well-entrenched power structures, Latin America has often resorted to armed insurrections to deal with social grievances. Unfortunately, the outcomes of violent insurrections have often reproduced new repressive forms of social control. Non-violent popular struggles remain a viable option in Latin America because they allow the poor, excluded, and oppressed the opportunity to raise their voices and reassert their rights (McManus, 2004). Yet, as the MST demonstrates, non-violent actions, struggles, or resistance are not easy journeys: there are no assurances of success. Non-violence cannot always force repressive regimes to accept changes, particularly when they control the monopoly of force.

▶ BACKGROUND

Brazil is the largest, richest, and most populous country in Latin America, with a population of almost 197 million people and a gross domestic product of 2.25 trillion US dollars (World Bank, 2015). Brazil is also a country with enormous income inequality, where 10% of the population possesses 50% of the country's income and the 50% poorest possesses only 10%. Despite significant progress in reducing absolute poverty over the last decade,[2] Brazil still faces enormous socio-economic obstacles to become a more inclusive and just society. Certainly, this is the case in the countryside where skewed power relations have continued to buttress systemic socio-economic exclusion. Brazil is a country with an enormous concentration of farmland in the hands of a few. In 2006, 1% of landowners controlled 44% of the total Brazilian farmland (Table 7.1), between 18 and 20 million rural people were living in poverty, and more than 5 million families were considered landless. This situation has remained virtually unchanged over the last seven decades. The expansion of subsistence farming over this same period did not change the enormous concentration of landownership. Not surprisingly, the Gini index of land inequality[3] has remained

Table 7.1: Distribution of Agricultural Landownership in Brazil, 2006

Rural Property Size (hectares)	Number of Properties	Pct. of Properties	Area (hectares)	Pct. of Area
Less than 10 (Minifundia)	2,477,071	47.86	7,798,607	2.36
10 to less than 100	1,971,577	38.09	62,893,091	19.06
100 to less than 1000	424,906	8.21	112,696,478	34.16
More than 1000 (Latifundia)	46,911	0.91	146,553,218	44.42
Other producers, property size unknown	255,024	4.93	N/a	N/a
Total	5,175,489	100	329,941,393	100

Source: IBGE, *Censo Agropecuário 2006* (Brasília, DF: IBGE, 2009).

very high (Table 7.2). The persistence of high land inequality has stymied Brazil's social and human development. This unfortunate situation has also led to intermittent and often violent conflicts in the countryside. Since the 1960s these conflicts have intensified due to the adverse consequences of agricultural modernization (Mançano, 2000).

Over the last two decades, landless peasants have openly expressed their growing discontent with the status quo: they have contested the *latifúndia*[1] by carrying out massive occupations of private or public lands.

Table 7.2: Average Gini Index of Land Inequality in Selected Latin American Countries, 1970–2000

(0 = Absolute Equality; 100 = Absolute Inequality)

Country	Gini Coefficient
Argentina	85
Bolivia	77
Brazil	85
Chile	84
Colombia	84
Costa Rica	81
Ecuador	84
Honduras	72
Mexico	61
Nicaragua	72
Panama	86
Paraguay	91
Peru	89
Venezuela	90

Source: Florencia Torche and Seymour Spilerman, "*Household Wealth in Latin America.*" UNI-WIDER, Research Paper No. 2006/114. Table 4B, p. 14.

From 1988 to 2011 landless peasants carried out 8,536 land seizures nationwide (see Figure 7.1). The Landless Rural Workers Movement has been the main force behind these occupations.[5] With more than a 1.5 million members, the MST is the most important landless peasant movement in Latin America today (Carter, 2013). This movement has an immense capacity to empower the poor: it has a strong political base, effective organization, and extensive social networks. All of these strengths have enabled the MST to advance new visions and practices of political and economic democracy in Brazil and beyond.

Since the late 1980s this movement has advocated access to land as a fundamental human right. For the MST, the poor continue to face hunger, and their systemic lack of access to food stems principally from their systemic lack of access to land (Robles, 2001). It has also argued that growing landlessness has contributed to a situation of global food insecurity (or food vulnerability), which has disproportionally affected the poor. For these reasons, the MST has embraced a grassroots push for land reform to correct not only an historical injustice but also to advance human rights in Brazil. The MST has popularized a simple message to emphasize the importance of this process: land reform is a struggle for human life and dignity, and land reform is everybody's struggle. This message has resonated among the landless peasants.

The MST was established in 1984 in the city of Cascavel, in the state of Paraná. Under the capable and charismatic leadership of João Pedro Stédile,[6] the MST has transformed, and continues to transform, Brazil's rural landscape. Since its inception, the MST has achieved remarkable

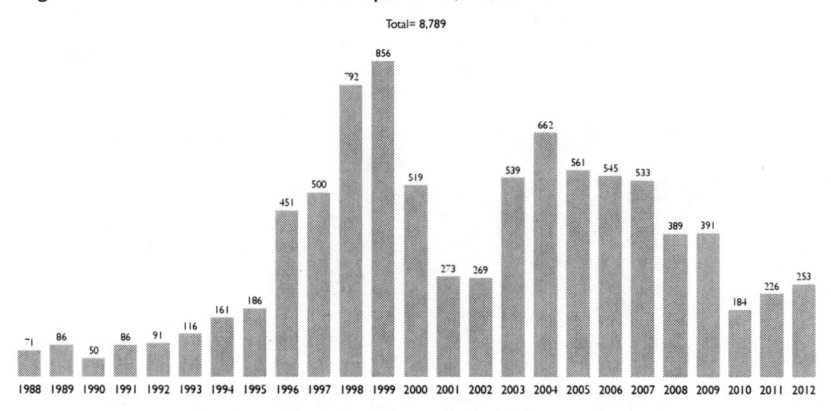

Figure 7.1: Number of Land Occupations, 1988–2012

Total= 8,789

Year	Occupations
1988	71
1989	86
1990	50
1991	86
1992	91
1993	116
1994	161
1995	186
1996	451
1997	500
1998	792
1999	856
2000	519
2001	273
2002	269
2003	539
2004	662
2005	561
2006	545
2007	533
2008	389
2009	391
2010	184
2011	226
2012	253

Source: DATALUTA, *Banco de Dados da Luta pela Terra*, 2012.
Note: There is no reliable available data of land occupations 1985–1987.

Table 7.3: Official Government Numbers of Land Reform Beneficiaries, 1964–2010

Period Military and Democratic Regimes	No. of Peasant Families Settled	Set Target	Total Area (millions hectares) Approximate	Average per Year
Military (1964–1984)	77,465	N/A	13.8	3,873
Sarney (1985–1990)	89,950	1.4 million	4.5	17,990
Collor and Franco (1990–1994)	60,188	N/A	2.3	15,049
Cardoso (1995–2002)	540,704	N/A	19.8	67,588
Lula (2003–2010)	614,000	400,0000 (first term)	48.3	76,750
Total	1,382,307		88.7	
Total (1985–2010)	1,304,842		74.9	

Source: Data collected from the following sources: "*Reforma Agrária: Compromisso de todos.*" Secretaria de Comunicação Social, Presidência da Republica, 1997; INCRA, *Resumo das Atividades do INCRA, 1985–94*; MDA, *Balanço 2003-2006: DESENVOLVIMENTO AGRÁRIO COMO ESTRATÉGIA*; and Journal INCRA, *Balanço 2003 and 2010*.

Notes:
1. Most of these families received land titles via colonization and settlement projects. Although during the 1995–2010 period there was a substantial increase in the granting of land titles, the total number fell short of the 1.4 million target set in 1985.
2. Cardoso and Lula's figures have been hotly contested.
3. Lula has settled peasant families mostly on public land.

results. First, the MST has compelled the Brazilian government to grant land titles to over 1.3 million landless peasants (Table 7.3). Currently, thousands more landless peasants are awaiting land titles. Second, the MST has established hundreds of agricultural settlements, several alternative media outlets, an extensive educational and social welfare system, and dozens of agricultural co-operatives. Finally, the MST has greatly contributed to the globalization of peasant struggles by actively participating in the formation and operation of the Vía Campesina[7] and the World Social Forum.[8]

▶ THEORIZING SOCIAL MOVEMENTS

The study of social movements has a long and rich history. It has been shaped by different intellectual traditions. Its has also been open to ongoing debate due to the complex and dynamic character of these movements. Social movements are in constant metamorphosis: they are continually embracing new forms of collective protest and popular struggle that challenge dominant theoretical perspectives. Since the 1960s the study of social movements gained momentum with the arrival of "new social movements."[9] The "new" social movements emerged in the particular historical conjuncture of the 1960s to 1980s: the arrival of "bureaucratic-authoritarian" political regimes, the collapse of organized political parties, the transformation of the Catholic Church, and the foreign "invasion" of non-governmental organizations (NGOs). The latter played a fundamental role in the formation and operation of grassroots development organizations by providing most of the funding for their activities. Unfortunately, most of these organizations have tended to function as local welfare agencies for the poor and destitute. With the exception of the Comunidades Eclesias de Base (CEBs), or Christian Base Communities,[10] these community-based movements have not been effective in bringing about structural change, because they lacked a unified strategy and broad vision of social change. Nevertheless, these movements reinforced community identity, redefined democratic values and practices, opened political spaces for women, and expressed conflicts beyond the sphere of economic production. Above all, they were localized social struggles not concentrated in the political realm of the state.

New social movements represented diversity and complexity: they represented new forms of collective action with new constituencies, new objectives, values, and ideologies. All of these questioned traditional categories in social movement theory. As a result, the study of these movements has undergone a number of paradigm shifts, from collective behaviour and social grievance approaches to resource mobilization, political process or framing, identity-oriented, and neo-Marxist approaches. Proponents and opponents of these opposing theoretical perspectives engaged in endless debates regarding the nature, character, and relevance of new social movements. In the mid-1990s these debates gained new momentum with the arrival of the anti-globalization and anti-corporate movements, which incited new forms of cross-border protest, solidarity, and resistance. Once again, theoreticians were challenged to re-evaluate social movements.

In the peculiar context of Latin America, new social movements are primarily engaged in the pursuit of substantive, participatory, inclusive democracy. This is in response to the formalist, exclusionary, and repressive nature of Latin America's political regime. New social movements are contesting this situation. These movements are functioning as both a catalyst for progressive social change and a form of healthy political therapy for dysfunctional social systems. In the current context of neo-liberal Latin America, these movements are vital instruments for organizing and equipping the poor to reassert their fundamental human rights. Despite their diverse origins and philosophies of action, these new social movements share a common objective: changing power structures that restrict democratic citizenship. These movements are playing a central role in redefining the interrelationships among democracy, development, and social justice. Despite some progress over the last decade, Latin America continues to maintain high levels of poverty and inequality. In response, new social movements are seeking new models of political and economic democracy that go beyond the restricted parameters of electoral politics and free-market economics. The MST is one of these movements.

▶ "Old" Social Movements

Social movements are not a new phenomenon in Latin America. In fact, these movements have a history that goes back to colonial times. Popular protests of one kind or another have occurred with unexpected consequences throughout the history of Latin America.[11] The authoritarian and discriminatory nature of the political regimes and the pervasive influence of Western powers all contributed to the formation of revolutionary and reformist movements that contested the political order by the use of force. Unfortunately, authoritarianism, dogmatism, personalism, and sectarianism undermined the social bases of these movements.[12] They were "bottom up" movements that operated through "top down" methods. Unfortunately, top down methods of political control tend to supress dialogue, tolerance, diversity, and creativity.

Social theorists have interpreted these "old" social movements (i.e., labour, peasant, and student movements) in terms of their macro-political and economic character (Eckstein, 2001). They were movements seeking broad-scale societal change by seizing state power by violent means.[13] The structural, ideological, and operational characteristics of these social movements were shaped by the evolving dynamics of capitalist development and the Cold War context of Latin America at the time.

Parsonian functionalist theory, the dominant school of thought during the 1960s, argued that these movements exposed dysfunctions provoked by strains in the social system.[14] That is, they were side effects of rapid socio-economic change that the system could not immediately absorb. In contrast, Marxist conflict theory, the predominant approach from the 1970s to the mid-1980s, contended that these movements were responses to capitalist economic exploitation. Other comparative theorists advanced alternative theories by elucidating the complex linkages among local, state, and international structures and relations that inhibited or promoted revolutions.

"New" Social Movements

Parsonian and Marxist theories were eventually contested as Europe, North America, and Latin America witnessed a "new wave" of social movements expressing a variety of social concerns and demanding immediate state attention. These movements did not explicitly embrace universal ideologies or clear social visions. In fact, their ideological, organizational, and operational characteristics have been marked by fragmentation, informality, and opportunism.

Social theorists have interpreted these "new" social movements in terms of their micro-political and cultural character (Alvarez, Dagnino, & Escobar, 1998).[15] They were movements seeking moderate rather than revolutionary change. The sociological interpretations of these movements have varied. Some argued that the utopian revolutionary ideologies of the old social movements had shifted to the more pragmatic and specific demands of political, environmental, and cultural rights. Others asserted that these movements were neither new nor isolated from class-based movements, because ethnic, Indigenous, slave, women's, and religious movements have existed for centuries. They have merely assumed new forms, incorporated news themes, and adapted to new socio-economic contexts.

During the last two decades, the theoretical armoury of new social movements has been enriched with the advance of postmodernism and poststructuralism. With their abstract and sophisticated language analysis, these theories shifted the study of these new social movements away from state and class politics and toward identity and cultural politics. In the process, Parsonian and Marxist theories lost ground. Nevertheless, the study of new social movements remains a contested terrain: the labyrinth of contemporary new social movements is a complex phenomenon that no single theory can comprehensively explain.

Interpreting the MST

There are many theories used to study the MST. Among these, the "political opportunity" and "neo-Marxist" approaches have been widely used. The political opportunity approach has been associated with, among others, the work of Eisinger, Piven, Cloward, and Tarrow (see Della Porta & Diani, 1999). This approach explains new social movements within the broader political-institutional environment in which these movements operate. These movements are understood as a form of mass politics and are viewed in relation to the state; that is, this approach focuses on the interaction between institutional political actors and social movements (Benford & Snow, 2000, pp. 611–639). Moreover, the political opportunity approach contends that the political context in which new social movements emerge influences, or frames, their success or failure.

Ondetti (2008) uses this approach to examine the highs and lows of the MST's political trajectory: its emergence (1974–84), growth (1985–94), take-off (1995–99), decline (2000–2), and resurgence (2003–6). The main argument is that the MST's trajectory was shaped by the changing political opportunities created by Brazil's transition and consolidation to democracy. Political opening facilitated the organization, operation, and strategy of this movement. The MST gained favourable public sympathy and support after the massacre of landless peasants in Corumbiara, Rondônia, in 1995, and Eldorado de Carajás, Pará, in 1996. These massacres exposed a serious crisis of political legitimacy, forcing the Brazilian government to speed up land reform. The MST took advantage of this political opportunity to intensify land occupations nationwide. Yet, the introduction of what were called "violent and destructive tactics" (actually isolated cases of vandalism in 2000–4) turned public opinion against the MST (Ondetti, 2008). This situation, in turn, constrained the political opportunities for the MST to advance its struggle. For Ondetti, the overall impact of the MST has been positive: the movement has provided political and economic opportunities for the poor to change their unjust situation.

Despite its strengths, Ondetti's approach has some weaknesses. First, he tends to overemphasize the political character of the MST, while giving scant attention to its cultural, economic, or religious dimensions. Second, Ondetti pays little attention to the contemporary dynamics of coalition building, network linking, resource sharing, and discourse construction between "old" and "new" social movements. The dynamic interaction of these movements created opportunities for diffusing collective action and for forming coalitions beyond institutional politics. These processes tended to strengthen or weaken the capacity of the MST to contest the state. Finally, Ondetti's analysis tends to downplay the power of the *latifúndia* in resisting the advances of the MST in the countryside. The latifundia are more than land concentration: latifundia area system of power that extends to all aspects of Brazilian society.

The neo-Marxist approach to new social movements has been associated with, among others, the work of Harvey (2001), Eckstein (2001), Omvedt (1992), and Petras and Veltmeyer (2005). Although these scholars explore new social movements from a critical Marxist perspective, they provide different, albeit complementary, explanations about the origins, roles, limitations, and strategies of these movements within the context of neo-liberal global capitalism. They all share the view that new social movements are best understood as anti-systemic movements whose struggles centre on both the state and society. These struggles encapsulate the contemporary spheres of political, economic, cultural, and ecological exploitation. Notably, these authors recognize that the effectiveness of these movements depends largely on their abilities to transcend particularism and localism. This can be achieved by formulating a relatively coherent and inclusive socio-political discourse that stresses justice, equality, and solidarity.

Using the neo-Marxist approach, I have argued (Robles, 2007) that the MST emerged out of a concrete historical struggle for land reform and has been influenced by progressive Catholicism. It is a complex movement that effectively promotes social, political, economic, and religious solidarity. This movement expresses the transformative power of the politics of non-violence. It has deliberately opted for non-violence as the most effective means of achieving its goals.[16] The MST has become an important conduit for reflection and action: it has linked academics, activists, artists, students, workers, peasants, women, and children to a broad-based reflection-action project that has stirred the consciousness of the nation. Notably, the MST has advanced a classed-based transformative pedagogy by linking *reflection* to *action* within a concrete social struggle. This pedagogy emerged out of necessity and eventually was adopted out of conviction.

▶ THE MST AND POLITICAL AND ECONOMIC ACTIVISM

For centuries, Brazil's poor have not been able to meet their basic needs because of socio-economic marginalization. This has particularly been the case in the countryside, where the landholding elite enjoys the monopoly of political and economic power. Even today, the political system remains exclusionary: the politics of production and reproduction of poverty, marginalization, and domination is well entrenched in Brazil. The state tends to favour the interests of the affluent and powerful at the expense of the poor and powerless. Oppression and exploitation, particularly in the countryside, lies at the heart of injustice-generating processes in Brazil. Political and economic exclusion themselves promote oppression and exploitation, and exit from these injustices depends largely on contesting unjust power structures.

This situation has to change in order to build a more inclusive and just society. The state has to play a fundamental role in this process: it has to become a vehicle for social justice. This, in turn, requires the transformation of the state through a genuine process of democratic participation. In the present context of neo-liberal ideological hegemony, the transformation of the state confronts serious obstacles. Yet, these obstacles can be overcome with intense and organized political mobilization channelled through social movements rather than political parties.[17] In addition, social movements must develop concrete strategies for social change: these movements often spearhead political change, but they seldom maintain the momentum to make a lasting impact. Moreover, the state tends to stifle the momentum of these movements by criminalizing their so-called illegal activities (i.e., collective protest, land occupations, etc.).

The MST is a movement with a well-defined strategy for progressive social change. Its aim is the democratization of Brazil's power structures. This strategy has two fundamental, interconnected principles: political and economic activism. The effectiveness of this strategy lies in its linking of local-level political processes (micro-politics) to national/international level political processes (macro-politics). This linkage has been instrumental in contesting power structures that buttress political domination, economic exploitation, and environmental destruction. The outcome is slowly, but firmly, transforming Brazilian society. In particular, the MST's political and economic activism reinforces the need to reconsider collective protest as a fundamental right to advance and defend genuine forms of participatory democracy. For the poor and powerless, political and economic activism is a fundamental tool to reassert their basic political and economic rights.

▶ Political Activism

The MST was established in 1984. However, its origin can be traced to a mobilization in 1976, when the military regime expropriated large tracts of peasants' land to construct the gigantic Itaipú Dam along the border with Paraguay. In response, the Catholic and Lutheran churches supported the peasants in their unsuccessful efforts to resist eviction. The military's failure to pay fair compensation further radicalized the peasantry.

Peasant revolt intensified in the following years, when landless peasants occupied idle lands in the southern, central-west, and northern regions of the country. In most cases, these occupations lasted only a few months. Nonetheless, they marked the beginning of the reopening of the agrarian question. These early experiences taught the landless peasants that a national organizational structure and broad political support were fundamental for successful land occupations. Specifically, they had to establish structures to link micro-politics to macro-politics.

The Catholic Church's Pastoral da Terra, or Church Commission on Land Reform, encouraged the landless peasants to reflect on the experiences of previous peasant movements to organize themselves. After much discussion, the landless peasants agreed to establish a national organization based on principles of decentralized grassroots democracy as the means of transforming restricted forms of political participation. They intended to avoid vertical forms of political control that fostered anti-democratic values. In 1984 landless peasants from across the country gathered in the city of Cascavel, State of Paraná, to create an organization dedicated to coordinating the struggle for land reform. The MST's organizational structure is highly decentralized (see Figure 7.2).

Figure 7.2: The MST's Structure

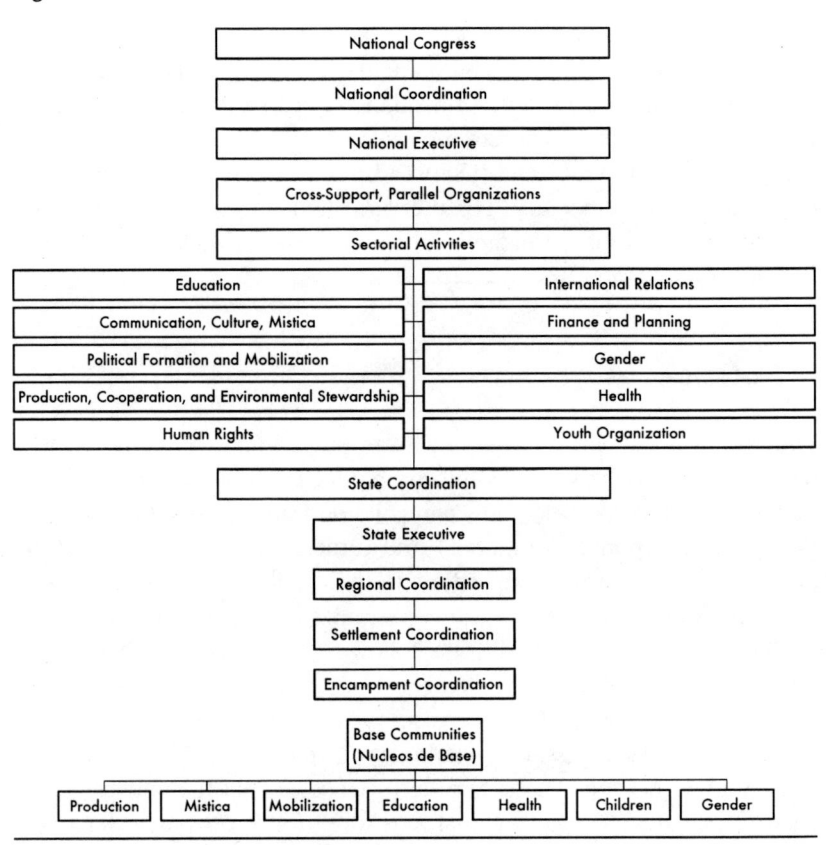

```
                        National Congress
                             |
                     National Coordination
                             |
                       National Executive
                             |
              Cross-Support, Parallel Organizations
                             |
                       Sectorial Activities
```

Education	International Relations
Communication, Culture, Mistica	Finance and Planning
Political Formation and Mobilization	Gender
Production, Co-operation, and Environmental Stewardship	Health
Human Rights	Youth Organization

```
                       State Coordination
                             |
                       State Executive
                             |
                     Regional Coordination
                             |
                    Settlement Coordination
                             |
                   Encampment Coordination
                             |
                       Base Communities
                      (Nucleos de Base)
```

| Production | Mistica | Mobilization | Education | Health | Children | Gender |

The MST has been consistently supported by the Catholic Church and the Partido dos Trabalhadores, or Workers Party (PT). This has enabled the movement to expand its national and international solidarity networks, thus facilitating its political mobilization. The fallout of globalization has also fuelled the MST's political engine. The movement has enlisted displaced rural workers, shantytown dwellers, and unemployed blue-collar workers. The MST has maintained a high level of political militancy. It has carried out land invasions, street demonstrations, nationwide marches, and occupations of government buildings. These actions have received the endorsement of church organizations, left-wing political parties, labour unions, student organizations, and other social movements. This support has facilitated the success of land occupations (Veltmeyer & Petras, 2002, pp. 79–96).

For the landless peasants, the first land occupation experiences shaped their conception of land reform. They faced fierce resistance from powerful groups vehemently opposed to land reform. The landless peasants soon understood that land reform was more than just a struggle for reclaiming a piece of land. Instead, land reform was a struggle for inciting the genuine democratization of society by non-violent means. Within this context, land occupation acquired a symbolic, powerful meaning: the first step toward regaining and exercising political citizenship as the precondition to overcoming systemic socio-economic exclusion. The MST has firmly held to this principle. Yet, it has been open to criticism. Many influential Brazilian academics have questioned the land occupation strategy, and hence the role of the MST in advancing democracy. For instance, Martins (2000) and Navarro (2002) consider the MST harmful to democracy because of its "fundamentalist," "anti-state," and "radical socialist" ideology.[18] Unfortunately, these authors fail to recognize that, because of unjust power structures, the landless peasants have no option but to resort to land occupation as the means of contesting socio-economic exclusion.

The MST has been instrumental in advancing democracy in Brazil. It has not only incorporated the disenfranchised into the democratic process, but also engendered new visions of democracy and development. However, as with any grassroots social movement, the MST has its limitations. Contrary to the paranoid fears of the right and the romanticized hopes of the left, the MST does not have the capacity to take power and establish socialism in Brazil. It is an organization operating with limited resources, confronting stiff political opposition, and facing internal problems. Despite these challenges, the MST has already demonstrated an enormous capacity to awaken the social consciousness of the poor in Brazil and beyond. Large-scale democratic transformation cannot take place without the changing of people's social consciousness.

Community-Level Politics

The MST's modus operandi reflects the praxis of the Christian Base Communities (CEBs) movement. This is not surprising given that both movements were influenced by Liberation Theology. The CEBs linked faith and politics to confront institutionalized injustice. During the 1970s and 1980s the radical character of these religious communities threatened powerful political and religious interests, particularly in Central America. Ultimately, the Vatican demobilized the CEBs to please conservative forces inside and outside the church (Robles, 2008). The rise of the MST coincided with the decline of the CEBs.

The MST's first step toward overcoming systemic social exclusion was to create community-based political units. These units conceived communities[19] as autonomous spaces, where the landless peasants learn how to organize and educate themselves to act against exclusionary power structures. These communities challenged the landless peasants to recreate, redefine, and re-energize effective forms of democratic mobilization beyond the micro-politics level. This, in turn, required redefining the theory and practice of class politics. The landless peasants embraced a broad vision of social change and solidified their ideological commitment to the cause. This was vital because social movements are prone to ideological fragmentation that contributes eventually to their political marginalization or co-optation.

National and International Level Politics

The second step was to link micro-politics to macro-politics. This was necessary in order to effectively pursue democratic change. In the macro-political arena, the landless peasants needed to have the ability to confront powerful political actors opposing changes to the status quo. Specifically, they had to confront the União Democrática Ruralista, or Rural Democratic Union (UDR), the powerful political arm of the landholding class.

The MST had then to forge political coalitions with other classed-based or non–classed-based movements without losing its political autonomy.[20] For the MST, the agrarian question was the microcosm of the social question; that is, it represented institutionalized injustice in Brazilian society. Overcoming this situation required social solidarity among all progressive sectors of society. This conceptualization paved the way for the building of multi-class political coalitions capable of responding to the demands for land, democracy, and social justice.

The MST has benefited from the politics of solidarity and the politics of mobilization to redefine its goals and strategies. It has created micro-

and macro-structures that facilitate active participation of intellectual, student, worker, and non-worker organizations in the struggle for land reform. Moreover, it has established links with transnational organizations to strengthen political solidarity. The building of strong political coalitions based on social solidarity has progressively transformed the MST: it has transformed itself into a vital conduit for reflection and action. The MST has brought together broad sectors of society to devise effective forms of collective action oriented toward changing skewed power relations in all spheres of human life.

The MST's co-operative experience demonstrates that incorporating the whole family in the productive process advances gender equity. Co-operative production provides men and women with opportunities to learn how cultural norms, values, and beliefs shape the unequal gender division of labour, and how this can be progressively changed though mutual understanding, respect, and collaborative work. Women's involvement in co-operative production also facilitates the re-evaluation of gender relationships in both the household and community. The MST's integration of gender issues has also contributed to its political effectiveness. It has openly promoted the active participation of women in the political process, reflecting the principle that democratic transformation requires overcoming cultural barriers that subordinate women in society. In the 1985 First National Conference, the MST adopted as one of its main objectives the active, egalitarian participation of women in society. This principle, reaffirmed in succeeding National Congresses, exhorted landless peasants to extend *concientização* (consciousness raising) to the private domain in order to progressively transform gender relations. Consciousness raising had to be practised as a holistic endeavour to unite both genders to the common project of overcoming oppression in the public and private spheres of human life.

▶ Economic Activism

Land reform is inherently a conflict-ridden process: it generates intergroup, interpersonal, and intrapersonal conflicts. This is because land reform disrupts skewed power relations, affects competitive positions or interests, and changes individuals' expectations. These conflicts are difficult to resolve, particularly when the key player in the process, the state, fails to adequately respond to the challenges of land reform. Land reform cannot succeed without an effective partnership between the state and community. History illustrates that state-led land reform initiatives without the active participation of peasant communities have frequently failed. History also points to the need for greater coherence in the roles, technical support, and financial commitments of the international and bilateral organizations. A multi-stakeholder approach is a necessity. Unfortunately, the state tends not only to frame but also to control the parameters of partnership with peasant communities. This uneven relationship undermines collaborative efforts to effectively advance land reform. In Brazil this type of relationship has led to increasing frustration with the pace and quality of land reform. The competing visions of land reform and sustainable rural development have intensified all types of conflicts. Despite its conflict-ridden character, land reform remains vital for addressing rural poverty.

The MST embraced co-operativism out of the need to address a crucial problem: How could peasants who had gained land titles survive in a capitalist agricultural economy oriented toward the international market? For João Pedro Stédile, the main political coordinator for the movement, this question required a pragmatic response: "Peasants must produce to commercialize" (in Veja, 1997, p. 47). Subsistence agriculture could not lift peasants out of poverty because isolating them from the market was a recipe for disaster. Given that government agricultural policies favour medium- and large-scale farmers, the MST established voluntary collective and semi-collective co-operatives to obtain access to agricultural credit, technology, and seeds. The landless peasants committed themselves to the difficult task of making the land productive to improve living conditions, to support financially the movement, and to transform socio-economic relations.

Co-operativism

In the early 1990s Stédile visited peasant movements in many countries to learn from their co-operative experiences. He returned to Brazil convinced that "peasants must not be afraid of the modernization of agriculture" (in Veja, 1997, p. 50). The co-operatives had to function as small business enterprises producing efficiently for the local markets in order to sustain their economic viability. Therefore, each co-operative had to operate autonomously so it could quickly adapt its business practices to the vicissitudes of the local markets. The autonomous character of the co-operatives has been one of the fundamental principles of economic activism. This principle has contributed to the spontaneous expansion of co-operatives in the settlements.

The MST's co-operative strategy responded to the economic realities of Brazil's rural communities. Large-scale farming required substantial amounts of capital and technology. This sort of agricultural practice was prohibitive for small-scale producers. In addition, these farmers were more vulnerable to the processes of rapid deforestation, soil erosion, and resource depletion. Capital-intensive agriculture was not the solution to these problems. The economic and environmental viability of small-scale farming depended on producing for the local markets using intermediate-scale agricultural technology.

The landless peasants did not object to a market-oriented co-operative strategy, despite their socialist political orientation. They understood that co-operativism was not the panacea for Brazil's economic woes and it was not intended as such. The landless peasants envisioned co-operativism not only as a source of income generation, but also as a tool to transform socio-economic relations. The co-operatives became learning communities whose members are reflecting and acting together to lay the foundations of a social economy that meets people's *needs* rather than *wants*. The objective is to construct a socially oriented conceptualization of the processes of material production, distribution, exchange, and consumption. This is essential to elaborate social standards for policy initiatives that promote the common good. The MST's co-operative strategy is integrating social, political, economic, ecological, and ethical values via continuing processes of direct interaction of people with land, capital, labour, market, and technology. The co-operativists are continuously learning to integrate theory into praxis, and praxis into theory in order to conceptualize a *normative* paradigm that goes beyond mere economic rationalization.

Over the last two decades, the MST's co-operative strategy has rapidly expanded. In 1992 the MST created the Confederação das Cooperativas de Reforma Agraria do Brasil (CONCRAB), or the Confederation of Brazilian Cooperatives for Land Reform, to coordinate the work of the agricultural, educational, financial, political, and research sections of the co-operatives. The objective was to provide services to the co-operative members through the exchange of resources, experiences, and strategies. CONCRAB encouraged landless peasants to search for alternative forms of socio-economic organization that meet their needs.

There are currently more than 500 agricultural, financial, and commercial co-operatives offering a variety of products and services to local communities. Notably, these co-operatives have become economically sustainable, with the most profitable co-operatives located in the southern region of the country (Leite et al., 2004). This achievement debunks the biased thinking that the poor are incapable of overcoming poverty through their own efforts.

▶ Education for Liberation

One of the main factors in the success of the co-operatives has been the MST's educational approach. The MST tackled the high level of illiteracy among the landless peasants with the delivery of educational programs tailored to their needs. These programs conformed to Paulo Freire's *education for liberation* pedagogy. This radical educational approach, banned during the military dictatorship, returned to its roots in the countryside. It soon "awakened" the creative capacities of the poor. By 2011 the MST was administrating a fully accredited primary school system providing education for more than 250,000 children, specialized adult literacy programs, and an innovative agricultural college to teach young peasants technical and managerial skills. The involvement of progressive intellectuals and institutions has been crucial in the planning and delivery of high-quality education. More than 50 Brazilian universities have established educational agreements with the MST to provide teacher training and extension education. The MST has benefited from this collaboration to strengthen its political base among the student population.

▶ THE IMPACT OF THE MST

The MST's political and economic activism is slowly transforming rural Brazil. It has had a positive impact on the countryside because it has stimulated *repeasantization*, or return to the countryside. From 1985 to 2011 the Programa Nacional de Reforma Agraria (PNRA), or National Program for Agrarian Reform, created a total of 8,906 land reform settlements (see Figure 7.3) benefiting over 1.2 million landless peasant families. These settlements have renewed, and continue to renew, the Brazilian countryside. In all regions of Brazil, land reform settlements have inserted new life into the countryside (see Figure 7.4). Even in remote *assentamentos* (settlements), such as those located in the rural districts of Rio Formoso and Condado in the State of Pernambuco, landownership has provided peasants with opportunities to reconstruct their communities by rediscovering their identities, re-establishing their livelihoods, and reconstructing social relations. As one settled peasant stated:

> I have worked on this land all my life. Two decades ago, this land started losing its people, particularly the youth. Most of them were moving to the big cities of Recife, São Paulo, or Rio de Janeiro. I thought then that the land would become a ghost place. Only the elderly were

Figure 7.3: Established Rural Settlements, 1985–2011

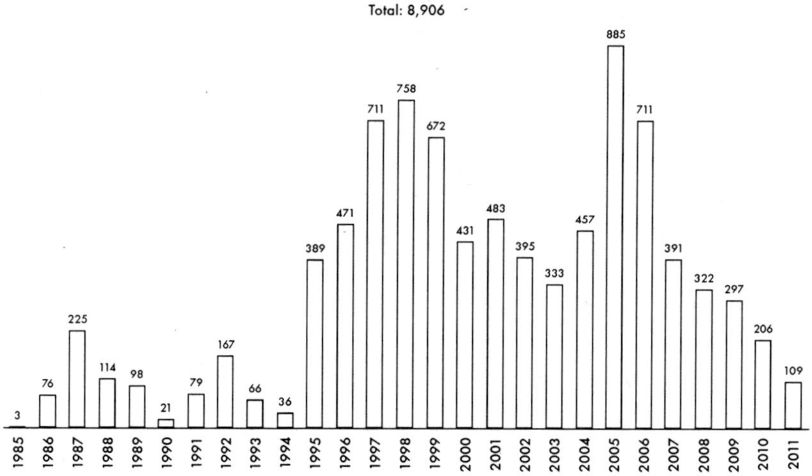

Total: 8,906

Bar values by year:
- 1985: 3
- 1986: 76
- 1987: 225
- 1988: 114
- 1989: 98
- 1990: 21
- 1991: 79
- 1992: 167
- 1993: 66
- 1994: 36
- 1995: 389
- 1996: 471
- 1997: 711
- 1998: 758
- 1999: 672
- 2000: 431
- 2001: 483
- 2002: 395
- 2003: 333
- 2004: 457
- 2005: 885
- 2006: 711
- 2007: 391
- 2008: 322
- 2009: 297
- 2010: 206
- 2011: 109

Source: DATALUTA, *Banco de Dados da Luta pela Terra*, 2011.

staying behind. I also thought about moving out, but I could not do so because I had to look after my extended family. Then, a decade ago we [the peasants] started to organize ourselves with the help of the MST and CPT [Comissão Pastoral da Terra or the Church Commission on Land Reform]. We wanted our own land. Other people outside the community joined the struggle. Some of them were children of peasants who had left this land a long time ago. The struggle for land was really tough but we all succeeded in the end. Now we have a piece of land and this community has been reborn. I am happy to see children playing again; we have weddings, festivals, and religious celebrations again. We are producing for local markets. Sure, life is still tough. Some people who came to these communities from the cities did not adapt well to the peasant rhythm of work. Peasant life is not easy. Even so it is very rewarding. Land reform has given us an opportunity to put food on the table on a daily basis. (Interview with Dom José Rosa, 11 Aug. 2004, *assentamento* Amaraji, Rio Formoso)[21]

Despite facing enormous obstacles, settled peasants are determined to create vibrant, sustainable communities in the countryside. Land reform has led to the creation of new communities and the revitalization of existing communities. This, in turn, has inserted new social, political, economic, and cultural dynamics into the countryside. Land reform has improved the social welfare of peasants. At its most basic level, land reform has

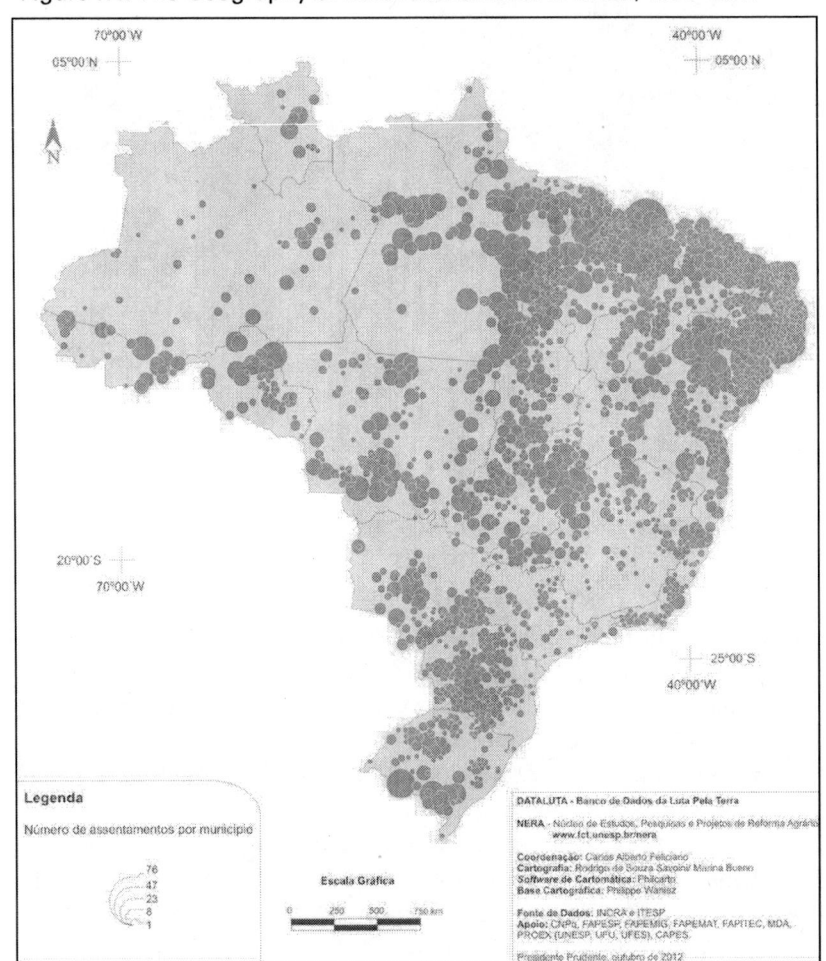

Figure 7.4: The Geography of Rural Settlements in Brazil, 1979–2011

enhanced food security in rural communities. This assessment is contained in an independent 2004 evaluation report. After evaluating key indicators of rural sustainability (access to credit, education, technology, and markets), the authors concluded that land reform has had an overall positive impact on the lives of the *assentados* (settled peasants). The following quote summarizes the report's key finding: "In practically all aspects, the settled peasants themselves have perceived a significant improvement in their present quality of life when compared to their previous situation. Despite their precarious nature, the settlements offer peasants a relatively promising future" (Leite et al., 2004, p. 75).

The precarious nature of the assentamentos refers to the living conditions confronting hundreds of thousands of peasant families, namely, lack of appropriate housing, potable water, sewage treatment, electricity, health, education, and social services. These problems were also identified in a 2003 land reform evaluation report funded by the Brazilian government (Sparovek, 2003).[22] In addition to identifying significant infrastructure problems, the 2003 and 2004 reports also recognized that settled peasants suffered from very limited educational skills and, in many cases, lack of farming experience.[23] Notably, these two reports clearly indicated that the precarious situation of the newly settled peasants is due primarily to limited government funding for settlement programs.

These studies also found that newly settled peasants had a remarkable capacity to overcome significant structural problems that inhibited their pursuit of sustainable rural livelihoods. Peasants had developed extensive socio-economic networks, which enabled them to make land reform socially, politically, economically, culturally, and environmentally sustainable. Socially, land reform has incorporated the previously dispossessed landless population into the ranks of small-scale producers. Small-scale farming has alleviated chronic poverty, advanced food sovereignty, and reduced urban migration. Politically, land reform has expanded democratic citizenship. Peasants have become politically active citizens in their communities. They have joined political parties, run for office, and, in many cases, been elected into office. Economically, land reform has re-energized local economies and created employment opportunities. Peasants have become producers, sellers, and consumers. Political and economic activism is slowly changing unjust structures of power that over the centuries have systematically marginalized the poor.

The creation of hundreds of new farmers' markets has opened alternative markets for small-scale agricultural producers. Culturally, land reform has stimulated the creation of new schools, arts centres, and community media channels. Environmentally, land reform has enabled peasants to become environmental stewards by practising small-scale organic farming. All of these changes have contributed to the slow but firm democratization of the polity and economy in the countryside. After more than two decades of struggle, the MST has progressively changed, and continues to change, rural Brazil. Yet, there is a long way to go to address Brazil's widespread systemic rural poverty.

Conclusion

After more than a decade of economic reforms, Brazil is entering again into a period of political uncertainty. In mid-2013 massive street protests caught the Brazilian democratic government off guard. Once again, the masses took to the streets to express their frustration with the quality of democracy at home. This is the fundamental truth about this unfortunate situation: political reforms have not kept up with economic reforms. Corruption, nepotism, and injustice remain rampant in the country.

Land reform, particularly Indigenous land claims, remains one of the most intractable social issues in modern Brazil. Land reform has a long way to go. This country continues to have one of the most unequal distributions of land in the world, and one of the highest levels of rural poverty in the world. The Gini index of land inequality remains high at 87, and 80% of the total rural population lives in abject poverty. Although more than 1.3 million peasants have received land titles to date, another 4–5 million are still landless. Over 80% of Brazil's total arable land belonging to the *latifundiários* (those who own farms over 1,000 hectares in size) remains uncultivated. The main reason for the persistence of skewed land concentration in Brazil is the inability or unwillingness of the government to address the issue. Political mobilization is necessary to address this issue. Yet, as the Landless Rural Workers Movement teaches us, political protest alone is not enough to bring about social justice. In an age of limited opportunities for the most disadvantaged groups in society, political and economic activism must go hand in hand in order to create a more just society. The MST has promoted political and economic activism in order to vigorously contest centuries of systemic socio-economic exclusion. The MST has practised the politics of land occupation to achieve access to land. It has also cultivated the politics of co-operativism to make land economically efficient and environmentally sustainable. This integrated approach to land reform has redefined and expanded democratic citizenship in the countryside. This movement demonstrates that there is an alternative path to social justice that goes beyond armed insurrection.

The MST's experience reveals important findings regarding peasant mobilization, land reform, and co-operativism. First, the MST is best understood in the context of five centuries of peasant subjugation. This movement embodies the aspirations of millions of landless peasants. It is a family-based peasant movement committed to the pursuit of a more just, egalitarian, and peaceful Brazilian society. Notably, this movement has used non-violent means to advance its objectives. The MST has transformed the politics of class by combining principles and practices of "old" and "new" social movements. The outcome has been the politics of hope that challenges the poor to become the objects and subjects of their own history.

Second, Brazil's current political system is inadequate to deal with contentious social issues, such as land reform, because this system is biased in favour of the affluent and powerful. As such, the poor and powerless are required to engage in land occupations in order to reassert their basic political and economic rights. The MST demonstrates the challenges of building inclusive democracy; the importance of engaging the poor and powerless in a broad project that secures common interests and goals; and the need to build social capital and improve the quality of society. The MST does all of this by articulating a culture of peaceful, non-violent protest that empowers rather than disempowers the poor and powerless.

Third, the MST is making land reform socially, economically, and ecologically viable. For the MST, the political "sustainability" of land reform is conditional on its economic productivity; that is, the efficient use of land is essential for enhancing food security, reducing poverty, and generating off-farming income. Accordingly, agriculture production must balance social, economic, and ecological factors through the selective use of modern scientific, technological, and technocratic expertise.

The MST has given millions of Brazil's landless peasants hope for a better future. Its approach to land reform is genuinely transformative. If properly supported by the state and the international community, the "scaling up" of this approach to land reform has great potential to improve the quality of life of rural communities while advancing environmental sustainability in Brazil. If Brazil is to become a truly just society, the Brazilian state must support the MST's efforts to undo one of the country's most unjust colonial legacies. Unfortunately, historical experience demonstrates that state forces rarely consider the concerns and efforts of the poor. Aware of this historical reality, the MST is nevertheless motivated to continue its historical struggle. In view of Brazil's well-entrenched power structures, land reform remains an unfulfilled promise, and the struggle for land reform is likely to continue for many more years, if not decades.

Notes

1 For the purpose of this chapter, "non-violence" refers to a method or tactic that avoids the use of armed violence for dealing with societal conflicts. Historically, non-violent action has been a powerful tool for social protest.
2 Brazil's Bolsa *Família*, or Family Allowance, program has been instrumental in reducing absolute poverty. The government of Luis Ignacio "Lula" Da Silva established this income-transferred program in 2004. According to Brazil's Ministry of Social Devel-

opment, there were almost 14 million families benefiting from the program in 2014 (MDS, 2015).
3. The Gini coefficient is the most commonly used measure of inequality. The coefficient ranges between 0 (which reflects complete equality) and 100 (which indicates complete inequality).
4. In Brazil, the *latifúndia*, or large landed estates, were established by Portugal during the sixteenth century to promote an export-oriented agriculture economy. Over the centuries, the development of the latifundia led to an enormous concentration of land in the hands of a few and the uprooting and impoverishment of peasants, tenant farmers, and rural labourers.
5. In Brazil, the word *camponês* (peasant) is not commonly used. Landless peasants identify themselves as *trabalhadores rurais sem terra*, or landless rural workers. Brazil has a long tradition of rural unions, which were historically subordinated to organized political parties. Although the MST maintains links to Brazil's Workers Party (PT), it is an autonomous landless peasant movement.
6. João Pedro Stédile is one of the main leaders of the MST. He was born in a family of Italian immigrants in 1953 in Lagoa Vermelha, Rio Grande do Sul, and was educated in Catholic schools. He is a trained economist and social activist. Stédile started his involvement with landless peasants working for the Catholic Church's Commission on Land Reform in the late 1970s.
7. The Vía Campesina is a movement made up of peasant organizations around the world. It advocates family farm–based sustainable agriculture and was the group that first coined the term "food sovereignty."
8. The World Social Forum is an annual meeting that brings together members of the anti-globalization movement. It tends to meet in January when the pro-globalization World Economic Forum is meeting in Davos, Switzerland.
9. At the most basic definition, "new social movements" refers to peace, anti-nuclear, animal rights, civil rights, ecological, urban, Indigenous, women's, religious, and gay/lesbian movements.
10. The CEBs were intrinsically linked to Liberation Theology. The latter was one of the most important theological movements in Latin America during the 1970s and 1980s. Whereas early critiques of development had little resonance outside academia, Liberation Theology had a far-reaching impact. For Gutiérrez (2010, what the poor needed was not *development* but *liberation*, which involved more than mere economic change.
11. Indigenous, peasant, student, and worker movements have been decisive agents of historical transformation, as transpired in the Haitian (1804), Mexican (1910), Bolivian (1952), Cuban (1959), and Nicaraguan (1979) revolutions.
12. Some of these movements included Zapatismo, Vargismo, Peronismo, and Castrismo.
13. These movements were also linked, in one form or another, to organized revolutionary, or reformist political parties with universalistic ideologies such as anarchism, socialism, communism, and nationalism.
14. In the 1960s the civil rights, peace, anti-war, and feminist movements reflected well these dysfunctions in American society. These struggles puzzled Parsonian sociologists, used to seeing American society as "stable" and "orderly," structured differently from those "unstable" and "disorderly" societies, such as those in Latin America.
15. This is a classic study that stressed the politics of identity and culture.
16. For Stédile (2002), the Gandhian approach is the best strategy in the present Brazilian political conjuncture. The disastrous experience of the Ligas Camponesas (Peasant Leagues), during the 1950s, has also cautioned Stédile not to resort to armed insurrection as an effective strategy.
17. In my view, political parties are not conducive to broad societal change because they do not provide effective avenues to express social discontent within the status quo.

Political parties are bound to vertical forms of power relationships. These inhibit the promotion of an inclusive democratic culture, which is fundamental for promoting democratic transformation.

18 Martins and Navarro are former advisers to the Brazilian Comissão Pastoral da Terra, or Church Commission on Land Reform (CPT) and MST. They left these movements due to ideological disagreements.
19 The concept of "community" is troublesome in the social sciences. In my view, communities constitute dynamic local spaces with complex forms of social control. They are also contested social spaces resisting or promoting change.
20 The MST was aware that in many Latin American countries land reform had failed to change the socio-economic conditions of the peasants, because they had little access to financial credit, agricultural technology, and markets. Furthermore, these peasants had not broken entirely with clientelistic and paternalistic forms of political control.
21 Dom José has eight children and 11 grandchildren. A very resourceful and hardworking small-scale farmer, he has been able to earn the equivalent of 3.5 times the minimum monthly wage by planting and selling food staples to the local markets.
22 Spavorek's research team interviewed 14,414 peasants on 4,430 settlements created between 1985 and 2001. Nearly every settled peasant family stated that their life was much better than it was before. However, the study recognized that land reform did not substantially increase the income of the settled peasants.
23 The average age of a land reform beneficiary is 39 years old. The average illiteracy rate is 30%, and in some regions, such as the north and northeast, it is 60% (Robles, 2007).

References

Alvarez, S., Dagnino, E., & Escobar, A. (Eds.). (1998). *Cultures of politics and politics of cultures: Re-visioning Latin American social movements*. Boulder, CO: Westview.
Benford, R., & Snow, D. (2000). Framing processes and social movements: An overview and assessment. *Annual Review of Sociology, 26*, 611–639.
Carter, M. (2013). *Challenging social inequality: The landless rural workers movement and agrarian reform in Brazil*. Durham, NC: Duke University Press.
Della Porta, D., & Diani, M. (1999). *Social movements: An introduction*. Oxford, UK: Blackwell.
Eckstein, S. (Ed.). (2001). *Power and popular protest: Latin American social movements*. Berkeley, CA: University of California Press.
Gutierrez, Gustavo (2010). *A theology of liberation*. Norwich, UK: SCM Press.
Harvey, D. (2001). *Spaces of capital: Towards a critical geography*. London: Routledge.
Holmes, R. (2004). *The Ethics of non-violence: Essays by Robert L. Holmes*. London: Continuum.
Leite, S., et al. (2004). *Impactos dos assentamentos: Um estudo sobre o meio rural Brasileiro*. São Paulo: Editora Unesp.
Mançano, B. (2000). *A formação do MST no Brasil*. Rio de Janeiro: Petrópolis, Editora Vozes.
Martins, J.D.S. (2000). *Reforma Agrária: O Impossível Diálogo*. São Paulo: Editora USP.

McManus, P. (2004). *Relentless persistence: Action in Latin America*. Eugene, OR: Wipf and Stock.

Ministério do Desenvolvimento Social (MDS). (2015). Prestação de contas ordinárias anual relatório de gestão – 2014, April.

Navarro, Z. (2002). O MST e a Canonização da Ação Coletiva: Reposta a Horacio Martins Carvalho. In B.D.S. Santos (Ed.), *Produzir para viver: os caminhos da produção não capitalista* (pp. 263–281). São Paulo: Civilização Brasileira.

Omvedt, G. (1992). *Reinventing revolution: New social movements and the socialist tradition in India*. New York: M.E. Sharpe.

Ondetti, G. (2008). *Land, protest, and politics: The landless movement and the sruggle for agrarian reform in Brazil*. University Park, PA: Penn State University Press.

Petras, J., & Veltmeyer, H. (2005). *Social movements and state power: Argentina, Brazil, Bolivia, Ecuador*. Ann Arbor, MI: Pluto.

Robles, W. (2001). The landless rural workers movement in Brazil. *Journal of Peasant Studies, 28*(2), 146–161.

Robles, W. (2007). *Peasant mobilization, land reform and agricultural co-operativism in Brazil: The Case of the Landless Rural Workers Movement, 1985–2004*. Doctoral dissertation, University of Guelph.

Robles, W. (2008). Liberation theology, Christian base communities, and solidarity movements: A historical reflection. In R. Harris and J. Nef (Ed.), *Capital, power and inequality in Latin America*, pp. 225–250. New York: Rowman and Littlefield.

Sparovek, G. *A qualidade dos assentamentos da Reforma Agrária brasileira*. São Paulo: Paginas e Letras, 2003.

Stédile, J.P. (2002). Landless batallions: The Sem Terra Movement of Brazil. *New Left Review*, 77, 77–104.

Veja. (1997). "O radical da tradição," 16 Apr., 20–24.

Veltmeyer, H., & Petras, J. (2002). The social dynamics of Brazil's Rural Landless Workers' Movement: Ten hypotheses on successful leadership. *Canadian Review of Sociology/Revue canadienne de sociologie, 39*(1), 79–96.

World Bank. (2015). *World Development Indicators*. Washington, DC: World Bank.

CHAPTER 8

Subversive Education in Ethiopia and Canada

Turning Coercive Encounters into Transformative Possibilities

Martha Kuwee Kumsa

In this chapter I position myself as a subversive social work educator and reflect on creative social actions that seek to turn coercive encounters into possibilities of personal and social transformation. Organizing the chapter into three parts, first I reflect on subversive education in an Ethiopian prison. Second, I reflect on my practices of subversive education in Canadian social work. I offer illustrative examples to instantiate my arguments in both contexts. I conclude the chapter by opening it up to further musings and questions to ponder. As the main thrust of my arguments, I contend that although the repressive totalitarianism in Ethiopia and the liberal democracy in Canada appear to be stark contrasts, the coercive encounters entrenched in both contexts reveal a "false" binary when it comes to subversive education and the pursuit of human rights and social justice. I frame subversive education as a creative social action that blurs the multiple false binaries between the West and the Rest, local and global, national and transnational, legal and illegal/paralegal, freedom and bondage, etc.

Three key concepts interweave in my analysis: the notion of encounters, the metaphor of pointing fingers, and the meaning of subversive education. I discuss these sequentially in describing my process. First, encounters offer me sites of meeting with others; then the shameful discovery of my pointing index finger happens along with the ensuing reflexive examination of my three fingers curling back and pointing back at me; and finally, I come to the process of reflexive sense-making and embracing the evanescent meanings of subversive education emerging from the specific context of my encounters.

Ahmed (2000) theorizes encounters as relational processes and necessary conditions for the emergence of bodies, identities, and subjectivities. As she argues, "the priority of encounters over identity suggests that it is only through meeting with an-other that the identity of a given person *comes to be inhabited as living*" (p. 8; original emphasis). She posits encounters as specific meetings of individuals that surprise by necessarily opening up the general and the collective. Elsewhere, Ahmed (2004) argues that individuals and collectives are inseparably intertwined and that emotions play a crucial role in the emergence of individual and collective bodies. She views emotions as relational processes located not in individual bodies but within relationships. Subjects, bodies, identities, and subjectivities do not exist prior to encounters. They are formed and transformed through the relational processes of encounters immersed in webs of inequitable power relations. Encounters are sites where boundaries blur between subjects and others, here and there, past and future, individuals and collectives, freedom/imprisonment and bondage, legal and illegal/paralegal. Encounters offer spaces of transgressive temporal and spatial practices through which these binaries are formed and transformed.

The metaphor of pointing fingers is the reflexive strategy I use to make visible my hidden embodied discourses. I often catch myself pointing my oppressive practices to others, only to find myself utterly surprised by the three fingers pointing them right back to me. Often these surprises are shameful and excruciatingly painful, but the pointing fingers make them bearable, indeed transformative, as they help me see shame not as something fixed in my body but as a malleable relational process between myself and others (Ahmed, 2000, 2004). If encounters are full of painful surprises, they are also full of creative possibilities. Those espousing anti-oppressive practice often know that the opacity of our embodied self (Butler, 2005) necessitates reflexive strategies. However, we find it easier to point outwards rather than point inwards and engage the murky waters of critical self-reflection. As social workers mediating between the state and vulnerable groups, we often point our oppressive practices of injustice toward the state and miss out on the priceless experiences of transformative disruptions and liberatory learning. We often think of subversion as subversion of states and not of our own practices. We, often conveniently, forget that we embody the policies of states, that we are the institutional arms of states both as individuals and as a social work collective.

When I say subversive education, I mean transgressive education. But who determines what is subversive and what is legitimate? I trace contemporary notions of legal and illegal to their roots in the laws of specific modern nation-states established through violent conquest and colonial aggression and legitimized by a global family of nations (Fanon, 1963; Taussig, 1987; Young, 1990). Their heterogeneity notwithstanding, these interwoven local and global systems of nations are all created and maintained through structural and cultural violence (Galtung, 1969, 1990). They exercise the power to determine who is a nation(al) and who is not, who is entitled to self-determination and who is not. They create boundaries of Self and Others and establish nested hierarchies of dominance and subordination globally and locally. These mystified and normalized boundaries are produced and reproduced in everyday encounters in international, intergroup, and interpersonal webs of power relations.

To me, subversive education is education that transgresses these legitimized, normalized, and invisiblized boundaries of Self and Other. It is education as the practice of freedom; it seeks not only to make visible these boundaries but also to transform them (Freire, 1970; hooks, 1994). It opens up space where boundaries blur between the legitimate and the subversive, the individual and the collective. In this chapter I place particular emphasis on interpersonal encounters because these are the sites where state policies are enacted and because they are the most hidden sites in critical social work. We often espouse the notion of education as a practice of freedom, but we rarely practise what we profess. Rather than transgress, we often embrace and defend the boundaries of Self and Other(s) with high emotionality (Ahmed, 2004). I seek to tease out the transgressive spirit of subversive education that engages these boundaries and opens up creative possibilities for change and transformation. For this, I use my personal experiences because they are the safest sites for me to explore these tensions.

▶ THE ETHIOPIAN CONTEXT

Imagine the 1980s Ethiopia, the decade I was in its dungeons. A military junta had consolidated itself on the ruins of the popular revolution that rocked Ethiopia from corner to corner and toppled Emperor Haile Selassie's monarchy in 1974. Globally, the Cold War with its East–West binary was in its last decade. Locally, the Cold War proxy of the Ethio–Somali war (1977–78) had just ended with the victory going to Revolutionary Ethiopia. From the perspectives of Oromo liberation, both Greater Somalia and Greater Ethiopia were fighting over their imperial ambitions to control Oromo land. Nonetheless, through this proxy war, Somalia and Ethiopia crossed the Cold War divide in opposite directions, one going from East to West and the other from West to East. The 1980s saw Ethiopia comfortably ensconced in the Eastern camp. The formation of the Workers Party of Ethiopia (WPE) was declared in 1984 on the tenth anniversary of the revolution and after years of tortuous groundwork through the ugliest bloodbath of Red Terror and White Terror. This national vanguard party was supposed to be civilian, but the military had simply dumped its uniforms and slipped into civilian clothes to stay in control.

The junta presented itself as *the* only authentic revolutionary vanguard and marked out other revolutionaries as counterrevolutionary, massacring tens of thousands and imprisoning the rest. The revolutionaries blanketed as counterrevolutionary were Marxists, Leninists, Maoists, communists, socialists, anarchists, anti-colonial liberationists, and various combinations of these, but each group saw itself as *the* only authentic revolutionary. There was an incredible diversity of profound ideological differences among them. For example, the goal of most communists and socialists was to modernize Ethiopia, while the goal of most anti-colonial national liberationists was to dismantle Ethiopia because they saw it as an empire, the prison house of nations.

When the Soviet Union and other sister socialist countries rallied behind the junta even as it was crushing popular revolution, those who saw themselves as genuine revolutionaries felt betrayed. Let down by the very forces they trusted, they doubted the authenticity of the vanguards of global revolution. "Revolution eats its own children" as the saying of the time warned. And disillusioned revolutionaries watched in utter disbelief as revolution literally ate up its own children. Corpses littered the streets of the cities and the fields of the country. When prisons were overcrowded with revolutionaries, confiscated private houses and basements of large government buildings were turned into makeshift prisons. The Addis Ababa Central Prison, Karchelle, was the largest storage house of revolutionaries. It was also home to a large number of the junta's puppets – either fallen from grace or disguised as inmates to inform on political prisoners.

The Prison School

As the largest prison in Ethiopia, Karchelle housed around 10,000 inmates, including revolutionaries of all political persuasions. Regardless of their deep ideological rifts, however, most revolutionaries in all political groups shared the burning passion of educating "the masses." And "the masses" were right there with them as Karchelle was full of unjustly convicted and unjustifiably held uneducated or inadequately educated inmates. Some did not even have literacy; others had some primary or high school but had not completed either. The inmates congealed into two radically different bodies lying side by side: on the one side was a body of mostly educated revolutionaries thrown in to rot there and perish; on the other was that of "the masses," hungry and thirsty for education and liberation. The condition was fully ripe for subversive education.

The passionate self-sacrificing force that stirred up the entire country and drowned it in a sea of revolution was now stirring up the prison. Political inmates were not allowed to talk or communicate with each other, let alone consult and work toward a common goal. The revolutionaries dared to do so anyway, at the risk of their lives. They were using every crack in the multiple facets of the heterogeneous junta. Comrades were being dragged out and summarily executed for no reason at all, but the remaining revolutionaries picked up the baton in defiance and continued their subversive actions anyway, until execution came for them, too. The harsher the regime struck, the brighter the revolutionary energy it ignited. This was the spirit in which the prison school was started. The masses must be educated and the regime could not stop the fiery spirit.

Schools started and flourished as opportunities opened up and even as summary executions continued. Eventually, three streams were firmly established – literacy, vocational, and academic – and it became a co-education school, allowing for men and women to learn together. The boundary separating political prisoners from those held or convicted as thieves, frauds, murderers, and criminals was also blurred. The prison buzzed with busy students and teachers who stood apart only in the classrooms but lay side by side on the floors of their cells. Then there were children growing up in prison. Some were born in bondage to mothers who conceived them in freedom; some were conceived through rape torture; others were thrown in with their mothers as they suckled at their mothers' breasts. These children needed kindergarten and the revolutionaries created a kindergarten for them. Finally, the revolutionaries also created a small space for those craving deeper philosophical explorations.

Revolutionaries refused to sit idle and rot; uneducated inmates refused to be left in the margins. The school was a salvation for both, and they worked against all odds to nurture it. Indeed, the prison school was ranked top in the entire country for many years in a row. Lo and behold the irony, though! High-ranking members of the junta as well as prison wardens and guards sought to send their children to prison in search of the best education! Evening classes were started for this new group of outsiders. The prison became school and the inmates turned the coercive encounters of prison into creative spaces of subversive education fostering change and transformation.

It is important to note, however, that this creative space of encounters is much more complex than what this unified face of revolutionaries depicts. There were encounters within encounters of subjects and subjectivities and subversive actions within subversive actions. The academic, vocational, and literacy streams of the unified school were also spaces differentiated mainly along the contours of political affiliation but also along social class, ethnicity/nationality, and level of education. Also, although the revolutionaries aiming to modernize Ethiopia dominated all three streams, those heading the academic stream did not mix well with those heading the vocational or literacy streams. And, although anti-colonial liberationists circulated well in all three streams, their subversive action was also focused on dismantling and transforming the very form and content of the colonial education that was taking root in all three streams. As a result, local skirmishes were everyday realities in the prison school.

Revolutionary Cheating

To illustrate an aspect of the complexity, I will reflect on my experience of a particular coercive encounter that opened up transformative possibilities. I participated actively in all three streams of the prison school and in the specialized space of philosophical explorations. As a good revolutionary with that peculiar self-sacrificing fiery spirit, I threw my whole being into the collective subversive actions with other revolutionaries on matters of educating "the masses." As an Oromo anti-colonial liberationist and a feminist, I also had equally self-sacrificing particular commitments within the general.

In one of the classes I taught in the academic stream, there was a student I name here as Abyot. It was rumored that Abyot was one of the regime's cadres, meaning that he was a specially indoctrinated and devoted member of the regime's Workers Party of Ethiopia. Everyone knew that Abyot was sent in to inform on political prisoners, but somehow the grapevines had missed me and I did not know. So I was the only fool messing with Abyot. This man challenged me on everything I stood for. Perhaps it was his way of making his *state-ly* presence felt. He was disruptive and disrespectful, and I did not know how to deal with him. One day I caught him cheating when he submitted another student's work as his own assignment. I took both students aside and gave them an earful. "No one pays me for teaching all these years," I said. "You know, my only reward is your success and I want you to succeed, for your sake and for mine." I told them the story of a thief and his mother:

When he was a child, this thief stole an egg and brought it to his mother and they ate it together. Then he stole a hen and the same thing happened. When he was a little older he stole a lamb; the same thing. As a grown man, he stole a bull, but this time he was caught. The police beat him as they dragged him through the marketplace for everyone to shame him. His mother was in the market and she screamed when she saw him. "Oh my son, my only son!" she cried. The son looked at her and said between groans, "Don't cry, Mother! If you had hit my hand gently when I stole that egg, the police would not be beating me so hard now."

As both students listened intently, I said, "I do not want to collude with you now and cry for you later. I do not know if I will get dragged out and killed tonight or if I will live to grow older. But my deepest desire is to pick up a newspaper and read about you, my students – not being shamed for stealing but being honoured for inventing something brilliant and doing something great." I shared this scenario with other teachers, and they told me to be very careful with Abyot. Apparently people were afraid of him because they believed he had such a twisted sense of power that he would have them tortured or executed for petty personal reasons. Those concerned about me advised me to just pass him and keep quiet. "No way," I said, "upon my dead body!" Now it became a question of my own integrity. Knowing that he was the regime's cadre made me even more furious. The regime cheated us out of our revolution, and now it tries to cheat us out of our own souls! I felt the coercive arms of the state all over my being. Abyot's counterrevolutionary *state-ly* hands were on my throat to snuff out my revolutionary spirit. I was more determined than ever to fight it.

As I became more vigilant, Abyot became even more disruptive in the class. His grades went tumbling down as he could no more cheat under my watchful eyes. One day he confronted me and demanded that I give him the same mark as other students. I told him to put in the same quality of work as them and he retorted, "It is socialism! We should all get the same mark!" I could not believe my ears. I looked at him open-mouthed with surprise, quietly begging him to tell me he was joking. But he really meant it! I thought I was struck by lightning. I felt his stabbing knife go right through my heart. It struck at the core of my values and I said, "It is the likes of you who make socialism stink!" I was referring to the Ethiopian state, the junta, and all sister socialist countries that were courting it. For me, deceiving people, living off someone else's work, and stealing someone else's labour signify the tenets of capitalism, not socialism. In socialism, everyone's work is valued equally – but everyone must work in the first place. Indeed, work is revered with a spiritual touch in socialism because it is work that makes us human. Socialism is for equity and justice in *working* relationships. I looked Abyot in the eye and roared, "What do *you* know about socialism? Get out of my class now! And never come back!"

After I threw him out of my class, Abyot still made sure that I saw the fiery anger in his eyes. When it was time for my class to start, he would linger about until I came into the door and made sure that he gave me a shove as he left and I entered. This continued for a few classes before it stopped. My comrades were very scared for me. They expected Abyot to do something sinister and tensely waited for when I would be called in the middle of the night for the ultimate. I was very scared, too, but I would rather die and sacrifice my life than sacrifice my integrity – the motto of true revolutionaries at the time. This philosophy, this readiness to take a life-and-death risk to achieve one's integrity and humanity goes back through Marxist dialectics (Afanasyev, 1980) all the way to the Hegelian dialectics of Self and Other (Hegel, 1967). Deeply immersed in that philosophy, I was ready to take on Abyot if and when he wreaked havoc.

On the last day of class, we organized our end-of-year party, and guess who showed up? Abyot! Everyone was taken aback, expecting a major disruption. But this was a completely transformed, softened, and humbled Abyot. He acknowledged that he was not supposed to be there and asked for my permission to tell a story. I surprised myself when I heard my own voice saying, "Welcome, Abyot! Please take a seat." Abyot told the class the most beautiful story of his revolutionary cheating, the lessons he learned from it, and why he would start classes all over again with a new spirit. He told the story of the thief and his mother. He had made it his own story in such a beautifully transformative way. The whole experience was profoundly moving for me, and I cried. I felt a deep sense of validation and triumph over some counterrevolution treading in the guise of revolution.

I celebrated my triumph over Abyot then but Abyot's triumph over me is only now revealing itself as I am processing it after almost three decades. As Ahmed (2000) would argue, that seemingly simple interpersonal encounter is never an encounter between just two individuals but one between two subjects embodying two radically different discourses of revolution. It is never an encounter simply in the here and now either but one that necessarily reopens other encounters from other times and other places. Nor is it simply a specific encounter but an encounter that, by its very specificity, necessarily opens up into the general, into broader societal relations and weaves in multiple other Others of multiple collectives. That simple encounter is a particular relational site of encounters between differing ideologies/discourses, nationalisms, genders, educational levels, and social classes to name but a few. It is an encounter between my illegal Oromo nationalism and Abyot's Ethiopian nationalism sanctioned by the global family of nations, my embodied anti-colonial discourse and his embodied colonial desire. Interpersonal encounter is a dynamic relational site where broader Subjects and Others engage in forming and transforming each Other.

This simple interpersonal encounter is also a highly emotionally charged constitutive site of Self and Other, as Ahmed (2004) would argue. It is a site that makes visible our deeply hidden embodied structures/discourses; so encounters are also full of surprises. Both Abyot and I were surprised, and we defended the integrity of our respective Selves and subject positions with high emotionality. We were angrily pointing to each Other's wrongdoing from our individual places of righteousness. This realization immerses me in the emotion of shame even now. The encounter is definitely a playground where the differences and boundaries of Self and Other come into play and open up into broader webs of power and inequitable relations that shape our likes and dislikes, happiness and sorrow, shame and pride. However, as long as I dig in my heels in my righteous indignation and point my index finger at Abyot and celebrate how *I* transformed *him*, I will not be able to examine my three fingers pointing back at me and realize how Abyot transformed me. As Palmer (1997) argues, a good teacher teaches with the whole undivided integral self. And I believe I am a good teacher with solid integrity. Digging in my heels, however, I will not be able to see that my integrity, the integral boundaries of this uncompromising Self and Subject position that I defended with such highly charged emotions, is not a given essence but a malleable and transformable relational process.

A reflexive examination of these emotions reveals the key role that a liberating subversive education plays in such mutually transformative processes, as it offers a site where state policies are engaged and transformed. As Shor and Freire (1987) argue, subversive education is not only a liberating political process, but also a creative process that calls reality into life where the "unveiling gives the object 'life,' calls it into 'life,' even gives it a new 'life'" (p. 118). I take this "unveiling" to be a simultaneous struggle that we wage against outside structures/discourses and our internalized versions of them. Subversive education does not just point toward *them* (Abyot, the state, the junta, the oppressor); it also points toward *us*. If normalizing education seeks to embody and invisiblize oppressive structures/

discourses, subversive education seeks to make them visible and transform their relations of domination.

Indeed, subversive education is a practice of liberation and creativity engaging boundaries of Self and Other. Now I can see the fragility of the oppressed–oppressor, revolution–counterrevolution, colonial–anti-colonial dualisms that mark our boundaries. Now I can see the surge of power that enabled me to yell at Abyot and throw him out of what I considered *my* class, doing back to *them* (Abyot and his state) what *they* did to me and, in the process, becoming the very thing I despised. Now I can see Abyot's fragility even with his male prowess. I can see his vulnerability even with the solid backing of the totalitarian state and its absolute power over my life and death.

▶ The Canadian Context

I fled the land of my people and came to Canada in 1991. Globally, the world was a radically different place from what I had known. The Cold War had just ended with the fall of the Berlin Wall, heralding not only the dissolution of the global East–West dualism but also the "failure" of socialism. Although this did not imply that capitalism was better for humanity, it did mean that unfettered capitalism was now unleashed in the entire world. There seemed to be no place for revolutionaries. I found myself in the belly of the beast, engulfed by all its digestive juices. Locally, Canada was in the aftermath of the Oka Crisis, where Indigenous Mohawks rose up to protect the land of their ancestors and the government used its military to quash them. I encountered a different face of colonialism yet intimately entwined with the type that forced me out of the land of my own ancestors. Two decades later, I witnessed government forces quashing the G20 protests. It's a different face of repression but, again, inseparably entwined with the totalitarian force that quashed revolutionaries in the land of my people. What?! The peacemaker abroad is making wars at home? O Canada!

I did come with bags full of dreams. After all, the West is the land of liberal democracy and human rights! After all, my human rights were violated in the socialist East, and it was the West that "rescued" me from the "communist" junta. Indeed, it was the promise of human rights that lured me to Canada. But the honeymoon did not last more than a few years. After that, even the most radical of progressives who saw themselves as open to critical dialogue seemed to tell me, "Turn a blind eye on injustice and fit in or critique it and marginalize yourself. There is no bipolar world anymore. Reconcile yourself with the reality of a capitalist world. There may be some good in it after all." As my hope for critical dialogue and better global vision was dashed and a harsh reality started to grind, a sense of disillusionment set in slowly — ever so slowly, so that even after 20 years it still seeps deep down into my bone marrow drop by drop and into the tiniest pores of my soul.

The state is democratically undemocratic here and it is exceptionally deceptive. Of course I knew that all relations of domination, conquest, and colonization require disorienting myths and deceptions (Fanon, 1963; Freire, 1970; Gramsci, 1971; Young, 1990, 2001), but this is the most sophisticated deceit I have ever seen. Professing one thing and doing the exact opposite! Worse still, this deception bleeds into the broader culture as its structural violence turns into cultural violence and trickles down into the everydayness of life (Galtung, 1990; Gramsci, 1971). It is so hegemonic that people are wilfully and consensually deceived. I am told that, here, people do not mean what they say and do not say what they mean. Alas! I am left alone in a strange land to deal with the meaning of my displacement and the displacement of my meaning simultaneously. Looking for a place of solace, I identify social work as a space of healing, personal liberation, and social transformation. I seek to make it a home for my burning passion of subversive social action.

Subversive Social Work

Lo and behold! The incredible deception of the broader culture permeates all facets of everyday social work relations, including administration, research, direct practice, and classrooms. Here progressives signal left and turn right – to my utter chagrin. Unwritten codes of ethics tell me to commit to non-judgmental ethics but be judgmental anyway; commit to gender-blind and colour-blind ethics but do gender and colour anyway; commit to non-violence and non-oppression but do violence and oppression anyway. One minute I am free to speak my mind; the next minute I am brutally muzzled. One minute we're all relational and we're all implicated in each other's well-being; the next minute it is all in my head, and I am solely responsible for my silences and utterances. One minute I have theoretical sophistication; the next minute I am only intuitive, Africans cannot theorize. In a reflexive moment, I am told not to leave myself out of the equation; the next moment it is not about me. In one poignant emancipatory minute I am told to blur the teacher-student binary; the next minute I am told I have boundary issues. One minute I am praised for transgressing oppressive binaries; the next minute I am scolded for being unprofessional. Social work drowns me in an incredible sea of mixed messages, and sets my head spinning with confusion. I seek clarity in subversive education. I engage in deceiving and subverting the world that deceives and subverts me.

I remember my very first course in social work teaching. It was a graduate course, and I was determined to transform the coercive disciplined space (Foucault, 1977) into a liberated space where the student–teacher binary was blurred and we learned from each other in the spirit of collegiality. I was confident that I would create the kind of liberated space I had always desired in a graduate school but seldom experienced as a student. In the very first class, I sat among students and waited. When it was almost time for class to start, I heard some students ask, "Where is the instructor; it's almost time." I raised my hand and said, "Here I am! I am the facilitator!" I heard some "Ohs" and "Ahs" before I greeted everyone and introduced my philosophy of liberatory education (Freire, 1970; Gramsci, 1971; hooks, 1994; Shor & Freire, 1987). I said that students were not going to "click click" and download their money's worth of education from the teacher; they were going to produce knowledge through dialogue with the teacher in an egalitarian collegial relationship. Sitting among students was my way of demonstrating my commitment to such egalitarian collegiality from Day One.

Far beyond removing hierarchical structures from the physical classroom, I also created space for student–teacher closeness in the content and process of learning. While most students loved the philosophy of what I preached as liberatory education, in practice, they resisted it with all the power they could exert. It is hard for me to believe. Who does not want liberation? Who does not want egalitarian relationship? To my chagrin, it was the students espousing critical approaches that resisted and subverted it with incredible emotional intensity. Yet they had no awareness of their resistance or subversion. In their minds, they embraced these values wholeheartedly. What is it that makes people believe one thing and practice the exact opposite? Is it simply the broader culture or is something else at play here? By the end of that course, I was thoroughly confused and dismayed.

It took me years to regain my confidence, but I continued to subvert normalized student–teacher binaries in every possible way that I could. I continued to believe, even more strongly, that education is an ideological apparatus of the state (Gramsci, 1971; Freire, 1970), a coercive institutional arm of the state and a technology of normalization and regulation (Foucault, 1977). I used every opportunity to name and make visible this hidden aspect of education. Whenever possible within institutional constraints, students transformed the emotional and spatial spirit of the classroom. They participated in weaving together their learning objectives and the course objectives in ways that were meaningful for them. They participated in selecting course materials that were meaningful for their objectives and learning styles. They set the marks they wished to achieve and worked toward their goals. They participated in evaluating their work and determining their marks. I believe that my subversive education has radical potential in both its political and creative processes. Although not many students appreciated my efforts, it took incredible reflexive energy from me to play with the vulnerabilities of relinquishing power.

Prison Education

Recently, I had the opportunity to take a social work course that I called "Human Rights in a Glocalizing World" into a Canadian prison through the Inside-Out prison exchange program. Inside-Out is a transformative educational program where students from regular colleges or universities and from prisons learn together as peers. The program has a strong standing in the United States, but recently opened its doors for the first time in Canada, where it has become the Walls to Bridges program. A colleague who is one of the pioneers invited me to teach a course and I grabbed the opportunity. I was allured by the program's educational philosophy crystallized in the motto of the American Inside-Out Center: "moving beyond the walls that separate us – social change through transformative education." It resonated very well with my personal motto of engaging the multiple boundaries constructed between Self and Other. I was particularly fascinated by a poignant quote from a core member of the Center, Tyrone Werts, who said, "That wall isn't there just to keep me in, but to keep you out." He inspires me to think of Self and Other as inseparable relational processes produced and reproduced by the same historical, socio-economic, and political processes.

"Getting beyond the walls that separate us" and walking through the inside spaces of the local Canadian prison for the first time, I was impressed by the setting. It was radically different from the prisons I had known. I could not help but exclaim, "Wow! This looks like a neighbourhood in the outside community!" I heard a voice around me say, "Not terribly bad, eh?" Another one warned, "Don't be deceived by the appearance." *Aha!* The ubiquitous deception! How could I have forgotten that? In fact, I was aware of how this prison reform came about as a result of anti-prison grassroots activism and how the retributive ideology of the state was firmly re-entrenched in the name of reform (Faith, 2000). I wondered what it was like for the inmates within those walls. I was also aware of the dangers of how the "schools not jails" movement grew in the United States and how it lost its radical roots when it was co-opted by the state (Acey, 2000). What I saw in Inside-Out/Walls to Bridges is an opportunity for transforming prisons into schools. Indeed, the "schools not jails" movement rekindled the spirit of my revolutionary prison school.

The Inside-Out syllabus was quite structured, but it also allowed for creative ways of engaging both the content and processes of learning. We sat in circles with Inside and Outside students interlacing to remove the walls that separate us and create an egalitarian classroom. To remove the invisible walls, we made them visible by talking about transforming the disciplined spaces of the prison (Foucault, 1977) and how to turn this classroom into a dynamic space of encounters (Ahmed, 2000) where our settled beliefs and subjectivities were unsettled. We explored how such transformative disruptions may be painful but necessary for liberating education. Despite all the talks, however, the class was not going as well as we expected. I watched as the initial overwhelming enthusiasm died. Although we revisited the content and process, this did not rekindle the initial fiery energy. The course was not meaningful to students. Simple! I did not realize this until a student confronted me, ever so gently, and said, "This is the only course where I feel forced to hold back ... where I cannot speak about the violations of my human rights." And this is a human rights course! I wanted to scream. What a shame! I thought I was facilitating the most subversive learning.

The student was right. We talked about all kinds of human rights violations in the entire world. We even discussed the Prison–Industrial Complex and how it fits into this glocalizing world, but we completely avoided the huge elephant in the room. We successfully failed to name and make it visible, call it to life. The political process may be in place, but the creative process was severely compromised (Shor & Freire, 1987). It was not making sense to students, especially after we agreed to move beyond the walls that separated us and unsettle our settled beliefs about Self and Other. By invisiblizing the elephant in the room, we reinforced the very boundary of Self and Other and put the Other back in its place. My immediate defences were that we could not rock the boat. We could not jeopardize the program. Many good people in the Inside-Out program, in the universities, and in the prisons, have worked hard on just getting these doors open. How can I discount their efforts? What about the personal agencies of Inside students who desire to move beyond the objectifying prison programming and take some university courses? The subversiveness of the learning was limited to the fact that a human rights course could come into the prison, that Outside students could cross the walls and get into the prison and learn with their Inside peers. But learn what?

Now I realize that I lined up all these defences so as not to hold myself accountable to the students, not to take responsibility for my practice of exclusion and Othering. Indeed, social work voices tell me, "It is not about you; don't make it about yourself; don't take it personally." But it *is* every bit about me as it is about students. Taking my Self out of the encounters is an unethical abdication of responsibility, a denial of the inseparable relationality of Subjects and Others (Ahmed, 2000). Taking it personally, I can see my Self in the mirror this student held up for me. I am the ugly coercive arm of the state. I *am* the state. And the three fingers pointing back show me that the shameful deception I pointed away from my Self to Others is now mine many times more. It is woven into the deepest fabric of my being. It is not an outside entity but an external coming from the depth of my own soul. All my robust self-righteous defences notwithstanding, I *am* deceptive! For sure the defences show that I did the right thing, that I was being pragmatic and realistic. But that is precisely how hegemony works (Gramsci, 1971)! Now that I intimately know how I deceive, I can be generous enough to understand all those I despised as deceptive. That is how the state works – through self-righteous individuals like me, individuals with solid integrity!

Now I can see how I was deceiving myself and the students in my regular social work classes, too. I promise egalitarian and collegial relationships in the same breath as I tell students they are not going to "click click" and download knowledge from the teacher. I, the Subject, tell the Other objects, what we do and what we do not do instead of arriving at it through dialogue/multilogue. I seek to blur the student–teacher binary and remove the distance between us, but I reinforce that very distance and reinscribe that very binary by putting students right back in their places of Otherness. What is the use of sitting among students if I still wield such coercive power over what should and should not happen in the classroom? In my self-righteous integrity, however, I had no room to doubt that mine was a liberating approach to learning, and I had no room to allow student dissent. What is the use of allowing students to define their mark and helping them to work toward achieving it if in the end I judge them by my version of the truth? Shor and Freire (1987) argue: "Many in a left position are convinced *religiously* that they received a mandate from God, in spite of not believing in God! To *save* the students, to *save* the people. They think they have *the truth* in their hands" (p. 81, original emphasis).

Shamefully, this is the practice I discover when I examine the three fingers pointing back to me. Right now "liberation" and "help" have become stale and dirty words in my mouth but, to be honest, I do not have better visions to replace them.

This leaves the meaning of subversive education, indeed the very notion of subversion, in a precarious position. We cannot exercise coercive power to discipline spaces in the name of liberating disciplined spaces. Two wrongs cannot make a right. The utopia I imagined in my simplistic desire for social work to be a healing space of unveiling and redressing injustice has waned on me. I realize that social work is co-opted and professionalized by the state (Moffatt, 2001), but it is also a complex space. As de Montigny (1995, p. 225) deciphers, "Safe social work remains inside regulated boundaries of the [professional] code. Liberating social work is dangerous. It takes risks.... Social work must risk taking a stand with the clients.... We need a social work that is subversive. We need to eat away at the inside of the beast. We must distort policies to favour clients."

Such risk taking needs to break out of its nationalist mould and speak to the neo-colonial and imperialistic face of social work that is being unleashed in the world through the globalization of social work (Gray, 2010; Lyons, 2006). In this face, social work hangs on to the skirt of its birth mother, the nation-state, and follows her as she follows market interests and roves throughout the world. It eschews places of inequity, injustice, and vulnerability to the works of charity and handouts and follows the market to establish its professional identity in places of potential economic gains. Social work needs to wean itself from its mother's breasts and chart its own paths within and beyond the nation-state.

The notion of encounters (Ahmed, 2000) brings this right home to social work as it calls on us to engage not only our inseparable relationality with the rest of the world but also the perpetual nature of mutual constitution and mutual transformation. Social work scholars engage such dynamic in-betweenness of social work. They invite us to the notion of unsettled social work (Rossiter, 2011) and rethinking our classroom spaces in terms of process and in-betweenness (Irving & Young, 2004). This kind of subversive social action goes beyond the domains of social work, but the basic question remains: If power is inescapable and if its complexities are so deeply hidden, how subversive can subversive social action be to effect the social change we desire?

▶ Longing Back, Looking Ahead

As a person who lived through two revolutions and got disillusioned by both, and as a person who experienced the reform of liberal democracy and got disillusioned by it, too, I seek an in-between space that engages the complexities of both reform and revolution. This is increasingly hard in a world where capitalism is the only player performing a historical amnesia – completely forgetting how it came to power through bourgeois revolution and marking any kind of revolution as illegitimate. The parallel with how the totalitarian regime in Ethiopia appropriates revolution and bans any other movement as counterrevolution comes into sharp relief. The righteousness in both countries is incredible. They both have the ultimate truth in their hands. The parallel in how we at the micro-(individual) level hang on to our righteousness and point to everyone else as wrong also comes into clear view for me. I believe this is a chronic illness of our time. We may fight against the external structures but we also need to fight against our internalized structures/discourses to create real change in the world.

From what I learned the hard way, oppositional struggles (structure versus agency, oppressed versus oppressor, East versus West, human rights versus social justice) work more to maintain the status quo rather than change/transform it. Socialism is not out to liberate and capitalism is not out to plunder. They both hang on to their own righteousness and they both deceive in their own ways. The challenge for us is to cut through the rhetoric. For me, both the Canadian liberal democracy and the Ethiopian revolutionary totalitarianism kill, albeit very differently. The Ethiopian regime kills swiftly by physically liquidating its Others. The Canadian liberal democracy kills its Others slowly by eroding their confidence, breaking their spirits, maximizing their suffering, and sapping the juices out of their lives – ever so slowly that people choose to take their own lives rather than lose their minds or their sense of who they are and what they stand for. Oppositional struggles do not allow us to explore the complexities of such killing. They only create utopia on their side and dystopia on the side of their Other. We need in-between spaces similar to what Foucault (1986) imagines as heterotopia in order to cut through the rhetoric and imagine subversive transformative social actions.

The era of oppositional collective struggles as I knew it is over. What I see currently, however, is that a dichotomy is setting in between heterotopic poststructural spaces and modernist structural spaces of struggle. It is disheartening to see these flip back into oppositional binary, thus allowing the status quo to continue blissfully. This is what makes me long back as I look ahead. In Canada the message is that we have reached the end of history. Capitalism is the best humanity can become. We need only little reforms here and there. O Canada! What heartache! Back in the then-Ethiopia the revolutionary spirit was the fiery spirit of reaching out for the best, reaching out for the stars. And this was not just desire; people were ready to put their lives on the line to achieve their desire. In Canada people want to eat their cake and have it as well. People are ambivalent and ambivalence preserves the status quo; it does not change it! If we really want to see change, we need to start paying the necessary sacrifices. My heart longs back to the raw passion, brutal honesty, and spirit of self-sacrifice among revolutionaries.

References

Acey, C.E.S.A. (2000). This is an illogical statement: Dangerous trends in anti-prison activism. *Social Justice, 27*(3), 206–211.
Afanasyev, V.G. (1980). *Marxist philosophy.* (4th ed.). Moscow: Progress Publishers.
Ahmed, S. (2000). *Strange encounters.* London: Routledge.
Ahmed, S. (2004). Affective economies. *Social Text, 22*(2), 117–139.
Butler, J. (2005). *Giving an account of oneself.* New York: Fordham University Press.
de Montigny, G.A.J. (1995). *Social working: An ethnography of front-line practice.* Toronto: University of Toronto Press.
Faith, K. (2000). Reflections on inside/out organizing. *Social Justice, 27*(3), 158–167.
Fanon, F. (1963). *The wretched of the earth.* New York: Grove.
Foucault, M. (1977). *Discipline and punish: The birth of the prison.* Translated by Alan Sheridan. New York: Vantage Books.
Foucault, M. (1986). Of other spaces. Translated by Jay Miskowiec. *Diacritics, 16,* 22–27.
Freire, P. (1970). *Pedagogy of the oppressed.* Translated by Myra Bergman Ramos. New York: Continuum.
Galtung, J. (1969). Violence, peace, peace research. *Journal of Peace Research, 6*(3), 167–191.
Galtung, J. (1990). Cultural violence. *Journal of Peace Research, 27*(3), 291–305.
Gramsci, A. (1971). *Prison notebooks.* Edited and translated by Joseph A. Buttigieg. New York: International Publishers.
Gray, M. (2010). Indigenization and knowledge development: Extending the debate. *International Social Work, 53*(5), 613–627.
Hegel, G.W.F. (1967). *The phenomenology of mind.* Translated by J.B. Baillie. New York: Harper & Row.
hooks, bell. (1994). *Teaching to transgress: Education as the practice of freedom.* New York: Routledge.
Irving, A., & Young, T. (2004). "Perpetual liminality": Re-readings of subjectivity and diversity in clinical social work classrooms. *Smith College Studies in Social Work, 74*(2), 213–227.
Moffatt, K. (2001). *A poetics of social work: Personal agency and social transformation in Canada, 1920–1939.* Toronto: University of Toronto Press.

Lyons, K. (2006). Globalization and social work: International and local implications. *British Journal of Social Work, 36*(3), 365–380.

Palmer, P. (1997). The heart of a teacher: Identity and integrity in teaching. *Change,* Nov./Dec., 15–21.

Rossiter, A. (2011). Unsettled social work: The challenge of Levinas's ethics. *British Journal of Social Work, 41,* 980–995.

Shor, I., & Freire, P. (1987). *A Pedagogy for Liberation: Dialogues on Transforming Education.* Westport, CT: Bergin & Garvey.

Taussig, M. (1987). *Shamanism, Colonialism, and the Wild Man: A Study in Terror and Healing.* Chicago: University of Chicago Press.

Young, R. (1990). *White Mythologies: Writing History and the West.* London: Routledge.

Young, R. (2001). *Postcolonialism: An Historical Introduction.* Oxford: Blackwell.

CONCLUSION

Rights, Justice, the Law, and Extralegal Action

Nilan Yu

▶ RIGHTS, JUSTICE, AND THE LAW

Although the words rights, justice, and law are often spoken in the same breath, they do not necessarily go hand in hand. Rights and justice are not inalienable considerations in the formulation of law. At certain points in Western history and in various parts of the world today, laws have been and are made to abrogate the rights of certain populations and institute unjust relationships. In such contexts, to insist on equal rights and the just treatment of people would be to act beyond or even against the law.

On the first of December 1955, a 42-year-old African-American woman named Rosa Parks boarded a bus on her way home after a day's work and changed the course of US history. At that time, municipal bus services were racially segregated, and the law required African Americans to sit at the back of the bus and give up their seats to white passengers as the need arose. When asked to do so on that day, Rosa refused to move even after the bus driver threatened to have her arrested. She was escorted out of the bus by police and jailed. It was a brave act of defiance of the law by a seamstress who knew that being jailed was certain and being beaten while in police custody was a distinct possibly.

By her own account, Rosa did not start the day intending to do what she did. But it would be naive not to see it in the context of her then decade-long involvement with the National Association for the Advancement of Colored People. She refused to give up her seat not because she was physically too tired to stand up as much as she had grown tired of being unfairly treated. Her challenging of the law allowed for the testing of implicit assumptions and assertions embodied in the law. According to Rosa, she asked the policeman who accosted her, "Why do you push us around?" And all he could say was "I don't know. But the law is the law and you are under arrest." The incident sparked the Montgomery bus boycott which lasted 381 days until December 1956 when the US Supreme Court ruled that the segregation law was unconstitutional, and Montgomery bus services were desegregated.

Conceivably, American society would have eventually changed even if Rosa Parks did not hold her ground. But, in all likelihood, the changes would not have come that soon. Could the same changes have been achieved in other ways without Rosa breaking the law? Perhaps. But why must the pursuit of rights and justice be predicated on "lawful" action, especially in the context of a society founded on unjust laws and social relations? And where do we draw the line in insisting on such principle in situations where the meaning of "lawful" action is defined and redefined at will by those in positions of power? In a sense, certain conceptions of rights and justice and of the work that needed to be done in society – social work, in the general sense of the term – necessitated Rosa Parks's challenging of the law.

▶ Surveying the Boundaries of Social Work

Certain conceptions of social work lay a bold claim. The International Federation of Social Workers (IFSW) defines social work as follows: "Social work is a practice-based profession and an academic discipline that promotes social change and development, social cohesion, and the empowerment and liberation of people. Principles of social justice, human rights, collective responsibility and respect for diversities are central to social work" (2014). The key elements also found in other definitions of social work speak of empowerment, the liberation of people, and social change in the pursuit of social justice and human rights.

These elegant words, cloaked in philosophical sophistication, have proven useful in expanding the claims of the discipline. But these words can be ascribed very different meanings and implications in different geographical and historical contexts. In contemporary Western liberal democracies, social change, empowerment, and liberation can be conveniently conceptualized within the realm of interpersonal relationships, institutional practices, and policy concerns in broader societal contexts that are seen as having sufficient democratic space and reasonably equitable distribution of power to allow for the fair negotiation of issues of rights and justice. This allows for the conceptualization of social work as a professional activity that can be undertaken well within the confines of the politico-legal framework.

But such an assumption does not hold true for other contexts exemplified by Rosa Parks's experience in the racially segregated United States and Gandhi's struggle in colonial India. If the profession were to stand by the claims laid with discourses on empowerment, liberation, and social change, then we should be prepared to explore what these claims mean where there is institutionalized exclusion, oppression, and discrimination. It can, in fact, be argued that it is in these contexts, marked by much more limited democratic spaces and inequitable distribution of power, where the true test of such claim lies. It is easy to speak of empowerment, liberation, and social change where relatively smaller power differentials are involved and where the societal order allows for such processes. Where people are systematically disadvantaged or excluded as an essential feature of the economy of the established order, what does it mean to speak of empowerment, liberation, and change?

Most definitions of social work found in social work texts are deceptive in that they speak of social work as if it were a single entity, perhaps composed of various parts but still making up one integral unit. What such definitions fail to portray are the varied and sometimes competing traditions and perspectives that inform and make up what we call social work. Such definitions hide from view the ideological differences that have hounded social work throughout its history (see, e.g., Haynes, 1998; Specht & Courtney, 1994; Margolin, 1997; and Mullaly, 2007). The term "social work" is used to name a range of practices that in very important ways profoundly differ from each other.

The forms of social work that we find today trace their roots to many and varied traditions. Western social work's history is generally traced to two grand traditions: case work and "friendly visiting," identified with the Charity Organization Society and Mary Richmond, and the settlement house movement, identified with Jane Addams (Hare, 2004). These traditions differ significantly, with the former focused on individual-oriented interventions and the latter on social reform (Margolin, 1997; Mullaly, 2007). While many definitions of social work espouse social reform and social justice as integral concerns of the profession, there are those who argue that social work does not live up to this selectively appropriated identity, with Margolin (1997, p. 4) suggesting that social workers "claim Jane Addams as their source of inspiration, but they do like Mary Richmond" (see Johnson, 2004; Specht & Courtney, 1994).

This difference in ideological perspectives is of great significance for how we conceptualize social work and how we go on to embellish it with such words as empowerment, liberation, and social change. An individual reform orientation, embodied by the tradition identified with Mary Richmond, does not require social workers to pay attention to the broader political-economic environment in their practice. The perspective does not necessitate and perhaps even counsels against the kind of actions that can put practitioners in conflict with the established order. Empowerment, liberation, and change are framed mainly within the confines of interpersonal relationships and, to a more limited extent, institutional practices. On the other hand, the profession's social reform tradition identified with Jane Addams requires practice to be oriented toward the broader political-economic system. The perspective requires a critical positioning in relation to the established order. Empowerment, liberation, and change are framed in the context of societal relations including race and ethnicity, class, and gender. In some of the most extreme circumstances, it points to a kind of practice exemplified by Gandhi's act of salt making in colonial India and Rosa Parks's refusal to give up her seat on the bus.

The tradition embodied in the work of Mary Richmond occupies a prominent place in social work (Margolin, 1997; Mullaly, 2007). It represents mainstream social work practice. The critical tradition exemplified by the work of Jane Addams occupies a much smaller space. The direction in which practice is undertaken is not just a matter of personal preference. The development of social work as a profession within particular political-economic orders orients it to a particular perspective.

▶ Professionalization and the Established Order

Although social work is at various stages of development across the world, there is a general thrust toward professionalization. Professionalization secures the place of social work by embedding it in broader society. In what Jones (2000, p. 156) calls the "aspirant" model of the profession, the goal is to achieve the characteristics of the traditional professions. These include having (1) a systematic body of knowledge, (2) recognized professional authority, (3) a code of ethics, (4) a shared professional culture, and (5) community sanction (Weiss-Gal & Welbourne, 2008). Community sanction comes in the form of professional licensing or registration in such countries as the United Kingdom, the United States, Canada, and the Philippines. The Australian Association of Social Workers has been actively campaigning for such a system to be put in place in Australia.

Licensing and registration are potent symbols of the recognition of social work as a profession. Registration can be seen as having an important role in securing a base for ethical practice by providing an institutional framework for the enforcement of practice standards (Orme & Rennie, 2006). But it is also a source of strength for the profession in the way it represents formal recognition by the state and accords legitimacy to social work (McDonald, Harris, & Winterstein, 2003). The lack of systems for professional recognition is seen by some as an indication of weakness in the advancement of the professionalization project (Orme & Rennie, 2006). Concerns over licensing and registration are manifestations of what can be seen as a more fundamental struggle: the drive toward the attainment of the status of the established professions.

There are, however, arguments against the professionalization project (see, e.g., Dominelli, 1996; and Hugman, 1996). The legitimate forms of practice and action by professionals are often defined within the bounds of the prevailing political-economic milieu. It is within the confines of given dispensations that professionals receive community/legal sanction to practise social work. On account of that, social work cannot exist and operate independently of and beyond the political-economic regime within which its professional identity is defined and from which it derives legitimacy and professional authority. Such conception of social work does not lend itself to practice that challenges the established order, implied in the definition cited above that makes mention of "social change" and "liberation." This, of course, is not so much of a problem within political-economic orders where there is enough democratic space that allows for the legitimate challenging of discrimination and disadvantage. But it presents a problem in restrictive political-economic regimes where the challenging of systemic disadvantage may be defined as being beyond the limits of legitimate professional action. In such circumstances, a strict professional conception of social work – that is, social work practice drawing legitimacy and authority from the state – would confine professional action within the policy and legal framework of the established order.

In the process of professionalization, social work becomes invested in the established order. Professionalization represents a claim of space within the broader societal context. The drive toward professionalization is a bid for legitimacy within that order. And for such legitimacy to be bestowed, it is necessary for social work to be painstakingly woven into the socio-political fabric. To be accorded legitimacy within the established order, social work must be securely nestled within its logic. This socializes the discipline to dominant knowledge and ways of thinking and impels social work to gravitate toward dominant ideology (Margolin, 1997;

Mullaly, 2007). In the case of the Philippines, the enactment of Republic Act No. 4373 in 1965, which instituted the licensing and registration system for social workers in that country, marked the investiture of social work within the framework of the Philippine state. This may partly explain the complicity with and legitimation of the Marcos dictatorship by the national professional association in the midst of the unprecedented scale and nature of human rights violations perpetrated by state authorities under martial law in the 1970s (Yu, 2006). Professionalization essentially embedded social work within Marcos's New Society, linking it with institutional systems that not only allowed for the regulation of the actions of practitioners but also bound the fortunes and interests of practitioners in the status quo. It was for this reason that some Filipino graduates of social work in the 1970s and 1980s who witnessed the atrocities of the Marcos dictatorship in the Philippines found it unconscionable to obtain professional registration, seeing it as the ultimate sign of one's selling out to the system.

Giving primacy to the legitimacy of actions as defined within particular politico-legal frameworks in the consideration of professional action would have implications for how we would go on to operationalize empowerment, liberation, and social change. How does one respond to issues of human rights and social justice? A strong professional framing would confine actions to what is allowed under the law. This should not be a problem for what might be considered peripheral issues in some political-economic orders that provide ample space for contestation. But it does present a problem in more restrictive political-economic orders.

Faced with growing resistance, the Marcos regime in the Philippines constructively crafted legislation to control dissent. Having consolidated executive, judicial, and legislative powers in his office, Marcos went on to issue decrees at will, with the view of containing dissent. It was made illegal to be a member of any organization and to sit in a meeting without national security clearance. The regime made it legally impossible for human rights advocates to investigate and document issues of human rights violations while unprecedented human rights abuses were being committed by members of the Philippine military, the police, and quasi-military forces receiving state funding. The apartheid policy in South Africa was imposed by the white minority. Racial discrimination, exclusion, and disadvantaging were collectively enforced in all corners of the state system – the legislature, the judiciary, and the executive. There was very little space for dissent on the part of members of the white minority who disagreed with the policy and even less for South Africa's black majority. How does one undertake "professional" practice in contexts where exclusion and disadvantage are institutionalized as part of the political-economic order? As argued earlier, a conception of social work that anchors professional intervention within the politico-legal framework of the context of practice would confine action to what is allowed under the law. In the case of martial law in the Philippines and in apartheid South Africa, this would have meant not being engaged in any work that sought to challenge the human rights atrocities of both of these regimes. Such a conception would have been inclined to counsel Rosa Parks to give up her seat and Gandhi not to pick up a clump of salt until such time when and if the laws changed to allow the challenging of the unjust practices and relationships they confronted.

Conceptions of social work that do not problematize the political-economic environment mainly rely on what Specht (1969, p. 6) called "collaboration approaches." Such approaches are based on the assumption that there is homogeneity of values and interests and issues of rights and justice can be resolved within the broader system. Other traditions in social work require a different positioning by practitioners in relation to the established order.

▶ OTHER TRADITIONS

Certain conceptions of social work – variously known as critical social work, progressive social work, structural social work, radical social work, political social work – focus on issues involving competing values and interests among different members of society (Mullaly, 2007). The perspective embodied in these traditions sees many of the problems that we find manifest in the everyday lives of people as rooted in societal inequality and the exclusion and disadvantage that arise out of unjust social relations. It argues that many of the problems found in the bodies and individual lives of people are mere manifestations of the exclusion, discrimination, exploitation, and oppression experienced by some members of society. The perspective recognizes the significant role played by intergroup and interclass politics in shaping the life chances of people by allowing the privileging of the values and interests of some over those of others. And while mainstream social work is oriented toward intervening at the individual level, addressing what Jamrozik and Nocella (1998) refer to as residual manifestations of broader societal problems with approaches that place heavy emphasis on individual change, critical social work is aimed at intervening at the social and societal level, addressing issues of interpersonal and societal politics. The key task is to challenge inequality, exclusion, discrimination, exploitation, and oppression.

While the challenging of exclusion, discrimination, exploitation, and oppression is often conceived of as being amenable to rational action and negotiation in the context of mostly Western democracies, such work becomes difficult in contexts where such practices are instituted as part of the economy of the established order. Confining African Americans to the back of buses was an essential trapping of the social order in the segregated United States, helping to maintain the privileged position of whites. The maintenance of its stranglehold on salt making and the local economy was crucial to the British Empire's interests in colonial India and its international imperial agenda. Such practices were not only consistent with dominant ideology, but also directly supported the interests of dominant members of the societies where they were instituted and enforced by law. Changes to these practices represented a significant threat to the interests, lives, and lifestyles of those in positions of privilege.

In such situations issues of rights and justice cannot simply be resolved within the logic and ground rules of the existing order. In the case of colonial India the success of the colonial regime was predicated on the continued subjugation of the general population. The suffering of the entire nation could not simply be eased through a deliberative process of negotiating for more reasonable colonial policies. It required the challenging of British imperial authority. In the case of the racially segregated United States racial segregation was vital to the maintenance of the emerging two-tiered nation. The daily experience of African Americans of being pushed to the back of the bus and of having the status of second-class citizens in law and in practice could not simply be stopped with exhortations for more equal and humane treatment. It required the outright challenging of racially discriminatory laws and practices. These experiences illustrate how discourses on empowerment, the liberation of people, and social change may, in certain contexts, require the challenging of institutionalized practices if not the established order itself, possibly with extralegal action.

Extralegal action can be seen as forming part of what Specht (1969, p. 8) calls "disruptive tactics." Disruptive tactics include actions that "move the other party toward some acceptable reconciliation" or "prevent the target from operating as usual" without physically injuring or harming them (p. 10). These tactics may involve (1) a clash of position; (2) the violation of normative behaviour through marches, demonstrations, boycotts, protests, vigils, strikes, and fasts; and (3) the violation of legal norms such as civil disobedience and non-cooperation and other violations of laws (pp. 10–11). Specht's conception of social action excludes the work of armed revolutionary groups who, in challenging the established order, engage in activities that are likely to cause physical harm to others. But it does not exclude extralegal action in the way Gandhi and Parks resorted to the wilful violation of the law in advancing their cause.

The mention of disruptive tactics would invariably bring to mind Alinsky (1971) and his model of social action. But while Alinsky's tradition is identified by political conservatives with radicalism, Ife (2010) points out how the approach is inherently conservative in the way it espouses a pluralist conception of power and advances the proposition that political adroitness on the part of disenfranchised populations, informed by knowledge of how the system works and how to work the system, can achieve important needed changes. Moreover, Ife (2012) also warns us about the human rights implications for practice of this tradition that unreservedly adopts militaristic language and operates on the notion that the ends justify the means. In contrast, Gandhi's approach to social action does not subscribe to the view that the ends justify the means; it links means and ends. The means, social action in the form of non-violent resistance embodied in the principle of *satyagraha* – the force of truth – was an important part of the ends. And yet the action was not conservative in that it went beyond the confines of the realm of possibilities provided by the political-economic order. Some of the battles fought by civil rights advocates in the United States, including Rosa Parks's in the bus, reflected this philosophy and framework.

▶ SOCIAL WORK AND EXTRALEGAL ACTION

Social workers lay rather bold claims in invoking discourses on empowerment, liberation, and social change. Their claims are not inadvertent considering how explicitly and clearly these are articulated. The Code of Ethics of the Australian Association of Social Workers (2010, p. 20) states, "Social workers will meet their responsibilities to society by engaging in action to promote societal and environmental wellbeing, advocate for equitable distribution of resources and effect positive social change in the interests of social justice" (5.1.3j). The US National Association of Social Workers' (2008) Code of Ethics declares, "Social workers pursue social change, particularly with and on behalf of vulnerable and oppressed individuals and groups of people." Social workers, according to the British Association of Social Work (2012, p. 9), "have a duty to challenge social conditions that contribute to social exclusion, stigmatisation or subjugation, and work towards an inclusive society," and "where distribution of resources, policies and practice are oppressive, unfair, harmful or illegal," social workers have a duty to bring this "to the attention of their employers, policy makers, politicians and the general public." Social workers are expected to "make a responsible effort" to resolve conflicts between social workers' ethical obligations and relevant laws or regulations "in a manner that is consistent with" professional values, principles, and standards (US National Association of Social Workers, 2008). Nevertheless, the overarching view is that "social workers must act in accordance with the law" (Australian Association of Social Workers, 2010, p. 40).

By virtue of their professional orientation, social workers are firmly positioned within the politico-legal framework of the state system. Thus, extralegal action exemplified by the work of Gandhi and Parks do not sit well with mainstream conceptions of social work, especially those that attach significance to social work's status as a legitimate profession that operates alongside the traditional professions. While the experiences of Gandhi and Rosa Parks are, on occasion, invoked in social work literature, the extralegal dimensions of such narratives are largely ignored, and very little consideration is given to their place in social work literature and professional practice.

Gandhi's salt march instigated the successful challenge to British colonial rule in India. The act of defiance by Rosa Parks catalyzed the civil rights movement in the United States. These actions embody many of the values and principles underpinning current definitions of social work that touch on the themes of social change, liberation, and empowerment. An important element in both cases is the challenging of the law in the process of contesting the legitimacy of the unjust practices and the social order. Those actions initiated the kind of changes that are alluded to in many articulations of professional social work principles, including the ones cited above.

This raises a number of questions for social work practice. What form does social work practice take within regimes that brazenly allow or instigate the violation of human rights and welfare? What defines legitimate action in such contexts? In state systems where injustice is institutionally sanctioned and legitimate avenues for dissent are systematically curtailed, where does professional practice begin and end? Should professional action be confined within the limits defined by the political-economic order in which it is practised? What defines the limits in the push for social change? How should social workers act if the legitimacy of particular social orders is in question? To what extent should practitioners allow the prevailing political-economic regime to dictate the limits of their range of action?

These are questions that are not well problematized in mainstream conceptions of social work. Mainstream conceptions that place social work squarely within the politico-legal framework of society do not, on the whole, provide space for these considerations. In the way that mainstream conceptions of social work are heavily informed by the assumption that the law represents the limits of professional action, it can be argued that social work, conceptualized as a legitimized profession, is mainly relevant to Western democracies or societies that provide a decent amount of political space to allow for the articulation and pursuit of social justice ends. But then it might be pointed out that there may be less relevance for such forms of practice in such contexts in the first place. After all, social inequality and injustice are conceivably easier to challenge where there is ample democratic space. Is this problematization of the realm of legitimate action in the face of social injustice mainly relevant to social work practice in non-Western societies? The questions raised here are not irrelevant to Western democracies. Contemporary Western democracies have their share of state-sanctioned discrimination and human rights violations as seen in the policy of mandatory detention of asylum seekers in Australia (Briskman, Zion, & Loff, 2012), the exclusion of people with disability and their families in the immigration policies of Canada (El-Lahib & Wehbi, 2011) and Australia (Yu, 2014), and the global push underpinned by the doctrine of unipolarism centred on the United States propounded by dominant interest groups (Midgley, 2006) that have led to the questionable treatment of prisoners at Guantanamo Bay and the deaths of civilians in Iraq and Afghanistan. Contemporary Western democracies have their share of state repression as seen in the government response to the G20 protests of 2010 in Toronto and the prosecution of whistleblowers like Bradley Manning, Edward Snowden, and Julian Assange on charges of espionage and treason. What is the role of social work – wrapped in the discourses on human rights, social justice, and social change – in relation to challenges like these? Is there a place for "salt making" in social work?

References

Alinsky, S. (1971). *Rules for radicals*. New York: Vintage.
Australian Association of Social Workers. (2010). *Code of ethics*. Canberra: Australian Association of Social Workers.
Briskman, L., Zion, D., & Loff, B. (2012). Care or collusion in asylum seeker detention. *Ethics and Social Welfare, 6*(1), 37–55.
British Association of Social Workers. (2012). *The code of ethics for social work*. Birmingham: British Association of Social Workers.
Dominelli, L. (1996). Deprofessionalizing social work: Anti-oppressive practice, competencies and postmodernism. *British Journal of Social Work, 26*(2), 153–175.
El-Lahib, Y., & Wehbi, S. (2011). Immigration and disability: Ableism in the policies of the Canadian state. *International Social Work, 55*(1), 95–108.

Hare, I. (2004). Defining social work for the 21st century: The International Federation of Social Workers' revised definition of social work. *International Social Work, 47*(3), 407–424.

Haynes, K.S. (1998). The one hundred-year debate: Social reform versus individual treatment. *Social Work, 43*(6), 501–509.

Hugman, R. (1996). Professionalization in social work: The challenge of diversity. *International Social Work, 39*(2), 131–147.

Ife, J. (2010). *Human Rights from below: Achieving rights through community development.* Sydney: Cambridge University Press.

Ife, J. (2012). *Human rights and social work: Towards rights-based practice.* (3rd ed.). New York: Cambridge University Press.

Jamrozik, A., & Nocella, L. (1998). *The sociology of social problems: Theoretical perspectives and methods of intervention.* Melbourne: Cambridge University Press.

Johnson, A.K. (2004). Social work is standing on the legacy of Jane Addams: But are we sitting on the sidelines? *Social Work, 49*(2), 219–322.

Jones, A. (2000). Social work: An enterprising profession in a competitive environment? In I. O'Connor, P. Smyth, & J. Warburton (Eds.), *Contemporary perspectives on social work and the human services* (pp. 150–163). Frenchs Forest, NSW: Addison Wesley Longman Australia.

Kurlansky, M. (2002). *Salt: A world history.* London: Vintage.

Margolin, L. (1997). *Under the cover of kindness: The invention of social work.* Charlottesville: University Press of Virginia.

McDonald, C., Harris, J., & Winterstein, R. (2003). Contingent on context? Social work and the state in Australia, Britain and the USA. *British Journal of Social Work, 33*(2): 191–208.

Midgely, J. (2006). International social work, globalization and the challenge of a unipolar world. *Journal of Sociology & Social Welfare, 33*(4), 11–17.

Mullaly, B. (2007). *The new structural social work: Ideology, theory, practice.* (3rd ed.). South Melbourne: Oxford University Press.

Orme, J., & Rennie, G. (2006). The role of registration in ensuring ethical practice. *International Social Work, 49*(3), 333–344.

Specht, H. (1969). Disruptive tactics. *Social Work, 14*(2), 5–15.

Specht, H., & Courtney, M.E. (1994). *Unfaithful angels: How social work has abandoned its mission.* New York: Free Press.

US National Association of Social Workers. (2008). *Code of Ethics.* Retrieved 28 Aug. 2013 from http://www.socialworkers.org/pubs/code/code.asp

Weiss-Gal, I., & Welbourne, P. (2008). The professionalisation of social work: A cross-national exploration. *International Journal of Social Welfare, 17*(4), 281–290.

Yu, N.G. (2006). Interrogating social work: Philippine social work and human rights under martial law. *International Journal of Social Welfare, 15*(3), 257–263.

Yu, N.G. (2014). Ableism and economic rationalism in Australian immigration. *International Journal of Social Welfare.* 23(3), 254–261.

About the Authors

Mary Lou L. Alcid, M.Sc. (Rural Development Planning)
Mary Lou is a professor of social work at the University of the Philippines Diliman. She obtained her Bachelor of Science in Social Work from the University of the Philippines, and her Master of Science in Rural Development Planning from the Asian Institute of Technology in Thailand. She has extensive experience in social development as a community organizer, trainer, founder, administrator, and trustee of non-government organizations engaged in promoting the rights and well-being of Indigenous Filipinos, fisherfolk, farmers, women, and overseas Filipino workers. She was part of pioneering initiatives in orienting social work academic programs toward practice in rural communities. She served as president of the National Association for Social Work Education from 2008 to 2012.

Ferzana Chaze, Ph.D. cand.
Ferzana is a doctoral candidate at the School of Social Work, York University, and teaches courses at the Chang School of Continuing Education, Ryerson University, and at Sheridan College. Prior to immigrating to Canada, she worked as a social work practitioner, educator, and researcher in Mumbai, India. Ferzana's research interests include immigrant settlement and the inclusion of new settlers in Canadian society. Her dissertation looks into the settlement experiences of immigrant South Asian women and how this relates to their mothering work in their new country.

Purnima George, Ph.D.
Purnima is an associate professor in the School of Social Work at Ryerson University. Prior to immigrating to Canada, she worked as a lecturer in the College of Social Work, Nirmala Niketan, Mumbai, and was engaged in community mobilization projects with slum and pavement dwellers in Maharashtra. Over the years Purnima has maintained her connection with India through partnership development with two colleges of social work in India. Her research interests include critical community practice and social advocacy, international social work practice, neo-liberalism, globalization, issues of South Asian communities in Toronto, and research as an anti-oppressive practice.

Alex Hundert

Alex is from Toronto (Mississauga Anishnabek Territory) and currently is living mostly in Asubpeeschoseewagong Netum Anishnabek Territory (Grassy Narrows First Nation). He is an organizer and activist who has spent most of the last ten years working with various groups and organizations, and on various social and environmental justice campaigns in southern Ontario. He is currently working in northwestern Ontario.

Martha Kuwee Kumsa, Ph.D.

Martha is a professor in the Faculty of Social Work, Wilfrid Laurier University. She is a former journalist, liberation struggler, and prisoner of conscience who reinvented herself as a subversive social work educator. While her teaching and research interests cut across and blur local and global as well as micro and macro levels of social work scholarship, she places particular emphasis on the challenges of reflexivity and the creative possibilities of social transformation through pedagogy, research, and direct practice. Her research interests include issues of identity, home(land), and belonging, violence and healing, spirituality and indigeneity, and most recently the Self–Other issue in the healing practices of racialized minority youth in Canada.

Deena Mandell, Ph.D.

Deena is an associate professor in the Lyle S. Hallman Faculty of Social Work, Wilfrid Laurier University. Prior to becoming an academic, she worked as a social worker in communities for many years. Her earlier research and writing focused on understanding individual and family problems in the context of systemic social relations, policies, and practices. More recently, her interest focused on reflexive practice, particularly fostering reflexivity through academic and field education. Her second book, *Revisiting the Use of Self: Questioning Professional Identities*, is used as a text in a variety of professional education programs. After witnessing the shocking treatment of G20 protesters in 2010, including the mass arrests and the incarceration of a number of people she personally cared about, Deena trained with the Inside-Out Prison Exchange Program in Philadelphia and subsequently taught a course on families and social systems in a Canadian women's prison, where the students were a mixed group from "inside" and "outside."

Manohar Pawar, Ph.D.

Manohar is a professor of social work at the School of Humanities and Social Sciences, Charles Sturt University (Australia). He is the president of the Asia-Pacific branch of the International Consortium for Social Development. He has over 30 years of experience in social work education, research, and practice in Australia and India. Manohar is the lead chief investigator of research funded by the Australian Research Council's Discovery Project that focuses on virtues and social work practice. His current areas of interest include international social work, development and social policy, social consequences of climate change and water, social work education, informal care and ageing, and NGOs and community development. His publications include: *Reflective Social Work Practice: Thinking, Doing, and Being* (Cambridge University Press, 2015), *Water and Social Policy* (Palgrave Macmillan, 2014), *Social and Community Development Practice* (Sage, 2014), and *International Social Work* (Sage, 2013); *Sage Handbook of International Social Work* (ed., Sage 2012); *Social Development: Critical Themes and Perspectives* (ed.); and *Community Development in Asia and the Pacific* (Routledge, 2010).

Venkat Pulla, Ph.D.

Venkat is a coordinator of social work discipline and senior lecturer in the Faculty of Health Sciences, Australian Catholic University. He was the founding head of the Department of Social Work, Northern Territory University, and more recently taught social work at Charles Sturt University and University of the Sunshine Coast. Venkat was a Tata Dorabji Merit scholar from the Tata Institute of Social Sciences (India). His research interests are in human coping and resilience, spirituality, green social work, and a strengths approach to social work. He is the founder of the Brisbane Institute of Strengths Based Practice. He has co-edited *Strengths-Based Practice* (Allied Publishers, New Delhi, 2013), *Theories, Experiences, and Challenges in Community Work* (Niruta Publications, 2014), *Advancing Social Work in Mental Health Through Strengths-Based Practice* (Primrose Hall, Australia, 2014), *Community Empowerment and Resilience* (Allied Publishers, New Delhi, 2015), and the *Lhotsampa People of Bhutan: Resilience and Survival* (Palgrave-Macmillan, 2015).

Wilder Robles, Ph.D.

Wilder is a Peruvian-born Canadian scholar educated in Brazil, the United States, and Canada. He is an Assistant Professor of rural development in the Faculty of Arts, Brandon University (Canada). His research interests include globalization, social and peasant movements, agrarian reform, community and rural development, food security, religion, conflict, politics, and peace and development. His current research is focused on land reform and agricultural co-operatives in Brazil.

Thérèse Sacco, D.Phil.
Terry is a Senior Research Associate at the Centre for Social Development in Africa, Faculty of Humanities, University of Johannesburg (South Africa). She is Executive Director of Mentoring and Empowering Program for Young Women, South Africa (MEMPROW SA). She teaches courses on reconciliation and pastoral care, works with refugees, and facilitates community educational development. Her research interests focus on reconciliation, social justice and transformation, and spirituality.

Jeanette Schmid, Ph.D.
Jeanette is a research fellow at the Centre for Social Development in Africa, University of Johannesburg (South Africa). She is a seasoned social worker who has practised in South Africa (her country of origin), Switzerland, and Canada in a range of areas, including developmental delay, early childhood intervention, trauma, oncology, restorative justice, and child welfare. Her work has been guided by a passion for social justice.

John Tomlinson, Ph.D.
John is a retired social work educator. He taught social policy and community work at universities and technical colleges in Western Australia, the Northern Territory, the Australian Capital Territory (ACT), and Queensland. Between 1987 and 1993, he was Director of the ACT Council of Social Services. He is a visiting scholar at the School of Social Work and Human Services, Queensland University of Technology (Australia). His Ph.D. investigated the political obstacles to the introduction of a guaranteed minimum income in Australia.

Nilan G. Yu, Ph.D.
Nilan is a Lecturer in social work at the University of South Australia. His main professional experience is in community development work. He has been teaching social work and social development for over 15 years. Nilan's teaching and research interests include critical social work practice and social policy, disability, labour migration, community work, and human rights. He is a member of the Asia Advisory Board of the journal Social Work Education and is an Editorial Reviewer of the *Asia Pacific Journal of Social Work and Development*.

Index

Page numbers followed by *fig* indicate a figure, by *t* indicate a table, and by *n* indicate an endnote

Aboriginal children, 34–35
Aboriginal identity, 38n2, 38n3
Aboriginal Inland Mission, 26
Aboriginal Legal Aid Service, 33
Abyot (student), 150–53, 154
activism: alliance of activists and social workers, 21, 22; arrest, 3, 10, 16, 18, 24n1; costs of involvement, 51–52; economic activism, 133–35; environmental activism, 5, 77, 78–79, 82, 90–91, 91*fig*, 95; marches and hunger strikes, 87–88; motives for activism, 52–54; of social work students, 17; of social workers, 19; perspectives on, 55–56; police actions, 13–14; policing, 3–4; political activism, 127, 129–33; radical activist, 7, 9; strategies to expand legal space for protest, 56–57; strategies used, 89; student activism, 62
Addams, Jane, 167, 168
Ad Hoc Committee (AHC) of College of Social Work in Bombay: achievements of, 109–10; action plan of, 105–7; collaboration with lawyers, 107–8, 110; critical reflections on action of, 109–15; ethical dilemmas of, 111–12; formation of, 99; legal actions of, 107–8; members profile, 114; protest march organized by, 108–9, 110; research on pavement dwellers, 106–7; safeguard measures for members of, 113
adivasi (Indigenous people), 78, 82
advocacy, 122
Agoncillo, Teodoro, 67
Ahmed, S., 146, 152
Alcid, Mary Lou, 5
Alinsky, Saul, 2, 66, 112, 173

Altman, J., 37
Ananda Marga ("Path of Bliss"), 65
apartheid: social workers' opposition to, 42; social work practice under, 44–46
asahakar non-violent method, 82
Assange, Julian, 175
Australia: Aboriginal children in foster care, 33–34; Aboriginal juvenile incarceration in, 35; Aboriginal population, 35; colonial intervention in Indigenous affairs, 37; Darwin city, 25, 26, 27; foster care in, 34–35; limit of Aboriginal Legal Aid's power, 33; national disability program, 36; national inquiry on separation of Aboriginal children, 26; policy of assimilation of Aborigines, 26; Racial Discrimination Act, 36, 37; racism toward Aborigines, 35; removal of Aboriginal children from Aboriginal communities, 34–35; social workers in, 4, 32, 35–36; "stolen generations" in, 26
Australian, The (newspaper), 31, 32, 38n4
Australian Association of Social Workers, 168, 173

Bantu Education system, 48
Barnard, Ferdi, 49
Bombay (Mumbai) city: characteristics of, 100; eviction and deportation of pavement dwellers, 5, 99, 102–4; migration to, 101; renaming of, 115n2; use of land in, 108
Bowdich, Jim, 38n4
Brazil: challenges of peasant mobilization, 140–41; Christian Base Communities (CEBs) movement,

132, 142n10; Church Commission on Land Reform (CPT), 143n18; commercial co-operatives in, 135; distribution of land in, 120, 121*t*; economic and social conditions in, 140; Family Allowance program, 141n2; geography of rural settlements in, 138*fig*; Gini index of land inequality, 140; illiteracy rate, 143n23; impact of land reform on rural settlements, 137–39; Landless Rural Workers Movement in, 6, 119; land occupation by landless peasants, 121–22, 122*t*; land reform beneficiaries, 123*t*, 143n23; land reform process in, 133–34, 139, 141; *latifúndia* (large landed estates), 142n4; massacre of landless peasants in, 127; National Program for Agrarian Reform, 136; political system in, 128, 140; population of, 120; Rural Democratic Union (UDR), 132; rural settlements, statistics of, 137*fig*; social inequality in, 120; status of peasants in, 142n5, 143n21; support of landless peasants by Catholic Church, 129–30; transformation toward democratic participation in, 128–29; weakness of political parties in, 142–43n17
Bringing Them Home report, 34
Browns foster family, 28, 29
Bryant, Gordon, 27, 29, 33, 34

Canada: perception of capitalism in, 161; social order and democracy in, 154–55; social protests in, 154; subversive education in, 145; Walls to Bridges program in, 157
Celi-Lansang, Flora, 68
Chambon, Adrienne, 20, 21
Chaze, Ferzana, 5, 100, 109, 110, 111, 113, 114
"Children under Repression" conference, 47
Christian Base Communities (CEBs) movement, 132, 142n10

cis-hetero, 12, 24n2
College of Social Work (Bombay), 99, 100, 104
community: concept of, 143n19
Concerned Social Workers (CSW): civic actions of, 46, 47; in coalition of progressive professional organizations, 50; compulsory registration with security police, 52; costs of involvement in activism, 51–52; goals and values of, 46, 53; involvement into anti-apartheid movement, 46; members' motives for activism, 52–54; opposition to apartheid, 42; origin of organization, 41, 45; partnerships, 47–48, 49; perspectives on activism, 55–56; research activities, 51, 56; security police and, 52; service to children and their families, 49; social work perspectives, 54–55, 57–58; strategies to expand legal space for protest, 56–57; tea parties, 49, 57; *In Touch* newspaper, 47
Confederation of Brazilian Cooperatives for Land Reform (CONCRAB), 135
conscientization: concept of, 47, 58n4
Constantino, Renato, 67

Dalits ("Untouchables") people, 82, 85
Darwin city, 25, 26, 27
David, Randy, 62
de Dios, A., 62
deportation, 115n1
Desai, Armaity, 99, 103
Detainee Education and Welfare (DEW), 49
Detainees' Parents' Support Committee (DPSC), 49
disruptive tactics, 172–73

Eckstein, S., 127
encounters: notion of, 145, 146, 150, 160; simple interpersonal, 152–53
Epstein, Laura, 20, 21

ethics. *See* social work, ethics in
Ethiopia: ideological differences in, 148; Karchelle prison, 148–49; political regime in, 147; school for political prisoners, 149, 150–51; Soviet support of junta, 148; subversive education in, 145; Workers Party of, 148
Evans, Ted, 29
Ewick, P., 64

Free the Children's Alliance, 48–49
Freire, Paolo, 46, 55, 64, 66, 136, 153

G20 Toronto Summit protests: academic discussions on, 3, 9, 13; arrests during, 10; policing for activist groups, 3–4
Gándhí, Mahátma: anti-British rebellion instigated by, 1; comparison with Medha Patkar, 84t; non-violent approach to social action, 5, 82–83, 173; salt march of, 1, 174; struggle against British rule, 2
George, Purnima, 5, 99, 105, 110
Gini coefficient, 142n3
Gooda, Mick, 35
Gutierrez, Gustavo, 66

Harrington, Penny, 37
Harvey, D., 127
Herbert, Xavier, 26
Hinkson, M., 37
Hundert, Alex: on activism of social workers, 19; on alliance of activists and social workers, 21, 22; arrest and detention, 3, 24n1; on breach of bail conditions, 14–15; charges related to G20 protests, 9–10; on feeling of being targeted, 12, 14; on lack of accountability among social workers, 20; on liberalism *vs.* radicalism, 20–21; on nature of law, 12–13; on notion of free speech, 14; on police actions during G20 summit, 13–14; on professionalism, 19; as radical activist, 7, 9; on *Reading Foucault for Social Work*, 20; relations and correspondence with Deena Mandell, 4, 11; on response of academia to law enforcement actions, 15; on role of academia in society, 14; on role of social work in maintaining social order, 21, 22; on social work as academic discipline, 20; on social work as career choice, 18–20
Hunter, John, 31

Ife, J., 173
India: causes of migration in, 101–2; challenges to human rights and social justice, 5; colonial regime, 172; eviction and deportation of pavement dwellers, 99; history of resistance in, 108; rebellion against British rule, 1; Right to Fair Compensation and Transparency in Land Acquisition, Rehabilitation and Resettlement Act, 90; social work in, 93–94, 114–15
Indigenous Australians: government intervention into communities of, 36–37; government investments in, 37; life expectancy, 36; practice of removing children from communities of, 30, 34–35; social security payments to, 36–37; "stolen generations" of, 26; story of injustice toward, 4; Whitlam government policy on, 26–27
injustice, 4
Inside-Out/Walls to Bridges program, 157, 158
International Federation of Social Workers (IFSW), 2, 166
In Touch (newspaper), 47
Irving, Allan, 20, 21
Iyer, Krishna, 110

Jack (father of Nola), 29, 31
Jamrozik, A., 171
Jan Vikas Sangharsh Yatra (Struggle March for People's Development), 87

184 Index

Jefferson, Thomas, 35
Juliano-Soliman, Corazon, 73
justice in relation to rights and law, 165, 166, 167

Kalin Compound, 26
Khanolkar, Vasant, 78
King, Martin Luther, Jr, 2, 7
Kurlansky, M., 1
Kumsa, Martha Kùwee: encounters with difficult students, 150–52, 154; life and work of, 6; on reform and revolution, 160–61; on subversion of student–teacher relations, 157–58; teaching experience in Canadian prison, 157–59; teaching experience in school prison in Ethiopia, 149–50; teaching philosophy of, 156, 159; view of Canadian liberal democracy, 154–55, 161–62

land distribution, 120, 121t; inequality, 140; occupation by landless peasants, 121–22, 122t; Right to Fair Compensation and Transparency in Land Acquisition, Rehabilitation and Resettlement Act, 90; use of, 108
landless peasants: Landless Rural Workers Movement in, 6, 119; land occupation by, 121–22, 122t; massacre of, 127; support of, 129–30
Landless Rural Workers Movement: achievements of, 122–23; advocacy of access to land as fundamental human right, 122; characteristics of, 119; community-based politics, 132; confrontation with Rural Democratic Union, 132; co-operative strategy, 134–35; democratic process and, 131; economic activism of, 133–35; goals and strategies of, 129; impact on rural communities, 136–37, 141; involvement in national and international politics, 132–33; land reform and, 131; membership, 6; organizational structure of, 130t; origin of, 122, 129–30; political activism of, 127, 129–33; promotion of education by, 136; promotion of participation of women in politics by, 133; spread of, 6; support from Catholic Church, 131; theoretical perspectives on, 126–27
land reform: beneficiaries, 123t, 143n23; Church Commission on Land Reform (CPT), 143n18; distribution of land, 120, 121t; impact of, 137–39; Landless Rural Workers Movement, 131; process, 133–34, 139, 141
Latin America: failure of land reforms in, 143n20; Gini Index of Land Inequality, 121t; non-violent popular struggles in, 120; social movements in, 125, 142n11, 142n12, 143n13
"lawful" action: meaning of, 166
law in relation to justice and rights, 165, 166, 167
liberalism: vs. radicalism, 20–21; as structural mechanism of capitalism, 21
Lovett, Elizabeth, 29, 31, 32

Mandela, Nelson, 7
Mandell, Deena: on activism of social work students, 17; on arrests in connection with G20 protests, 16, 18; as facilitator of panel discussion of G20 summit protests, 11–12; on fear of material and social safety, 16–17; on identity crisis of social workers, 22; on influence of social workers, 11; on manifestations of radicalism in neo-liberal society, 23; personal experience related to son's arrest, 9–10; on perspectives on democracy and freedom of speech, 16; as progressive social work educator, 9; questioning in Court, 12; relations and correspondence with Alex Hundert, 4, 11; on social

work as profession, 17–18, 23; on theory and practice of social work, 23; on university response to police actions, 15
Manning, Bradley, 175
Mao Tse Tung, 66
Marcos, Ferdinand E., 61, 69, 74
Martins, J.D.S., 131, 143n18
Maruyama, E., 65
Marx, Karl, 66
Mendes, P., 111
Montgomery bus boycott, 166
Montigny, G.A.J. de, 160
Movimento dos Trabalhadores Rurais Sem Terra (MST). *See* Landless Rural Workers Movement
Mumbai. *See* Bombay

Narmada Bachao Andolan (Save Narmada Movement): current status of, 89–90; drowning in rising Narmada River action, 88; formation of, 87; marches and hunger strikes, 87–88; Medha Patkar as organizer of, 78, 82; media on, 91; petition in the Supreme Court of India, 89; poem inspired by, 96; profession of social work and, 93–94; strategies used by, 89
Narmada River, 79, 80*fig*, 95
Narmada Valley: constructions of dams on, 79; hydroelectric projects in, 80*fig*; Indigenous peoples in, 78; Jan Vikas Sangharsh Yatra (Struggle March for People's Development) march, 87; mobilization of local population against dam construction, 85; opposition to dams in local communities, 82; supporting and opposing arguments on development project in, 81*t*
Narmada Valley Development Project/Plan (NVDP), 79, 81–82, 83, 87, 89
Narmada Water Disputes Tribunal, 79
National Alliance of People's Movements (NAPM), 90

Navarro, Z., 131, 143n18
Nehru, Jawaharlal, 77, 82–83
"new" social movements: characteristic of, 124–25; definition of, 142n9; neo-Marxist approach to, 127–28; social theories on, 126
Niekerk, W.A. van, 50
Niketan, Nirmala, 99
Nocella, L., 171
Nola (Aboriginal girl): birth and illness, 28; disputes over reunification with natural family, 29–30; government officials' involvement in case of, 29; life among Aboriginal people, 32; media about, 31–32, 33; return to natural parents, 25, 31; search for foster family for, 28; story of, 4; termination of fostering agreement, 31
non-violence, 119, 141n1; use of non-violent methods by, 92–93
Nuremberg Judgment, 35

Omvedt, G., 127
Ondetti, G., 127

Palmer, P., 153
Parks, Rosa, 165, 166, 174
Patel, Leila, 56
Patkar, Medha: biography of, 78–79; comparison with Ghandi, 84*t*; dialogue with inhabitants of Narmada Valley, 84–85; education of, 78, 90; environmental activism of, 5, 77, 78–79, 82, 90–91, 91*fig*, 95; hunger strike of, 88; ideology and goals of, 92; impact on social work thinking, 94–95; leadership of Narmada Bachao Andolan, 83, 87; mobilization of population in Narmada Valley, 85; on Nehru's perception of dams, 77; opposition to Sardar Sarovar Project, 87; protests organized by, 85–86, 87–88; Right Livelihood Award, 79; on role of state in protection of people's rights, 93; use of non-violent methods by, 92–93; work in Gujarat, 83

Pauw, Jaques, 49
pavement dwellers (Bombay): employment and income of, 101; eviction and deportation of, 99, 102–4; legal norms and, 112–13; living conditions of, 100, 102; mass deportation of, 99; non-citizenship status of, 101, 111; plan of mobilization of, 106; population of, 100; public education and awareness of lives of, 107; resistance strategy of, 5–6
Pawar, Manohar, 5
Petras, J., 127
Philippine Association of Social Workers, 62, 72
Philippines: dictatorship regime in, 69; legislation to control dissent in, 170; martial law in, 61, 62–63; poverty in, 63, 69; social work study in, 63, 64–66, 67, 69–70; student activism, 62
pointing fingers: metaphor of, 145, 146
political system, 128, 140; transformation toward democratic participation in, 128–29; weakness of political parties in, 142–43n17
politics: community-based, 132; involvement in national and international, 132–33
Poor Fellow My Country (Herbert), 26
praxis: notion of, 55
Pulla, Venkat, 5
Purificacion (Puri) Pedro, 72

Rabbit-Proof Fence (film), 34
Racial Discrimination Act, 36, 37
racial segregation in United States, 166–67, 172
racism, 35
Recto, Claro M., 67
resistance: history of, 108; strategy, 5–6
Richmond, Mary, 167, 168
rights in relation to justice and law, 165, 166, 167
Robles, Wilder, 6
Ryan, Bill, 29, 30, 31, 33

Ryerson University, 13

Sacco, Thérèse, 4
salt-making, 1, 7; salt march of Gandhi, 1, 174
Sardar Sarovar Project, 79, 83, 85, 86, 87, 88–90
satyagraha non-violent campaign, 77, 82–83, 86, 173
Schmid, Jeanette, 4
School of Social Work at the University of the Witwatersrand, 45
Sharp, Gene, 83
Shor, I., 153
Silbey, S., 64
Sison, Jose Maria, 67
Snowden, Edward, 175
social action models, 172–73
social inequality, 120
socialism, 151–52, 154, 161
social justice, 2
social movements, 123–25, 142n14
social work: as academic discipline, 20; arguments against professionalization of, 169; in comparative perspective, 114; conceptions of, 2, 18, 168, 174–75; definitions of, 2, 7, 66, 166, 167; dependence on government funding, 11; ideological perspectives on, 168; as inspiration, 155–56; in India, 93–94, 114–15; non-professionals in, 7; notion of unsettled, 160; political-economic environment for, 171; in relation to environmental activism, 93–94; role in maintaining social order, 21; roots of, 167; safe *vs.* liberating, 160; "salt making" in, 1, 7; study, 63, 64–66, 67, 69–70; theory and practice of, 23; traditions of, 171; Western democracies and practice of, 174, 175; views of nature of, 69
social work, ethics in: codes of ethics of US National Association of, 173–74; ethical and legal challenges, 112
social work, professionalization of: process of professionalization of,

169–70; as profession, 2, 3, 10–11, 17, 18–20, 23, 93–94, 168–68
social workers: identity crisis of, 22; licensing and registration of, 169; in political-legal framework of state system, 174; social activists and, 21, 22
social workers, professionalization of: codes of ethics of US National Association of, 173–74; ethical and legal challenges, 112;
social workers in Philippines: activism of, 65, 74; age and gender of, 65; backgrounds of, 74; education of, 62, 65, 66, 67, 68–69; field work of, 67–68, 70; government prosecutions of, 71, 72; ideas of, 66–67; licensing and registration for, 170; under martial law, 5, 62, 63–64, 70–73, 74; in national government agencies, 73; in non-governmental organizations, 73; prominent representatives of, 71–72; radicalization of, 61; subversive actions of, 5, 149, 150; under surveillance of officials, 68; suspicions of subversion, 70; views of nature of social work by, 69; women as, 66–67
social workers in South Africa, 4–5, 44–45, 55–56
South Africa: children detention in, 48, 50; Detainee Counselling Service (DCS), 50; end of apartheid in, 41; label of race, 58n1; National Party in power, 42; notion of black people in, 58n2; post-apartheid Constitution, 50; power of white minority in, 42; practice of detention in, 44, 58n3; security forces in, 42–43; social workers under apartheid, 44–45, 170–71; states of emergency, 43, 45; United Democratic Front (UDF), 46; violence in, 43–44; world media attention to, 48
Spavorek, G., 143n22
Spech, H., 2, 171, 172

Springs, Ali
Stédile, João, 142n15
stolen generat, inquiry on s nal children, Aboriginal ch nal communiti
subversive actions, subversion of st relations, 157–58; subversion, 70
subversive education, 153–54, 160; subver dent–teacher relatio

Taguiwalo, Judy, 71–72
Tomlinson, John: on best of Aboriginal people, 3 in social work, 29, 30; a Department of Social Sec Brisbane, 27; education o on injustice toward Indige peoples, 4; publications op intervention into Indigenous munities, 37, 38n5; public se charges against, 32; at Welfare Branch in Darwin, 25, 27, 37n

University of the Philippines in Dili man, 62, 64, 72
University of Toronto, 10, 16

Veltmeyer, H., 127
Vía Campesina movement, 123, 142n7

Webster, David, 49
Werts, Tyrone, 157
White, Ken, 33, 34
Wilfrid Laurier University, 13
Willesee, Gerri, 32
Witwatersrand, University of the, 45, 47, 49
World Social Forum, 123, 142n8

Yu, Nilan, 7
Yu, Peter, 36